Essentials of Health Policy and Law

Essentials of Health Policy and Law

Maverick MacMillan

MURPHY & MOORE
www.murphy-moorepublishing.com

Murphy & Moore Publishing,
1 Rockefeller Plaza,
New York City, NY 10020, USA

ISBN: 978-1-63987-209-1

Cataloging-in-Publication Data

Essentials of health policy and law / Maverick MacMillan.
p. cm.
Includes bibliographical references and index.
ISBN 978-1-63987-209-1
1. Medical laws and legislation. 2. Medical policy. 3. Health. I. MacMillan, Maverick.

K3601 .E77 2022
344.041--dc23

For information on all Murphy & Moore Publications
visit our website at www.murphy-moorepublishing.com

MURPHY & MOORE

Contents

Preface VII

Chapter 1 Health Law: Nature and Scope 1

Chapter 2 The Fundamental Right to Health 19

Chapter 3 Right to Health: Current Challenges 32

Chapter 4 Right to Health: Solution to Challenges 66

Chapter 5 Laws Regarding Public Health and Health Rights 87

Chapter 6 Laws Regarding Mental Health 114

Chapter 7 Health Care Professionals and their Regulation 139

Chapter 8 Malpractices in Healthcare 173

Chapter 9 Fundamental Rights of Patients 193

Chapter 10 Research on Human Participants 209

Permissions

Index

Preface

It is the responsibility, and moral and political mandate of the states to protect their populations from threats to health. The two most important mechanisms that assist in this task are public health policy and public health law. Public health policy can be defined as the process of consultation, negotiation, and research that leads to a plan of action that sets out a vision of identified public health goals. Public health law refers to the power and duty of the state to ensure the conditions for people to be fit and healthy. This book is a compilation of chapters that discuss the most vital concepts and emerging trends in this field. Also included herein is a detailed explanation of the various topics and applications of health policy and law. This book will provide comprehensive knowledge to the readers.

After months of intensive research and writing, this book is the end result of all who devoted their time and efforts in the initiation and progress of this book. It will surely be a source of reference in enhancing the required knowledge of the new developments in the area. During the course of developing this book, certain measures such as accuracy, authenticity and research focused analytical studies were given preference in order to produce a comprehensive book in the area of study.

This book would not have been possible without the efforts of the authors and the publisher. I extend my sincere thanks to them. Secondly, I express my gratitude to my family and well-wishers. And most importantly, I thank my students for constantly expressing their willingness and curiosity in enhancing their knowledge in the field, which encourages me to take up further research projects for the advancement of the area.

Maverick MacMillan

1

HEALTH LAW: NATURE AND SCOPE

1 Introduction

1.1 Understanding the concepts 'health' and 'law'

Before attempting a working definition of health law and mapping out the scope of the subject, it is necessary to understand the meaning of the two main concepts: 'health' and 'law'. Though these words are used in everyday conversation and in many different ways, they are not easy to define. For example, World Health Organisation (WHO) defines 'health' as a 'state of complete physical, mental, and social well-being and not merely the absence of disease and infirmity'.[1] In the Ottawa Charter for Health, the WHO explained that health is not just a state, but also 'a resource for everyday life, not the object of living. Health is a positive concept emphasizing social and personal resources, as well as physical capabilities'.[2]

Health status is affected by a number of factors including income and social status, physical and social environments in which we live, education and literacy, genetics, life styles, health care, social security, gender and culture. According to the UN Committee on Economic, Social and Cultural Rights (Committee on ESCR), other determinants of health include, resource distribution, gender differences, violence and armed conflict,[3] and

> access to safe and portable water and adequate sanitation, an adequate supply of safe food, nutrition and housing, healthy occupational and environment

1 WHO *The Constitution* (1948) Preamble.
2 WHO *The Ottawa charter for health promotion* (1986) http://www.crrps.org/download/ottawaCharter.pdf (accessed 13 May 2013).
3 Committee on ESCR 'The Right to the highest attainable standard of health' (Art 12 of the International Covenant on Economic and Cultural Rights) UN Doc E/C.12/2000/4 (2000) General Comment 14, para 10.

> conditions, and access to health-related education and information, including sexual and reproductive health. A further important aspect is the participation of the population in all health-related decision-making at the community, national and international levels.[4]

From the foregoing, it can be seen that health is a broad and holistic concept, which covers physical and mental health and social well-being. So, what is health? What does it mean to be healthy? Can a person be in a *complete* state of health free from any physical, emotional and mental defects? Health is a general condition of a person in all respects. The WHO definition of health is an ideal worth working for, but it may be difficult to attain.[5] However, a number of strategies, including laws and policies, may be employed to ensure that individuals and populations attain a level of health that ensures their survival and well-being.

It should be pointed out that governments have the responsibility to promote and protect health. As the Committee on ESCR has pointed out,

> [t]here are a number of aspects which cannot be addressed solely within the relationship between states and individuals; in particular good health cannot be ensured by a state, nor can states provide protection against every possible cause of human ill health. Thus, genetic factors, individual susceptibility to ill health and the adoption of unhealthy or risky life styles may play an important role with respect to an individual's health.[6]

Consequently, individuals and communities also have a responsibility to control their health. There are things which the government is expected to do while others may be beyond its scope. For example, people should avoid life threatening conditions such as abuse of drugs and bad eating habits, which may lead to health challenges such as obesity, high blood pressure and heart disease. An individual should avoid unsafe and reckless sexual behaviour, which may lead to him or her contracting HIV and other sexually transmitted infections. Although the government may not invade the privacy of your home to ensure that you do not drink excessive alcohol or have unprotected sex, it does have an obligation to ensure that the information on the diseases and conditions that might emerge from indulging in such behaviour is available and accessible to the public.

A parent or guardian should ensure that he or she has enough food to feed the family, unless prevented by circumstances beyond his or her control. If the government provides a health centre, the parent or guardian is expected to take children for immunisation and other health care services. The government is obliged to ensure that services such as health

4 n 3 above, para 11.

5 For a critical analysis of the WHO definition of health, see: M Huber et al 'How should we define health?' (2011) *British Medical Journal* 343; L Breslow 'A quantitative approach to the World Health Organization definition of health: Physical, mental and social well-being' (1972) 1 *International Journal of Epidemiology* 347.

6 Committee on ESCR (n 3 above) para 9.

personnel, equipment, drugs and other services are available, accessible, affordable and of good quality. Thus, ensuring good health involves many actors: the government, individuals, communities and other private actors such as pharmaceutical companies, non-governmental organisations (NGOs) and religious organisations.

This brings us to the next question: what is law? Like many other concepts, 'law' has attracted various definitions. The Oxford Dictionary defines law as 'the system of rules which a particular country or community recognizes as regulating the actions of its members and which it may enforce by the imposition of penalties'.[7] It is a system of rules and guidelines, which are enforceable through social institutions for the purpose of governing behaviour.[8] Law shapes economics, politics and other spheres of life and serves as a social mediator of relations between people. As Corley et al have observed, law is,

> an instrument of social, political and economic change. Law is both an instrument of change and a result of changes that take place in our society. The law brings about changes in our society; society brings about changes in the law. The law - responding to the goals, desires, needs, and aspirations of society - is in a constant state of change. Sometimes the law changes more rapidly than the attitude of the majority in society. In this event, the law provides leadership in bringing out changes. At other times our society is ahead of the law in moving in new directions, and changes in the law are brought about by the people ...[9]

Law is thus a critical tool in the development and good governance of society. It causes changes in society, including the advancement or deterioration of health. Law regulates people's health behaviour. For example, law prohibits and punishes certain acts such as the deliberate spread of diseases, nuisances, the sale of adulterated food, abuse of drugs and other acts that may be deleterious to the health of individuals and populations. Law may also be used to encourage or force parents or guardians of children to take them for immunisation in order to promote their health. It should be noted that not all laws attract punishment or sanctions for non-observance. For example, doctors may observe the law regulating their profession not simply for fear of sanctions but because it is ethically right to do so. Such laws governing health professionals usually provide an indication of good practice.

It should however be noted that law may be a double edged sword: it may be an instrument of change and an obstacle to change. In some cases it may be an instrument of oppression. For example, a law that provides for mandatory testing for HIV without sufficient safeguards such as

7 Oxford Dictionaries http://oxforddictionaries.com/definition/english/law (accessed 21 March 2013).
8 As above.
9 R Corley et al *Fundamentals of business law* (1982) 4.

counselling, privacy and confidentiality may not only undermine the human rights of persons living with HIV/AIDS (PLHA) but may actually undermine public health efforts to tackle HIV prevalence in the country. Many PLHA may be driven underground and may not be meaningfully engaged with by public health officials. Similarly, a law that enforces family planning or population control measures such as forced sterilisation of women or mandatory contraceptive use oppresses women by violating their human rights, including privacy, human dignity, autonomy and bodily integrity. Thus, this book subjects the relevant health laws to serious scrutiny in order to determine the extent to which they address contemporary and emerging health challenges without unduly undermining and limiting the human rights and freedoms of individuals and populations.

1.2 The scope of health law

The question now is: what is 'health law' and what is its scope? Health law is that branch of the law that is essentially concerned with the health of human beings. According to Belanger,[10] health law

> is understood today as being a branch of law in its own right. It is itself divided into (sub) branches of increasing complexity … two sets: a classical set, represented by medical law and another set bringing in emerging disciplines.[11]

Some aspects of the health law course have for long been taught in universities and colleges. For example, health rights have been covered under international and human rights law; legal construction of quarantines and other enforcement powers of the state in public health law; and medical negligence in the law of torts. However, serious initiatives towards the development of health law as a distinct course within university programmes may be traced to the 1960s and 1980s in countries such as Canada, the United States of America and France and later in countries of the South such as Senegal.[12] However, during this period, medical law was the predominant discipline in health law.[13]

Health law refers to those enforceable laws established by government, central and local, and applied to people for the purpose of building a healthy society. It also covers rules and regulations established by other key stakeholders in the area of health promotion such as business, communities and health professionals' associations. It deals with the legal aspects of promoting public health, which is largely concerned with the state's duties and powers to assure the conditions of the people to be

10 M Belanger *Global health law: An introduction* (2011) 15.
11 Belanger (n 10 above) 19.
12 Belanger (n 10 above) 18.
13 As above.

healthy without unduly constraining key human rights and freedoms such as autonomy, movement, privacy, liberty and property.[14] Health law is also concerned with the legal aspects of health care, which cover availability, accessibility, acceptability, and quality of health facilities, goods and services. Thus, health law is multifaceted: it encompasses not only health care delivery but other areas of study that focus on the intersection between law and health.

It is important to note here that health law involves civil law and criminal law aspects. Civil law provides for the rights and obligations of individuals and seeks to compensate the victim of a wrong, for example a tort or breach of contract. For instance, in cases of medical negligence, the patient may seek damages from a doctor who wrongly performed an operation. On the other hand, criminal law aims at punishment of the offender in order to reform him or her and perhaps satisfy the public expectation that wrong should be met with retribution. The punishment may take the form of imprisonment, a fine or community service. For example, where a doctor in a rash or negligent manner 'gives medical or surgical treatment' to a patient, he or she commits an offence and may be liable to imprisonment not exceeding three years.[15]

The scope of health law is vast. It covers a complex array of laws such as the Constitution, treaties, statutes, rules, regulations, ordinances, guidelines, decrees, bye-laws, statutory instruments, case law and other legal instruments governing public health and the health care industry. Because of the broad nature of health law, this book does not promise to cover every aspect of the subject. It deliberately focuses on specific aspects of health law that are applicable in the Ugandan context: health rights, public health law, health professional regulation, malpractice litigation, consent to treatment, and research on human subjects. Given the multi-disciplinary nature of the subject, the book inevitably refers to various policy frameworks and ethical[16] principles and guidelines that have a bearing on health.

14 LO Gostin 'State public health law: Assessment report' (2002); LO Gostin *Public health law: Power, duty and restraint* (2000).

15 Sec 228(e) of the Penal Code Act, Cap 120.

16 According to Fremgen, ethics 'is the branch of philosophy related to morals, moral principles, and moral judgments. Morality is the quality of being virtuous or practicing the right conduct ... Medical ethics concerns questions specifically related to the practice of medicine. This branch of ethics is based on principles regulating the behaviour of health care professionals, including practitioners such as physicians, nurses and allied health professionals. It also applies to patients, relatives and the community at large'. See BF Fremgen *Medical law and ethics* (2009) 8. One can also add to this list researchers who conduct clinical research as illustrated in Chapter 10 of this book.

1.3 Sources of health law

Like other branches of law in Uganda, health law is derived from the Constitution, principal legislation, subsidiary legislation, common law or case law, international law and customary law. These sources are explained below.

1.3.1 The 1995 Constitution of the Republic of Uganda

Unlike the 1962, 1966 and 1967 Constitutions, the 1995 Constitution was a product of wide consultations carried out by the Constitutional Commission, whose report was debated by the Constituent Assembly leading to the promulgation of the new Constitution on 8 October 1995.[17] The Constitution is the 'supreme law of Uganda and shall have binding force on all authorities and persons throughout Uganda'[18] and where 'any other law or any custom is inconsistent with any of the provisions of the Constitution, the Constitution shall prevail, and that other law or custom shall, to the extent of the inconsistency, be void'.[19] In simple terms, this provision means that the Constitution takes precedence over all laws in the country. Thus, all health-related laws must conform to the provisions of the Constitution, short of which, they may be declared void or nullified by the Constitutional Court.[20] The Constitution contains some provisions with a direct bearing on health rights issues as illustrated in Chapter 2 below.

The Constitution recognises the doctrine of separation of powers whereby the powers, duties and responsibilities of the three arms of government are clearly laid out. One arm is the executive, which is headed by the president of Uganda who shall be the head of state and shall be vested with executive authority.[21] This authority may be exercised either directly or through subordinate officers such as ministers.[22] The executive has powers to develop policies and other administrative measures, including in the field of health. It also has powers to initiate bills for consideration by parliament of Uganda, which is vested with the power to make laws. Parliament has powers 'to make laws on any matter for the peace, order, development and good governance of Uganda'[23] and '[e]xcept as provided in this Constitution, no person or other body shall have power to make provisions having the force of law in Uganda except under authority conferred by an Act of Parliament'.[24]

17 Republic of Uganda (1995) Constitution of the Republic of Uganda (as amended).
18 Art 2(1) of the Constitution.
19 Art 2(2) of the Constitution.
20 Art 137 of the Constitution.
21 Art 98(1).
22 Art 99(4).
23 Art 79(2).
24 Art 79(2).

The other arm is the judiciary, which is in charge of the administration of justice and shall exercise judicial power over cases of a civil and criminal nature 'in the name of the people and in conformity with the law and with the values, norms and aspirations of the people'.[25] The Constitution guarantees independence of the judiciary and in the exercise of judicial power, the courts 'shall not be subject to the control or direction of any person or authority'.[26] The courts in Uganda comprise of: the Supreme Court; the Court of Appeal, which also sits as the Constitutional Court; the High Court, which are superior courts of record;[27] and such other courts as Parliament may by law establish.[28] The Supreme Court is the final court of appeal. Appeals from the Court of Appeal go to the Supreme Court while those from the High Court are lodged in the Court of Appeal.[29] It should be noted that when hearing matters involving the interpretation of the Constitution, the Court of Appeal sits as a Constitutional Court.[30] The High Court has unlimited original jurisdiction[31] and also handles appeals from lower courts such as magistrates courts.[32] As shall be explained in the course of this book, the judiciary can play a critical role in advancing health. Violations of health rights may be challenged in courts of law.

The Constitution establishes the Uganda Human Rights Commission,[33] a quasi-judicial body, which is critical in the protection of health rights. The Commission has a broad mandate, including 'to investigate, at its own initiative or any complaint made by any person or group of persons against a violation of any human right [including health rights]',[34] and to monitor the Government's compliance with its obligations under international law.[35] In the exercise of its powers, the Commission has powers of the High Court.[36] Unlike the courts, where a person whose health rights have been violated has to go through the rigorous procedure of filing a suit and paying the prescribed fees, the procedure before the Commission is informal. This informal procedure is important given the high levels of illiteracy and poverty in the country where the costs for instituting legal proceedings are usually high. It is worth noting that the Commission has a right to health unit, which handles complaints regarding health rights issues.

25 Art 126(1).
26 Art 128(1).
27 Art 129(2).
28 Art 129(1)(a) - (d).
29 Art 134(2). See also sec 10 of the Judicature Act, Cap 13.
30 Art 137(1).
31 Art 139(1). See also section 14(1) of the Judicature Act, Cap 13.
32 Art 139(2).
33 Art 51(1).
34 Art 52(1)(a).
35 Art 52(1)(h).
36 See sec 20 of the Uganda Human Rights Commission Act, Cap 24.

1.3.2 Principal legislation

Principal or primary legislation refers to statutes passed by the Parliament of Uganda and formally assented to by the President.[37] Examples of statutes relevant for health include the Public Health Act, Cap 281; Mental Treatment Act, Cap 279; Food and Drugs Act, Cap 278; Venereal Diseases Act, Cap 284; the Water Act, Cap 152; National Medical Stores Act, Cap 207; National Drug Policy and Authority Act, Cap 206; National Environment Act, Cap153;the Medical and Dental Practitioners Act, Cap 272; the Nurses and Midwives Act, Cap 274; and the Allied Health Professionals Act, Cap 268. The procedure of making principal legislation is that bills are presented to parliament by the government through the sector minister.

It is important to note that once introduced in parliament, a bill must go through a number of stages before it becomes an Act. The minister delivers the bill to the clerk of parliament, who tables copies to all members. The bill must be accompanied by a certificate of financial implications.[38] Every bill shall also be accompanied by an explanatory memorandum outlining the policy and principles of the bill, the defects in the existing law, if any, and the remedies proposed to deal with such defects.[39] This certificate is to ensure that the proposed law shall not create a financial burden on the government. Except for urgent bills, all bills shall be published in the gazette.[40] The bill is then put on the order paper, which is the agenda of parliament, by the clerk on instructions of the speaker of parliament for the first reading.[41]

It should also be noted that every bill must be read three times before it is passed.[42] At the first reading, the clerk reads out aloud the short title of the bill.[43] The speaker forwards the bill to the relevant committee of parliament for detailed scrutiny. The committee conducts an inquiry in order to obtain the views of the relevant stakeholders on the purpose and contents of the bill. At the second reading, the chairperson of the relevant committee presents the report on the bill to parliament for debate on the merits and principles of the bill.[44] After the second reading, parliament resolves itself into a committee of the whole house, which scrutinises the bill clause by clause.[45] Immediately after the report of the committee of the whole house, the bill may be read for the third time and passed. After the bill is passed by parliament, it is sent to the president, who may either

37 Art 91(1).
38 Rule 102(1) of the Rules of Procedure of the Parliament of Uganda, 2006.
39 Rule 101(2).
40 Rule 101(1); rule 103.
41 Rule 22(1) - (5).
42 Rule 107.
43 Rule 112.
44 Rule 114(1) - (4).
45 Rule 116(1).

assent to it or refuse and return it to the speaker with suggestions that parliament should reconsider the whole bill or a specific provision(s) of it.[46] The Rules contain safeguards against undue pressure from the executive. For example, where the president: (a) refuses to assent to a bill twice; or (b) returns the bill twice; or (c) refuses to assent to the bill within 30 days without returning it to parliament, the speaker shall cause the bill to be laid before parliament, and the bill shall become law without the assent of the president.[47]

In addition to government legislation, a member of parliament may move a private member's bill.[48] A member moving such a bill shall be afforded reasonable assistance by the relevant government department whose area of operation is affected by the bill.[49] The bill shall be introduced by way of motion, and if the motion is passed, the bill shall be published.[50] Upon publication, the procedure to be followed shall be like that of the government bill outlined above. An example of legislation that was introduced by a member of parliament and supported by government is the Prevention of Female Genital Mutilation Act,[51] which is critical for women's health. Female genital mutilation (FGM) has severe consequences for women's physical and mental health. According to the WHO, the immediate consequences include severe pain, shock, haemorrhage or bleeding, tetanus or sepsis or bacterial infection, urine retention, open sores in the genital area and injury to nearby genital tissue. The long term consequences include: recurrent long term bladder and urinary tract infections, cysts, infertility, an increased risk of childbirth complications and new-born deaths and the need for later surgeries.[52] Thus, once passed by parliament, the bills are known as Acts of Parliament and while they are under discussion by parliament, they are called bills. All Acts of Parliament must not contravene the Constitution.

1.3.3 Subsidiary legislation

Subsidiary or secondary legislation, which is also at times called delegated legislation, means any regulation, rule, proclamation, notice, bye-law, or other instrument made by virtue of or under the authority of the Constitution or parliament. Examples of health related regulations include the National Environment (Noise Standards and Control) Regulations of 2003, which recognise noise as a public health problem and recommend

46 Rule 127(1).
47 Rule 127(10) (a) - (c).
48 See also rule 105(1).
49 Rule 105(2).
50 Rule 106(1) & (3).
51 Acts Supplement 3 of 2010.
52 See WHO 'Female genital mutilation' http://www.who.int/mediacentre/factsheets/fs241/en/ (accessed 1 March 2014). See also African Women.Org 'Consequences of FGM' http://www.africa-women.org/FGM/consequences.php (accessed 1 March 2014).

different permissible noise levels for day and night, and the National Environment (Control of Smoking in Public Places) Regulations of 2004, which regulate smoking in public places. Thus, subsidiary legislation is the law brought into operation by authorities, persons or bodies other than parliament.

Subsidiary legislation has a number of advantages. Although parliament has the authority to pass laws, it is a very busy institution: it only has the time to discuss the bill before it thereby leaving procedural and other subordinate matters to ministers and their departments. In any case, the subject matter of most modern legislation is highly technical and may not be included in a bill to be discussed in Parliament. Delegation to ministers enables them to consult technical and expert advisors and relevant stakeholders while the regulations are at the draft stage. Another advantage of subsidiary legislation is that it is flexible: changes can be made from time to time in the light of contingencies and local conditions without the necessity of amending the Act of Parliament. In case of an emergency such as an outbreak of a new disease, Parliament does not have time to sit and pass a bill introduced by the Minister responsible for health to stop, control or manage the disease. In such circumstances, the Minster is empowered to make regulations to deal with the emergency. In fact, most health-related statutes contain a provision empowering the relevant minister to make regulations for attaining the objectives of the particular law.

It should be pointed out that Uganda follows a decentralised system of government where the exercise of legislative power in certain areas is shared between central and local governments. The powers of local governments to make laws are derived from the Constitution and were operationalised by the Local Government Act.[53] Local governments have powers to make laws, which are not inconsistent with the Constitution and any other national laws in the areas that have been decentralised such as agriculture, education and health care.[54] Thus, local governments may pass bye-laws or regulations for the promotion of health in their jurisdiction. Like with principal legislation, all subsidiary legislation must conform to the Constitution.

53 Cap 243.

54 See secs 38(1) and 39 of the Local Government Act, Cap 243, which empower district and local councils to make laws which are consistent with the Constitution and laws made by Parliament.

1.3.4 International human rights law

Treaty based law

Uganda is a party to many treaties, which are rich sources of health law. The most significant of these is the International Covenant on Economic, Social and Cultural Rights (CESCR),[55] which provides for the right to the highest attainable standard of physical and mental health.[56] Another important source of health law, especially in relation to women's health is the Convention on the Elimination of all Forms of Discrimination against Women (CEDAW).[57] Other treaties, which contain provisions critical for the protection of health include the Convention on the Rights of the Child (CRC),[58] the Convention on the Rights of Persons with Disabilities (CRPWD),[59] the African Charter on Human and Peoples' Rights (ACHPR),[60] the African Charter on the Rights and Welfare of the Child (ACRWC),[61] and the Protocol to the African Charter on Human and Peoples' Rights on the Rights of Women in Africa (Women's Protocol).[62]

Another important source of health law at the regional level is the Treaty for the Establishment of the East African Community (EAC),[63] which enjoins partner states to co-operate in the area of health.[64] According to the treaty, the states undertook, amongst other things, to co-operate in the areas of the prevention and control of communicable and non-communicable diseases, management of health delivery systems, drug polices, harmonisation of national health policies, exchange of information, and promotion of research.[65] A number of initiatives have also been developed in the area of health such as the East African Community HIV and AIDS Prevention and Management Act, 2012. The EAC has also developed a policy to guide partner states on how their national intellectual property legislation can be adjusted in order to enable them to fully utilise the public health-related World Trade Organization

55 UN Doc A/6316(1966), 993 UNTS 3, entered into force 3 January 1976.
56 Art 12(1) of the CESCR.
57 1249 UNTS 13 http://www.refworld.org/docid/3ae6b3970.html (accessed 1 March 2014).
58 1577 UNTS 3 http://www.refworld.org/docid/3ae6b38f0.html (accessed 1 March 2014).
59 GA res 61/106 of 13 December 2006; A/RES/61/106, Annex 1http://www.refworld.org/docid/4680cd212.html (accessed 1 March 2014).
60 CAB/LEG/67/3 rev 5, 21 ILM 58 (1982) http://www.refworld.org/docid/3ae6b3630.html (accessed 1 March 2014).
61 CAB/LEG/24.9149 (1990) http://www.refworld.org/doid/3ae6b38c18.html (accessed 1 March 2014).
62 CAB/LEG.66.6 (2000) http://www.unhcr.org/refworld/docid/3f4b139d4.html (accessed 1 March 2014).
63 'Treaty Establishing the East African Community (EAC)' http://www.eac.int (accessed 12 November 2013).
64 Art 118.
65 Art 118(a) - (i).

(WTO) Trade Related Aspects of Intellectual Property Agreement (TRIPS) flexibilities.[66]

'Soft law' instruments

Health law can also be derived from what are known as 'soft law' instruments. These instruments take the form of declarations, resolutions, charters, codes, recommendations and guidelines. Over the years, soft law instruments have played an important role in international law-making in various fields such as environmental law, health and human rights. Unlike 'hard law' instruments such as treaties, soft law instruments have been said not to be legally binding.[67] However, they have a number of advantages, which largely revolve on their flexibility, adaptability, speed and simplicity.[68]

Soft law instruments allow states to gradually become familiar with the proposed standards in the instrument before they are confronted with the adoption of enforceable rules at the international or national levels. States are usually reluctant to give away part of their sovereignty in legally enforceable agreements whose breach may lead to the imposition of sanctions. Soft law instruments differ from the so-called hard law instruments because they do not undergo the rigorous process of ratification by states. The instruments can easily be employed to address environmental or health problems, whose deleterious consequences for human health should be handled expeditiously rather than waiting for the lengthy process of ratification and amendment. The use of these instruments helps to promote legislative responses to emerging challenges, which may not wait for the more elaborate and lengthy processes of treaty law-making. They play a significant role in filling gaps in existing treaty law and in interpreting particular treaty provisions.[69]

It should be noted that although soft law instruments may not be legally binding as such, they may have such effect in the long run. Where the norms in soft law instruments such as the Universal Declaration of

66 'EAC Regional intellectual property policy on the utilization of public health-related WTO-TRIPS flexibilities and the approximation of national intellectual property legislation' http://www.cehurd.org/wp-content/uploads/downloads/2013/05/EAC-TRIPS-Policy.pdf (accessed 20 February 2014).

67 See D Shelton 'Soft law' in D Armstrong (ed) *Handbook of international law* (2008) 68; H Hartmut 'A fresh look at soft law' (1999) 3 *European Journal of International law* 499; A Boyle 'Some reflections on the relationship of treaties and soft law'(1999) 48 *International and Comparative Law Quarterly* 901.

68 As above.

69 On the role of soft law in responding to the deleterious health consequences of depletion of the ozone layer, see eg BK Twinomugisha 'The development of the law relating to the protection of the ozone layer with particular reference to the position of developing countries' unpublished LLM thesis, Makerere University, 1996 80.

Human Rights (Universal Declaration) and Siracusa Principles[70] have been subjected to intensive state practice, they have become part of customary international law, which is directly binding on states.[71] The UN Guidelines on HIV and AIDS have influenced the development of HIV/AIDS related legislative and policy frameworks in many countries. The WHO, which was created in 1948 by member states of the UN as a specialised agency with various responsibilities and functions in the field of health, including assisting governments in strengthening health services and the development of international conventions and agreements on health matters, has also developed a number of instruments to promote public health.[72] For example, instruments such as the 1978 WHO Primary Health Care Declaration of Alma Ata and resolutions of the World Health Assembly (WHA)[73] have guided countries in the development of legal and policy frameworks in the area of health promotion and protection. The African Union has also developed a number of instruments such as the Abuja Declaration on HIV/AIDS, Tuberculosis and other Related Infectious Diseases,[74] and the Libreville Declaration on Health and Environment in Africa.[75] The European Union has also used soft law instruments in health policy making and implementation.[76] Thus, the influence of norms created by soft law instruments on state behaviour in matters of health ought not to be underestimated.

The legal status of international law

Before leaving the question of international law as a source of health law, it is necessary to comment on its legal status in Uganda. The Judicature Act[77] does not recognise international law as a source of law. Yet, as illustrated above, critical aspects for the protection of health such as health

70 The Siracusa Principles on the Limitation and Derogation Provisions in the International Covenant on Civil and Political Rights, E/CN.4/1985/4 http://www.umn.edu/humrts/instree/siracusprinicples.html (accessed 1 March 2014). The application of these principles in the context of public health is discussed in Chapter 5.

71 On custom as a source of law as a result of intensive state practice, see art 38 of the International Court of Justice (ICJ) Statute http://www.icj-cij.org/documents/index.php.pl+4&p2+2=p3+0& (accessed 10 September 2013).

72 On the mandate of the WHO see art 2 of the Constitution of the World Health Organisation, adopted by the World Health Conference held in New York from 19 June to 22 July 1946. WHO operations are executed by three organs: the World Health Assembly, the Executive Board, and the Secretariat. According to art 4, membership of the WHO is open to all states.

73 See eg WHO 'International code of marketing of breast milk substitutes' WHA 57.17 (21 May 1981); WHO 'Global strategy on diet, physical activity and health' WHA 57.17 (22 May 2004).

74 For the Abuja Declaration, see http://www.un.org/ga/aids/pdf/abuja-decration.pdf (accessed 19 March 2015).

75 For the Libreville Declaration, see, http://www.idrc.ca/EN/Documents/LibrevilleDeclarationEN.pdf (accessed 19 March 2015).

76 For a discussion of the use of soft law in the field health in the European Union, see SL Greer & B Vanherke 'The hard politics of soft law: The case of health' http://www.euro.eho.int_data/assets/pdf_file/0004/138154/E94886_ch04.pdf (accessed 19 March 2015).

77 Cap 213.

rights are contained in international instruments. So, the question is: what is the legal status of international law in Uganda? For a treaty to be applicable in Uganda, it should be ratified in accordance with the Ratification of Treaties Act.[78] Some commentators have argued that in addition to ratification, the treaty should be domesticated by an Act of Parliament.[79] Others are of the view that through signing and ratification, the state is bound by the treaty. For example, Tumwine-Mukubwa is of the view that once a treaty is ratified, it is sufficient if it is laid on the table of parliament.[80] He argues that this position is fortified by the Constitution, which provides that the foreign policy of Uganda shall be based on amongst other things, respect for international law and treaty obligations.[81]

Courts in Uganda have used international law as a guide to the interpretation of the Constitution. For example, in *Tinyefuza v Attorney General*,[82] Egonda-Ntende J observed that court may use international instruments in the interpretation of the Constitution. In *Charles Onyango Obbo & Another v Attorney General*,[83] the court referred to various international instruments such as the European Convention of Human Rights in finding that section 50 of the Penal Code Act, which criminalises publication of false news, is unconstitutional since it infringed article 29 of the 1995 Constitution on freedom of expression. In *Col (Rtd) Dr Kiiza Besigye v Yoweri Museveni Kaguta*,[84] the Supreme Court applied the principles enshrined in articles 21 and 25 of the Universal Declaration and the International Covenant on Civil and Political Rights (ICCPR) respectively. In *Attorney General v Susan Kigula & 417 Others*,[85] the court made extensive reference to international instruments such as the Universal Declaration, ICCPR, ACHPR as a guide to the interpretation of the right to life.

From the above analysis, it may be concluded that the government must comply with the obligations in health related treaties to which it is a party. Like other states parties, Uganda is presumed to have willingly signed and ratified these treaties and should therefore be bound by the obligations therein. These treaties are part of Ugandan law and serve as a guide to the interpretation of the Constitution. However, like national legislation, they are subsidiary to the Constitution, which is the supreme law of Uganda.

78 Cap 204.
79 See B Kabumba 'The application of international law in the Ugandan judicial system: A critical inquiry' in M Killander (ed) *International law and domestic human rights litigation in Africa* (2010) 83.
80 GP Mukubwa 'International human rights norms in the domestic arena' (1997) *East African Journal of Peace and Human Rights* 33.
81 NODPSP XXVIII(i)(b).
82 Constitutional Petition 1/1996.
83 Constitutional Petition 2/2002.
84 Election Petition 1/2001.
85 Constitutional Appeal 3/2006.

1.3.5 Common law and equity

Common law and equity are principles of English law applied in Uganda to supplement the existing written law. Common law is that part of English law based on the concept of *stare decisis*, which literally means to stand by decisions and not to disturb what has been settled. The concept means that a judicial decision has established a precedent. Where a court of competent jurisdiction has decided a controversy and has in a written opinion, set forth the rule or principle that formed the basis of its decision, that rule or decision will be followed by the court in deciding subsequent cases. Subordinate courts will be bound by the rule set forth in the decision. In Uganda, the superior courts of record set precedents. Decisions by the Supreme Court are binding on all lower courts[86] including the Court of Appeal while those of the Court of Appeal are binding on the High Court and all subordinate courts.

Equity refers to the expressions of values that promote fairness, justice and reasonableness in social relations. Equity developed to address the unfairness and inadequacies in the application of common law. According to the Judicature Act, common law and doctrines of equity shall be applied in the administration of justice in Uganda 'only insofar as the circumstances of Uganda and of its people permit, and subject to such qualifications as circumstances may render necessary'.[87] As shall be illustrated in this book, most if not all case law on health related issues in Uganda especially on the doctor-patient relationship have a foundation in common law and doctrines of equity.

1.3.6 Customary law

There is no single definition of customary law agreed upon by lawyers, jurists, and anthropologists.[88] Customary laws are derived from the morals, values, and traditions of indigenous ethnic groups. These norms and values have passed on from one generation to the next. Customary law includes customs and traditions of the people, which play a crucial role in shaping their culture. Culture encompasses a system of beliefs, languages, and laws that give individuals their unique character.[89] Accordingly, customary law in Uganda has been defined as

86 Art 132(4) of the Constitution provides as follows: 'The Supreme Court may, while treating its own previous decisions as normally binding, depart from a previous decision when it appears to it right to do so; and all other courts shall be bound to follow the decisions of the Supreme Court on questions of law'.

87 Sec 14(2)(b)(i) & (3) of the Judicature Act. See also sec 11(1) of the Magistrates Courts Act, Cap 16.

88 On the difficulties of defining customary law, see CMN White 'African customary law: The problem of concept and definition' (1965) 9 *Journal of African Law* 86.

89 BK Twinomugisha 'African customary law and women's human rights in Uganda' in J Fenrich et al *The future of African customary law* (2011).

> a rule or set of rules, established, accepted and binding on the members of a given society in their social relations. Customary law may exist and operate on its own or side by side or complementary to another different nature of law.[90]

Customary law refers to rules of conduct which govern relationships as established by custom or usage and which do not form part of the common law or laws enacted by Parliament or other written law.[91]

Customary law represents law that originates with the people in the most direct sense. The customary law system gives a sense of ownership to the people who subscribe to it. Customary law is largely unwritten and its validity is mainly a question of social practice to be tested by social observation. It should be noted that customary law in Uganda is not uniform. Uganda has diverse ethnic and social groupings, with a wide range of customary laws and practices that they ascribe to and which may influence their health care seeking behaviour. For example, traditional medicine, which is largely governed by cultural values and practices and serves the health needs of communities in Uganda, may be administered alongside some aspects of modern or conventional health care services.

One advantage of customary law is that it is flexible and changes with time and circumstances. Customary law itself and the culture in which it is based are not static; it is influenced by the evolution of the social, economic, and political conditions in which it operates. For instance, for a long time, the provision of maternal health care services in rural areas was exclusively handled by traditional birth attendants (TBAs) in accordance with the customary values and practices of the society where the pregnant women lived. However, with the emergence of modern medicine and increased formal education, although many women still utilise the services of TBAs for economic and cultural reasons, they also visit modern health centres for antenatal, labour and delivery care in order to avoid complications.

According to the Judicature Act, the High Court shall have power to enforce 'any existing custom, which is not repugnant to natural justice, equity and good conscience and not incompatible either directly or by necessary implication with any written law'.[92] Most importantly, customary legal systems relevant for health must conform to the Constitution, which promotes only positive customary norms, values and

90 JMN Kakooza 'The application of customary law in Uganda' (2003) 1 *Uganda Living Law Journal* 23.
91 As above.
92 Sec 15(1) of the Judicature Act, Cap 13.

practices that do not for example undermine human rights, including equality and non-discrimination.[93]

1.4 Policy frameworks

Uganda has many policy frameworks in the area of health for example, the National Health Policy,[94] the HIV/AIDS Strategic Plan,[95] and the Health Sector Strategic Plan (HSSP).[96] The HSSP recognises health as a fundamental human right and lays down administrative strategies through which health rights may be achieved. Although technically these frameworks are not sources of law as such and are not legally binding, they contain benchmarks, standards and targets against which the performance of government in the area of health may be measured. In any case, although legislative measures and case law may be apposite for the realisation of health rights, international human rights law recognises the important role played by administrative measures, including policy frameworks.[97]

In some jurisdictions, the courts have referred to relevant policy frameworks as part of the socio-economic context in which a particular law was developed. For example in the Kenyan case of *Patricia Asero Ochieng & Others v The Attorney-General & Another*,[98] in which it was held that sections 2, 32 and 34 of the Anti-Counterfeit Act, 2008 violated the fundamental rights to life, human dignity and health guaranteed under the 2010 Kenyan Constitution in so far as the sections affected access to affordable and essential drugs and medication particularly generic drugs, the High Court directly referred to the Kenya National AIDS Strategic Plan 2004-2009, the 2010 Country Report to the United Nations General Assembly Special Session on HIV and AIDS, the 2007 Kenya AIDS indicators Survey and the 2010 Kenyan National HIV and AIDS Estimates.

1.5 Chapter synopsis

The book is divided into ten chapters. Chapter 1 is the introduction, which provides the contextual foundation for the book by mapping out the health law: nature and scope in Uganda. The sources include the Constitution, principal and subsidiary legislation, common law and

93 See Twinomugisha (n 89 above); S Tamale 'The right to culture and the culture of rights: A critical perspective on women's sexual rights in Africa' (2008) 16 *Feminist Legal Studies* 47.
94 Republic of Uganda *National health policy* (2010).
95 Republic of Uganda *National strategic plan for HIV/AIDS 2011/12-2014/15* (2012).
96 Republic of Uganda *Heath sector strategic plan* 2010/11-2014/15 (2010).
97 See for example para 1 of UN Committee on Economic, Social and Cultural Rights (Committee on ESCR) General Comment 9: 'The domestic application of the covenant' (Nineteenth Session, 1998), UN Doc E/C.12/1998/24 (1998).
98 Petition 409/2009 (High Court of Kenya).

equity, treaty based law, soft law instruments, and customary law. Chapter 2 maps out the nature, scope and content of the right to health at the international, regional and domestic levels and Uganda's obligations to realise the said right. Chapter 3 examines some of the major challenges to realisation of the right to health in Uganda, thereby laying a foundation for Chapter 4, which looks at possible strategies for realising the right in question. Chapter 5 looks at the meaning of public health and the role of law in its protection. With the aid of comparative case law, the chapter proceeds to examine existing public health legislation with the view of determining its potential to meet the challenges of public health without unnecessarily burdening human rights. Chapter 6 looks at the mental health situation in Uganda and maps out the scope of protection of mental health rights at the international, regional and domestic levels.

Chapter 7 examines legislative and ethical frameworks regulating health professionals in order to find out whether they adequately govern the training, practice, conduct and discipline of these professionals in light of the requirements of modern health practice. Chapter 8 examines the basis on which health professionals may be held accountable through litigation. Chapter 9 specifically discusses patients' rights and the question of capacity to consent to or refuse treatment. Chapter 10 examines legal and administrative frameworks, which govern research involving humans as participants. The chapter considers the mechanisms available for the scrutiny of this type of research with the view of finding out the extent to which they address the inherent risks and burdens for research participants. The chapter looks at how the mechanisms address questions of informed consent, fraudulent research, compensation and the general question of accountability of researchers and sponsors.

2

THE FUNDAMENTAL RIGHT TO HEALTH

1 Introduction

In the previous chapter, I explained that legal and policy frameworks play a critical role in the promotion of health. I also noted that the right to health has been recognised in a number of international and regional instruments. The need for legal recognition of a right need not be over emphasised. By legally recognising health as a right, legal instruments view good health not merely as a need but an entitlement, denial of which may attract accountability of state and non-state actors.

The WHO was the first international instrument to explicitly recognise the right to health. Its Constitution affirms that 'the enjoyment of the highest attainable standard of health is one of the fundamental rights of every human being without distinction of race, religion, political belief, economic or social condition'.[1] Over the years, the right has been reiterated in various international and regional human rights instruments, such as the Universal Declaration,[2] the American Declaration on the Rights and Duties of Man,[3] European Social Charter,[4] CESCR,[5] CEDAW,[6] CRC,[7] CRPD,[8] ACHPR,[9] ACRWC,[10] and Women's Protocol to the ACHPR.[11] As pointed out in the previous chapter, Uganda is a party to some of these human rights instruments that provide for the

1 Preamble.
2 Art 25.
3 Art 33.
4 Art 11.
5 Art 12.
6 Art 12 & 14.
7 Art 24.
8 Art 25.
9 Art 16.
10 Art 14.
11 Art 14.

right to health.[12] The Ugandan Constitution also contains provisions that have a bearing on this right. There are also health related policy frameworks aimed at ensuring that citizens enjoy good health.[13] Against this backdrop, this chapter provides an overview of the nature, scope and content of the right to health at the international, regional and domestic levels and Uganda's obligations to realise the said right.

2 The normative content of the right to health

2.1 The right to health at the international level

The Universal Declaration entitles everyone to the enjoyment of economic, civil, social, political and cultural rights and affirms various health related components.[14] According to the Universal Declaration,

> [e]veryone has the right to a standard of living adequate for the health of himself and of his family, including food, clothing, housing and medical care and necessary social services, and the right to security in the event of unemployment, sickness, disability, widowhood, old age or other lack of livelihood in circumstances beyond his control.[15]

According to the Universal Declaration, '[m]otherhood and childhood are entitled to special care and assistance'.[16] It guarantees everyone the right to life,[17] liberty and security of the person,[18] and stresses non-discrimination in the enjoyment of the rights set forth in the Declaration.[19] The norms in the Universal Declaration have been subjected to intensive state practice and may be said to be part of international customary law with direct application to nations, including Uganda.[20] As Kinney has observed,

> [c]ustomary international law holds promise as an important source of international law with respect to human rights. International customary law is interesting for it can legally bind nations regardless of treaty ratification … Customary international law is promising when it comes to establishing a binding international human right to health in the nations of the world.[21]

12 Uganda ratified CESCR, 993 UNTS 3 on 21 January 1987; ICCPR 999 UNTS 171 on 21 June 1995; CEDAW1240 UNTS 13 on 22 July 1985; CRC1577 UNTS 3 on 16 September 1990; ACHPR on 10 May 1986; the CRPD on 25 September 2008; and the Women's Protocol on 22 July 2010.

13 See for example Ministry of Health *Health sector strategic plan, 2010/11-14* (2010).

14 Art 25(1) of the Universal Declaration.

15 As above.

16 Art 25(2).

17 Art 3.

18 As above.

19 Art 2.

20 See S Bruno & P Alston 'The source of human rights law: Custom, jus cogens, and general principles' (1992) 12 *Australian Law Book of International Law* 82.

21 ED Kinney 'The international human right to health: What does this mean for our nation and world?' (2001) 34 *Indiana Law Review* 1457 1468.

The CESCR, which provides for the 'right of everyone to the highest attainable standard of physical and mental health',[22] outlines the following steps to be taken by state parties to achieve the full realisation of this right:

- The provision for the reduction of the still birth rate and infant mortality and for the health development of the child;
- The improvement of all aspects of environmental and industrial hygiene;
- The prevention, treatment and control of epidemic, occupational and other diseases; and
- The creation of conditions which would assure to all medical service and medical attention in the event of sickness.[23]

Emphasising the interdependence and indivisibility of rights, the UN Committee on Economic, Social and Cultural Rights (Committee on ESCR), which monitors state compliance with the CESCR, has elaborated on this right and noted that '[h]ealth is a fundamental human right indispensable for the exercise of other human rights'.[24] On the interdependence of health and other human rights, it has observed as follows:

> The right to health is closely related to and dependent upon the realization of other human rights, as contained in the International Bill of Rights, including the rights to food, housing, work, education, human dignity, life, non-discrimination, equality, the prohibition against torture, privacy, access to information, and the freedoms of association, assembly and movement.[25]

The right contains a number of interrelated and essential elements: availability and accessibility, which includes physical, economic and information accessibility; and acceptability and quality of health facilities, goods and services.[26] In this vein, public health and health-care facilities, goods and services, including safe and potable drinking water and adequate sanitation facilities, hospitals, clinics, essential drugs, and well remunerated health personnel, should be available in sufficient quantity.[27] The health facilities, goods and services should be physically and economically accessible to everyone without discrimination within the country.[28] There should also be information about these facilities, goods and services.[29] Accessibility also requires that people should have 'the right to seek, receive and impart information concerning health issues'.[30] Health facilities, goods and services must be respectful of medical ethics

22 Art 12.
23 Art 12(2)(a) - (d).
24 Committee on ESCR General Comment 14: 'The right to the highest standard of physical and mental health' HRI/GEN/1/Rev 9 (Vol I) (2000) para 1.
25 Para 3.
26 Para 12(a) - (d).
27 Para 12(a).
28 Para 12(b).
29 As above.
30 As above.

and culturally appropriate.[31] The facilities, goods and services must also be scientifically and medically appropriate and of good quality.[32]

Like with other human rights, the state has three types of obligations: to respect, protect and fulfil the right to health.[33] The obligation to respect requires the state to refrain from interfering directly or indirectly with the enjoyment of the right. This obligation requires the state, amongst other things, to abstain 'from imposing discriminatory practices relating to women's health status and needs'[34] and 'to refrain from prohibiting or impeding traditional preventive care, healing practices and medicines'.[35] The obligation to protect requires the state to take measures that prevent third parties from interfering with the enjoyment of the right. The state should 'adopt legislation or take other measures ensuring access to health care and health-related services provided by third parties'[36] and 'to ensure that privatization of the health sector does not constitute a threat to the availability, accessibility, acceptability and quantity of facilities, goods and services'.[37] The state is also obliged to ensure that harmful social or traditional practices such as female genital mutilation do not interfere with women's access to reproductive health services.[38] The obligation to protect also requires the state to ensure that third parties do not limit people's access to health-related information and services.[39]

Finally, the obligation to fulfil requires the state to adopt appropriate legislative, administrative, budgetary, judicial, promotional and other measures towards the realisation of the right. The state is obliged

> to give sufficient recognition to the right to health in the national political and legal systems, preferably by way of legislative implementation, and to adopt a national health policy with a detailed plan for realizing the right to health.[40]

The obligation to fulfil includes the obligation to facilitate, which requires the state to 'take positive measures that enable and assist individuals and communities to enjoy the right to health'.[41] It also includes the obligation to provide a specific component of the right to health 'when individuals or a group are unable, for reasons beyond their control, to realize that right themselves by means at their disposal'.[42] The obligation to fulfil also

31 Para 12(c).
32 Para 12(d).
33 Para 33. On the typology of human rights obligations, see H Shue *Basic rights: Subsistence, affluence and US foreign policy* (2nd ed, 1996).
34 Para 34.
35 As above.
36 Para 35.
37 As above.
38 As above.
39 As above.
40 Para 36.
41 As above.
42 As above.

requires the state to promote the right to health by undertaking actions that create, maintain and restore the health of the population.[43]

According to the Committee on ESCR, the state's obligations are to be realised progressively in accordance with the available resources.[44] However, the Committee on ESCR has observed that while the CESCR provides for progressive realisation and recognises constraints due to the limits of available resources, there are obligations, which are of immediate effect: the guarantee that the right will be exercised without discrimination of any kind;[45] and the obligation to take steps towards the realisation of the right.[46] The steps must be deliberate, concrete and targeted towards the realisation of the right.[47] The concept of progressive realisation should not be interpreted as depriving the state's obligations of any meaningful content. States have a specific and continuing obligation to move as expeditiously as possible towards the full realisation of the right to health.[48] Retrogressive measures are not permitted unless the state justifies that it took the decision 'after the most careful consideration of all alternatives'.[49]

The Committee on ESCR has also established what are called 'core obligations'. States have a core obligation to ensure the satisfaction of, at the very least, minimum essential levels of the right to health.[50] According to the Committee on ESCR, some of these core obligations include:

- To ensure the right of access to health facilities, goods and services on a non-discriminatory basis, especially for vulnerable and marginalised groups;
- To ensure access to minimum essential food which is nutritionally adequate and safe, to ensure freedom from hunger for everyone;
- To ensure access to basic shelter, housing and sanitation, and an adequate supply of safe and potable water;
- To provide essential drugs, as from time to time defined under the WHO Action Programme on Essential Drugs; and
- To ensure equitable distribution of all health facilities, goods and services.[51]

43 As above.
44 Art 2(1) of CESCR.
45 Article 2(2) of CESCR; para 30 General Comment 14.
46 Article 2(1) of CESCR; para 30 General Comment 14.
47 Para 30.
48 Para 31. See also para 9 General Comment 3.
49 Para 32. See also para 9 General Comment 3.
50 Para 43, quoting General Comment 3 of 1990, where the Committee on ESR noted that states have a core obligation to ensure the satisfaction of, at the very least, minimum essential levels of each of the rights enunciated in the Covenant, including primary health care. CESCR, General Comment 3: 'The nature of states parties' obligations (Art 2 Para 2 of the Covenant)' 14 December 1990 http://www.refworld.org/docid/4358838e10.html (accessed 12 March 2014).
51 Para 43.

Another treaty, which specifically deals with women's human rights and contains provisions with a direct bearing on the right to health, is CEDAW. It obliges states parties to

> take all appropriate measures to eliminate discrimination in the field of health care in order to ensure, on a basis of equality of men and women, access to health care services, including those related to family planning.[52]

The Convention also enjoins state parties to 'ensure to women appropriate services in connection with pregnancy, confinement and the post-natal period, granting free services where necessary, as well as adequate nutrition during pregnancy and lactation'.[53] The Convention urges state parties to pay special attention to rural women and ensure that they amongst other things have 'access to adequate health care facilities, including information, counselling and services in family planning'.[54] The Committee on the Elimination of all forms of Discrimination against Women, which is mandated to interpret CEDAW and to make recommendations to state parties on issues affecting women, has interpreted article 12 of the Convention on women and health[55] and affirmed that access to health care, including reproductive health is a basic human right.[56]

The CRC, which specifically addresses children's rights, guarantees every child the right to the enjoyment of the highest standard of health and to facilities for the treatment and rehabilitation of health.[57] State parties are obliged to take appropriate measures to diminish infant and child mortality and to ensure children access to both preventive and curative health services.[58] The Committee on the Rights of the Child, which is responsible for monitoring implementation of the CRC by the states parties, has interpreted children's right to health and emphasised the fact that the right to health is indispensable to the realisation of other human rights and must be enjoyed without discrimination taking into account the best interests of the child.[59]

The CRPD guarantees persons with disabilities (PWDs) the right to the enjoyment of the highest standard of health without discrimination on the basis of disability.[60] It enjoins state parties to take all appropriate measures to ensure access for PWDs to health services that are gender sensitive, including health related information.[61]

52 Art 12(1) CEDAW.
53 Art 12(2).
54 Art 14(2)(b).
55 General Recommendation 24.
56 Para 1.
57 Art 24(1) CRC.
58 Art 24(2)(a) - (f).
59 General Comment 15.
60 Art 25 CRPD.
61 Art 25(a) - (b).

2.2 The right to health at the regional level

At the regional level, the ACHPR guarantees the right to the best attainable state of physical and mental health.[62] The ACHPR obliges state parties to 'take the necessary measures to protect the health of their people and to ensure that they receive medical attention when they are sick'.[63] The African Commission has, pursuant to its mandate under the ACHPR, which authorises it to 'formulate and lay down principles and rules aimed at solving legal problems relating to human rights',[64] developed General Comments, resolutions[65] to assist states parties to fulfil their obligations in respect of the right to health.[66] For example, the African Commission has observed that women and young girls are disproportionately affected by HIV due to multiple forms of discrimination such as sex, sexuality, sexual orientation, age, pregnancy, marital status, and socio-economic status.[67] The African Commission has affirmed that women in Africa have the right to health, which includes sexual and reproductive health and rights.[68] The Commission has called upon states parties to create enabling and supportive environments that empower women to be in a position to fully and effectively realise their right to self-protection and to be protected from HIV.[69] The Commission also stressed women's right to be informed of their health status, including providing information about their health.[70]

In a number of decisions, the African Commission has also elaborated on the normative framework of the right to health under the ACHPR. For example, in the *Free Legal Assistance Group* case,[71] the African Commission stated that the failure by the Government to provide basic services, such as safe drinking water and electricity, and the shortage of medicine amounts to a violation of the right to health under the ACHPR.[72] In *Sudan Human Rights Organisation and Another v Sudan*,[73] the African Commission stated that the right to health extends not only to timely and appropriate health care services but also to the underlying determinants of health such as access to safe and portable water, an adequate supply of safe food and

62 Art 16(1) ACHPR. Unlike CESCR, ACHPR does not qualify economic, social and cultural rights such as the right to health with respect to progressive realisation and resource constraints.
63 Art 16(2).
64 Art 45(1).
65 See for example Resolution on access to health and needed medicines in Africa' ACHPR/Res141 (XXXXIIII) 08; and Resolution on maternal mortality in Africa ACH[R/Res 135 (XXXXIIII) 08.
66 On the role of the African Commission in the interpretation of the right to health, see E Durojaye 'The approaches of the African Commission to the right to health under the African Charter' (2013) 17 *Law, Democracy and Development* 393.
67 General Comment on Art 14(1)(d) & (e) of the Protocol to the African Charter on the Rights of Women in Africa, para 5.
68 As above.
69 Para 10.
70 Para 13.
71 (2000) AHRLR 74 (ACHPR 1995).
72 Art 16.
73 (2000) AHRLR 153 (ACHPR 2009).

nutrition. In *Purohit & Another v The Gambia*,[74] the African Commission also observed that the right to health is crucial to the realisation of all human rights and freedoms.

The African Charter on the Rights and Welfare of the Child (ACRWC) guarantees every child the right to enjoy the best attainable state of physical, mental and spiritual health.[75] State parties are obliged to take measures to reduce infant and child mortality rates in addition to provision of appropriate health care for pregnant women and nursing mothers.[76]

In addition to providing for other rights such as non-discrimination,[77] human dignity,[78] life, integrity and security of the person,[79] the Women's Protocol, which is the only treaty that specifically deals with African women's human rights, obliges state parties to ensure women's right to health, including sexual and reproductive health rights (SRHR).[80] Women are also guaranteed the right to a healthy and sustainable environment.[81] According to the African Commission, women's health should be interpreted as per the definition of the WHO, as a state of physical, mental and social well-being and not merely the absence of disease or infirmity.[82] The SRHR include the right to control one's fertility, the right to decide whether to have children, the number and spacing of children, and the right to choose any method of contraception.[83] State parties are enjoined to take appropriate measures to, amongst other things, provide adequate, affordable and accessible health services including information, education and communication programmes especially for women in rural areas.[84] The African Commission has pointed out that these provisions 'are inextricably linked, interdependent and indivisible'[85] and thus should be interpreted broadly, taking into account other 'cross-cutting issues of women's human rights, including the right not to be discriminated against, the right to dignity, the right to integrity and security, access to justice and the right to education'.[86] In this vein, the African Commission has observed as follows:

74 (2003) AHRLR 96 (ACHPR 2003). For a detailed consideration in respect of mental health, see, Chapter 6 below.
75 Art 14(1) ACRWC.
76 Art 14(2).
77 Art 2.
78 Art 3.
79 Art 4.
80 Art 14(1). The African Commission on Human and Peoples' Rights has passed two General Comments. The first comment is on art 14(1)(d) and (e) on women's health, including their health status in the context of HIV. General Comment 2 is on art 14(1)(a), (b), (c) & (f) of the Protocol.
81 Art 18.
82 Para 7 & 38 General Comment 2.
83 Art 14(1)(a) - (g).
84 Art 14(1)(a) - (c).
85 Para 23 General Comment 2.
86 General Comment 2 (n 80 above) para 11.

> The right to dignity enshrines the freedom to make personal decisions without interference from the state or non-state actors. The woman's right to make personal decisions involves taking into account or not the beliefs, traditions, values and cultural or religious practices, and the right to question or to ignore them.[87]

The Women's Protocol is the first treaty to recognise legal and safe abortion under certain circumstances as a woman's human right, which she should enjoy without fear of prosecution. In this regard, state parties are enjoined to take all appropriate measures to

> protect the reproductive rights of women by authorizing medical abortion in cases of sexual assault, rape, incest, and where the continued pregnancy endangers the mental and physical health of the mother or the life of the mother or the foetus.[88]

According to the African Commission, women should be informed of safe abortion related products, procedures and health services.[89] Women's right to be free from discrimination, which is guaranteed under the Protocol also means that

> [they] must not be subjected to criminal proceedings and should not incur any legal sanctions for having benefited from health services that are reserved to them such as abortion and post abortion care. Furthermore, it entails that the health personnel should not fear neither prosecution nor disciplinary reprisal or others for providing these services, in the cases provided in the Protocol.[90]

State parties should ensure that women who seek reproductive health services such as family planning or safe abortion and post abortion care 'are not treated in an inhuman, cruel or degrading manner',[91] since the ACHPR prohibits cruel, inhuman and degrading treatment.[92] In any case, forcing a woman to keep a pregnancy resulting from sexual assault, rape or incest 'constitutes additional trauma which affects her physical and mental health'.[93]

2.3 The right to health at the domestic level

The right to health is not explicitly provided for in the Bill of Rights of the Constitution of the Republic of Uganda. However, it contains a number of provisions with a bearing on health. The Constitution enjoins the state to promote the social well-being of the people and in particular to ensure that all Ugandans enjoy rights and opportunities and access, amongst other

87 General Comment 2 (n 80 above) para 24.
88 Art 14(2)(c).
89 General Comment 2 (n 80 above) para 31.
90 General Comment 2 (n 80 above) para 32.
91 Para 36.
92 Art 5.
93 Para 37.

things, to education, health services, clean and safe water, food security and adequate housing.[94] The state is also enjoined to take all practical measures 'to ensure the provision of basic medical services to the population'[95] and 'to promote a good water management system at all levels'.[96] The Constitution also urges the state to 'encourage and promote proper nutrition through mass education and other appropriate means in order to build a healthy State'.[97] The state shall also take all possible measures to prevent or minimise damage and destruction resulting from pollution.[98]

It is arguable whether the National Objectives and Directive Principles of State Policy (NODPSP) in the Constitution are justiciable since they do not appear in the main body of the Constitution, especially the Bill of Rights. The Constitution simply provides that the NODPSP

> shall guide all organs and agencies of the State, all citizens, organizations and other bodies and persons in applying or interpreting the Constitution or any other law and in taking and implementing any policy decisions for the establishment of a just, free and democratic society.[99]

In *Zachary Olum & Another v Attorney-General*,[100] the court observed that although the NODPSP form an important part of the Constitution and are crucial canons in the interpretation of the Constitution, they are not justiciable. In *Tinyefuza v Attorney-General*,[101] although Egonda Ntende J observed that the NODPSP should guide all organs of the state including the judiciary in the interpretation of the Constitution, he fell short of saying that these objectives and directives are by themselves legally binding.

Through the 2005 constitutional amendments, a new article on national interest was introduced in the main body of the Constitution and it states as follows: 'Uganda shall be governed based on principles of national interest and common good enshrined in the national objectives and directive principles of state policy'.[102] The question is: does this clause render the NODPSP legally enforceable? Though some commentators such as Mbazira,[103] have argued that this provision renders the NODPSP justiciable, clause 2 requires Parliament to 'make laws for purposes of

94 National Objective and Directive Principle of State Policy (NODPSP) XIV of the Constitution.
95 NODPSP XX.
96 NODPSP XXI.
97 NODPSP XXII(c).
98 NODPSP XXVII(ii).
99 NODPSP I.
100 Constitutional Petition 6/1999.
101 Constitutional Petition 1/1996.
102 Art 8A(1).
103 C Mbazira 'Public interest litigation and judicial activism in Uganda: Improving the enforcement of economic, social and cultural rights' HURIPEC Working Paper (2008) 9.

giving full effect to clause (1) of this Article'.[104] Since Parliament has not made any law to this effect, it makes the situation a bit unclear and fluid.

In some jurisdictions, however, Directive Principles of State Policy (DPSP) have been creatively interpreted in order to achieve the ends of social justice. For example, in India, although article 37 of the Constitution explicitly declares that the DPSP shall not be enforceable by any court, the courts have, through a bold and creative interpretation, applied these principles. In *Keshavananda Bharati v State of Kerala*,[105] the Supreme Court stated that although article 37 of the Indian Constitution expressly provides that the DPSP are not enforceable by any court, they should enjoy the same status as traditional fundamental rights.

The Constitution contains a number of human rights and freedoms, which are critical for the protection of the right to health, given the interdependence, indivisibility and interrelationship of human rights. These include equality and freedom from discrimination,[106] the right to life,[107] respect for human dignity and 'prevention from torture or cruel, inhuman or degrading treatment or punishment'.[108] Others include the right to education,[109] rights of women,[110] children rights,[111] rights of minorities,[112] participation in the affairs of government,[113] the right to a clean and healthy environment,[114] economic rights,[115] and the right of access to information.[116]

There has been an expansive interpretation of the right to life in a number of jurisdictions. For example, in the Ugandan case of *Abuki & Another v Attorney-General*,[117] the court held that the banishment of the petitioner from his home under the Witchcraft Act, thereby depriving him of shelter, food and essential sustenance, infringed his right to life in light of NODPSP XIV of the Constitution, which enjoins the state to ensure that all Ugandans have access to health services, food and shelter. In the Indian case of *Francis Coralie Mullin v The Administrator, Union Territory of Delhi & Others*,[118] the Supreme Court said that the right to life is

104 Art 8A(2).
105 (1973) 4 SCC 225.
106 Art 21 of the Constitution.
107 Art 22.
108 Art 24.
109 Art 30.
110 Art 33.
111 Art 34.
112 Art 36.
113 Art 38.
114 Art 39.
115 Art 40.
116 Art 41.
117 Constitutional Petition 2/1997.
118 (1981) 2 SCR 516

> the most precious human right ... which forms an ark of all human rights [and] must therefore be interpreted in a broad and expansive spirit ... [It] includes the right to live with human dignity and all that goes along with it, namely, the bare necessities of life such as adequate nutrition, clothing and shelter, [and covers] such functions and activities as constitute the bare minimum expression of the human self.[119]

In another Indian case, *Paschim Banga Khet Samity v State of West Bengal,*[120] the Supreme Court used the right to life to secure the right to emergency medical care and concluded that such an essential obligation could not be avoided by pleading financial constraints. In *Consumer Education and Research Centre v Union of India,*[121] it was held that a worker's right to health forms an integral part of the right to life. In *Villagram Morales & Others v Guatemala,*[122] the Inter-American Court of Human Rights also ruled that the right to life includes more than the mere right of existence, and that it implicates the right to live with dignity.[123] The court found that restrictive approaches to the right to life are inadmissible and that the right includes the right 'not [to] be prevented from having access to the conditions that guarantee a dignified existence'.[124] In *Sudan Human Rights Organisation & Centre on Housing Rights and Evictions (COHRE) v Sudan,*[125] the African Commission observed that the right to life is a basic human right and that the '[t]erm life itself has been given a relatively broad interpretation by courts internationally, to include the right to dignity'[126] and that exposing victims to 'personal suffering and indignity' violates the right to human dignity.[127]

The Human Rights Committee (HRC) has also observed as follows:

> [T]he right to life has been too often narrowly interpreted. The expression 'inherent right to life' cannot properly be understood in a restrictive manner, and the protection of this right requires that states adopt positive measures. In this connection, the Committee considers that it would be desirable for states parties to take all possible measures to reduce infant mortality and to increase life expectancy, especially in adopting measures to eliminate malnutrition and epidemics.[128]

It should be noted that the Constitution contains an inclusive article, which provides as follows:

119 *Francis Coralie Mullin* (n 118 above) 518.
120 (1996) 4 SCC 37
121 (1995) 3 SCC 117 130.
122 ICACHR (19 November 1999) Ser C No 63.
123 *Villagram Morales* (n 122 above) para 139.
124 Para 144.
125 (2009) AHRLR 153 (ACHPR 2009).
126 Para 146.
127 As above.
128 See UN Human Rights Committee (HRC), CCPR General Comment 6, art 6 (Right to Life), 30 April 1982, para 5http://www.refworld.org/docid/45388400a.html (accessed 8 March 2014).

> The rights, duties, declarations and guarantees relating to the fundamental and other human rights and freedoms specifically mentioned in this Chapter shall not be regarded as excluding others not specifically mentioned.[129]

It may be argued that the above provision recognises other human rights such as the right to health, which though not specifically mentioned in the Bill of Rights, are contained in international and regional human rights instruments, which Uganda has ratified.

3 Conclusion

The aim of this chapter was to map out the nature, scope and content of the right to health. It was found that the right to health is now firmly established in international and regional human rights instruments. Although the right is not explicitly provided for in the Ugandan Constitution, this is not necessarily a bar to its adjudication and enforcement. The provisions in the NODPSP may be creatively interpreted by the judiciary in order to protect and promote the right to health in the country. In addition to applying principles of international human rights law, Uganda can also learn from other jurisdictions, which have expansively interpreted existing civil and political rights such as the right to life in order to protect the right to health. Uganda can also be guided by the jurisprudence of the various quasi-judicial bodies such as the Committee on ESCR, Committee of CEDAW and the African Commission, in implementing the right to health and its various components.

129 Art 45.

3

RIGHT TO HEALTH: CURRENT CHALLENGES

1 Introduction

In spite of the legal and policy frameworks for the realisation of the right to health, for the majority of Ugandans, the right remains elusive as evidenced by the worrying health related statistics. For example, malaria, which is the leading cause of morbidity and mortality in the country, accounts for between 70 000 and 110 000 deaths per year.[1] It accounts for 25-40 per cent of outpatient visits to health facilities; 15-20 per cent of all hospital admissions; and 9-14 per cent of all hospital deaths.[2] According to the WHO, Uganda's malaria mortality rate is seven times that of Kenya, 18 per cent more than that of Tanzania, and 9 per cent more than that of Sub-Saharan Africa.[3] Although treatment for malaria in form of artemisinin-based combination therapies (ACTs) is available, it is not economically accessible for the majority of the rural and urban poor.[4]

Maternal Mortality Ratio (MMR) is still high at 435 deaths per 100 000 births roughly translating into an estimated 16 women dying per day giving birth.[5] The national met need for emergency obstetric care (EmOC) is at only 40 per cent, yet this type of care is very critical for 15 per cent of

1 Ministry of Health *Uganda national malaria control strategic plan 2010/11-2014/15* (2010); Uganda Bureau of Statistics and IFC Macro *Uganda malaria indicator survey 2009* (2010); Ministry of Health 'The burden of malaria in Uganda' http://www.health.go.ug/malaria.htm (accessed 10 January 2013); USAID *Presidential malaria initiative Uganda, malaria operational plan* (2012).

2 As above. See also, Uganda 'Presidential malaria initiative' http://www.pmi.gov/countries/profiles/Uganda (accessed 5 June 2013).

3 WHO *World Health Statistics 2011* (2011). On the burden of malaria, see also G Ahaibwe & I Kasirye 'Reducing the burden of malaria among children in Uganda' http://www.eprc.or.ug/pdf_files/policybrief20.pdf (accessed 5 June 2013); GN Kiwanuka 'Malaria morbidity and mortality in Uganda' (2003) 40 *Journal of Vector Borne Diseases* 16.

4 P Moszynski 'New malaria drugs need subsidy, study finds' (2008) *British Medical Journal* 337; BK Twinomugisha (2008) 'Beyond social programmes: Protection of the right of access to malaria treatment in Uganda' HURIPEC Working Paper 22.

5 Ministry of Health (n 1 above) 11.

women who develop life threatening complications during pregnancy.[6] In fact, only 11,7 per cent of women deliver in fully functional comprehensive EmOC facilities.[7] Child morbidity and mortality are also high with neonatal deaths contributing to 38 per cent of all infant deaths.[8] Child Mortality Rate (CMR) is at 137 deaths per 1000 live births while Infant Mortality Rate (IMR) is at 75 per 1000 live births.[9] Many children die from AIDS, Tuberculosis (TB), diarrhoea, measles and malnutrition, with the number of stunted children ranging from 25-44 per cent.[10] HIV prevalence rate was estimated at 6,4 per cent in 2005, 6,7 per cent in 2008/2009 but rose to 7,3 per cent in 2012.[11] HIV prevalence amongst pregnant women attending antenatal care is estimated at 20-30 per cent.[12]

There are many challenges to the realisation of the right to health. However, because of the multifaceted nature of the right, it may be difficult to comprehensively discuss all of the challenges. Thus, out of necessity, this chapter pays specific attention only to some of the major challenges that affect the realisation of the right, with a view to advancing possible strategies to tackle them.

2 Mapping out the challenges

2.1 Muted recognition of the right to health and a reluctant judiciary

As pointed out above, the right to health is not expressly provided for in the Bill of Rights of the Constitution. There is also no law that specifically deals with the right to health. The available pieces of legislation, for example the Public Health Act and the Mental Treatment Act are either outdated or outmoded or piecemeal and simply inadequate in ensuring the enhanced protection of the right. Most of the issues concerning health are covered under policies, and in the NODPSP, whose justiciability requires a bold and creative judiciary, which is prepared to hold the state accountable for failing to meet its obligations in the area of health rights. Unfortunately, as the case of *Centre for Health, Human Rights and Development* below illustrates, the Constitutional Court has exhibited a rigid legalistic positivist approach towards socio-economic rights generally and the right to health in particular.

6 As above.
7 As above.
8 As above.
9 Ministry of Health (n 1 above) 8.
10 As above. See also UBOS *Uganda demographic and health survey 2011* (2012).
11 Uganda AIDS Commission (UAC) *Uganda AIDS indicator survey 2011* (2010).
12 Uganda AIDS Commission (n 11 above) 11.

In Uganda, apart from a few cases on violations of patients' rights[13] and those challenging violations of the right to a clean and healthy environment guaranteed under article 39 of the Constitution, there have been very few attempts to challenge the state over violations of other components of the right to health.[14] In *Centre for Health, Human Rights and Development & Others v Nakaseke District Local Administration*,[15] the plaintiffs brought an action on behalf of the deceased, who died at the defendant's hospital due to lack of emergency obstetric care. It was alleged by the plaintiffs that the deceased had an obstructed labour condition but did not receive the appropriate medical care and attention due to the absence of a doctor assigned to her. Kabito J visited the defendant's hospital in order to acquaint himself with some of the facilities such as the theatre and maternity ward, which were mentioned in the evidence. It was held that the deceased's right to basic medical care was violated. The defendant was found to have violated article 33(3) of the Constitution, which obliges the state to 'protect women and their rights, taking into account their unique status and natural maternal functions in society'. The defendant was also found to have violated article 34 of the Constitution, which protects children's rights.

In the ill-fated case of *Joyce Nakacwa v Attorney-General & Others*,[16] the petitioner alleged that by denying her medical and or maternity care, the state had violated her human rights under article 33(3), which obliges the state to 'protect women and their rights, taking into account their unique status and natural maternal functions in society'. The state raised a preliminary objection to the effect that the jurisdiction of the Constitutional Court was limited to matters, which fall under article 137 of the Constitution, which deals with constitutional interpretation. It was argued that since the allegations by the petitioner did not require constitutional interpretation, the petition should be dismissed. The Constitutional Court cited the Supreme Court decision in *Ismail Serugo v Kampala City Council & Another*,[17] to the effect that it has jurisdiction to entertain matters that would otherwise fall under article 50, which deals with enforcement of human rights, if this is done in the process of a constitutional interpretation under article 137 of the Constitution. The Constitutional Court decided that it had jurisdiction to entertain the petition and dismissed the preliminary objection. Unfortunately, as fate would have it, the petition abated because the petitioner died before it could be heard.

13 These are considered in chapter nine below.

14 For a discussion of some of the cases on the right to a clean and healthy environment, see BK Twinomugisha 'Some reflections on judicial protection of the right to a clean and healthy environment in Uganda' (2007) 3 *Law, Environment and Development Law Journal* 246.

15 Civil Suit 111/2012 (Unreported).

16 Constitutional Petition 2/2001 (CC).

17 Constitutional Appeal 1/1998 (SC).

In *Centre for Health, Human Rights Development & Others v Attorney-General*,[18] the petitioners petitioned the Constitutional Court seeking declarations to the effect that the non-provision of essential maternal health commodities in public health facilities and the unethical conduct and behaviour of health workers towards expectant mothers are inconsistent with the Constitution and a violation of their right to health and other related rights namely, women's human rights,[19] the right to life,[20] and freedom from torture, cruel, inhuman and degrading treatment.[21] The following were agreed upon as the issues to be determined by the Constitutional Court: (1) whether the right to the highest attainable standard of health is a constitutional right by virtue of article 45 of the Constitution; (2) whether the inadequate human resources for maternal health specifically midwives and doctors, frequent stock-outs of essential drugs for maternal health and lack of emergency obstetric care (EmOC) services at Health Centres III, IV and hospitals is an infringement of the right to health; (3) whether non-provision of basic maternal health care services in health facilities contravenes article 8A, NODPSP XIV and XX of the Constitution; (4) whether the Government's non-provision of basic maternal health care packages in government hospitals resulting in the death of expectant mothers and their children is a violation of the right to life as guaranteed under article 22 of the Constitution; (5) whether the health workers' failure to attend to expectant mothers subjects them to degrading and inhuman treatment and thereby contravenes article 24 and 44(a) of the Constitution; (6) whether the high rates of maternal mortality in Uganda contravene article 33(1), (2) and (3) of the Constitution; and (7) whether the families of two women who died in Mityana District Hospital and Arua Regional Hospital due to non-availability of basic maternal commodities are entitled to compensation.

At the commencement of the hearing, the Attorney General raised a preliminary objection based on the 'political question' doctrine.[22] She argued that the petition requires the Court to make a judicial decision involving and affecting political questions. That in doing so, the Court would in effect be interfering with the political discretion of other

18 Constitutional Petition 16/2011 (CC).

19 Art 33(2) & (3).

20 Art 22(1).

21 Art 24 & 44.

22 The political question doctrine originated from the United States of America. The doctrine is to the effect that courts of law should be restricted to handling legal but not political questions. That some political questions are best handled by the political process, especially by branches such as the legislature and the executive whose members are elected by the people. The doctrine is closely linked to the concept of justiciability. In the Supreme Court case of *Marbury v Madson* 5 US 137 (1803), Chief Justice Marshall stated that some actions of the Secretary of State such as advising the president on matters of policy could not be reviewed by the a court of law. See also *Baker v Carr* 369 US 186 (1962). For a discussion of the scope of the political doctrine, see JH Choper 'The political question doctrine: Suggested criteria' http://www.scholarship.law.duke/cgi/viewcontent.cgi?article=1258&content:dlj (accessed 15 March 2014).

branches, namely, the executive and the legislature. She further contended that in order to determine the issues in the petition, the Court has to call for a review of all the policies of the entire health sector and make findings on them, yet implementation of these policies is the sole preserve of the executive and the legislature. She prayed that the Court is prohibited from hearing the petition since the questions raised therein are non-justiciable. In reply, it was argued by counsel for the petitioners that the preliminary objection was misconceived as the petition is for the determination of whether the acts and omissions are in contravention of the Constitution and not the determination of a political question. The Constitutional Court stated as follows:

> Much as it may be true that government has not allocated enough resources to the health sector and in particular the maternal health care services, this court is ... reluctant to determine the questions raised in this petition. The Executive has the political and legal responsibility to determine, formulate and implement policies of government, for *inter alia*, the good governance of Uganda ... This court has no power to determine or enforce its jurisdiction on matters that require analysis of the health sector government policies, make a review of some and let on, their implementation. If this Court determines the issues raised in the petition, it will be substituting its discretion for that of the Executive granted by law ... From the foregoing, the issues raised by the petitioners concern the matter in which the Executive and the Legislature conduct public business, issues or affairs which is their discretion and not of this court. This court is bound to leave certain constitutional questions of a political nature to the Executive and the Legislature to determine.[23]

The Court upheld the respondent's preliminary objection and struck out the petition with no order as to costs since 'the petitioners were motivated by their respective concerns for the plight of maternal mothers, and not for personal considerations'.[24] The Court advised the petitioners to pursue alternative remedies in the High Court such as compensation and the prerogative remedies of prohibition, certiorari and injunction.[25]

It should be noted that the ruling of the Court is a threat to the justiciability of socio-economic rights in Uganda. By deciding that it cannot entertain claims involving political questions, the Court has denied citizens access to justice in respect of certain executive or legislative acts or omissions that contravene socio-economic rights, including the right to health. The Constitution is clear: judicial power shall be exercised in accordance with the values, norms and aspirations of the people.[26] Maternal health issues are legitimate concerns of the judiciary, which is charged with the administration of justice, including issues of social justice. Mothers, like other human beings, aspire for a dignified life free

23 *Centre for Health, Human Rights Development & Others* (n 18 above) 25.
24 *Centre for Health, Human Rights Development & Others* (n 18 above) 28.
25 The petitioners have appealed to the Supreme Court.
26 Art 126.

from premature mortality caused by failure on the part of the state to meet its constitutional and human rights obligations. Poverty issues such as maternal health care, which are largely in the socio-economic domain certainly form part of the values envisaged under article 126 of the Constitution and are therefore within the competence of the courts.

The judiciary in Uganda should learn from other jurisdictions that have exalted the need to protect maternal and child health. For example, in the Indian case of *Laxmi Mandal & Others v Deen Harinagar Hospital & Others,*[27] the court recognised the internationally protected right to maternal health care and ordered compensation for the violations experienced by two impoverished women and their babies during childbirth. The women died of clearly unavoidable deaths. One urban poor woman, who was severely anaemic and epileptic, was forced to deliver her child under a tree due to denial of maternal health services. The court found that there were violations of the fundamental right to life under the Constitution and the right to health. The court relied extensively on international law as well as national law to support its findings. The court for example cited General Comment 14 on the right to the highest attainable standard of physical and mental health; articles 12 and 14 of CEDAW, which enjoin states to eliminate discrimination against women in the field of health care; and articles 24 and 27 of the CRC, which outline the states' obligations to ensure the highest attainable standard of health for every child, and pre and post natal health care for mothers. The court stressed the indivisibility and interconnectedness of human rights especially the rights to life, health and food. It stated that the inalienable right to health is inherent in the right to life and observance of this right leads to enforcing the right to life. The state and its entities were ordered to compensate the women and their families to ensure the provision of food and medication to the two babies. The state and its entities were also directed to remedy deficiencies in, and improve monitoring of, public health programmes.

Judges need to know that socio-economic rights such as health care are particularly relevant for vulnerable and disadvantaged individuals and groups in society who may have limited access to basic needs in order to lead a dignified life. Courts in other jurisdictions have emphasised the importance of paying special attention to the needs of marginalised groups in society. For example, in the Colombian *Vaccination* case,[28] where there was a general failure by the state to provide vaccination to children, the Constitutional Court observed as follows:

> The negligent abstention by the State, its passivity regarding the marginalized and discriminated groups of society, does not meet its duty to put in place an equitable social order – which constitutes the basis for the legitimacy of the

27 WP (C) 8853/2008 (New Delhi High Court).
28 Decision (Sentencia) SU-225/98, May 20, 1998.

> welfare state under the rule of law. It also fails to comply with the constitutional provision proscribing marginalization and discrimination. In these circumstances, the role of the judiciary is not to replace public authorities which are liable for its abstention. It is rather to order the State to fulfil its duties, where it is clear that failure to act violates a fundamental constitutional right.[29]

It cannot be denied that there are genuine differences between civil and political rights on the one hand and socio-economic rights such as the right to health on the other. But these differences should not be exaggerated. Both categories of rights involve political decisions. As the Committee on ESCR observed,

> It is sometimes suggested that matters involving the allocation of resources should be left to the political authorities rather than the courts. While the respective competencies of the various branches of government must be respected, it is appropriate to acknowledge that courts are generally already involved in a considerable range of matters which have resource implications. The adoption of a rigid classification of economic, social and cultural rights [such as the right to health] which puts them by way of definition, beyond the reach of the courts would thus be arbitrary and incompatible with the principle that the two sets of human rights are indivisible and interdependent. It would also curtail the capacity of the courts to protect the rights of the most vulnerable and disadvantaged groups in society.[30]

On the question whether the inclusion of socio-economic rights in the South African Constitution would breach the separation of powers by permitting the court to dictate to the government how the budget would be allocated, the South African Constitutional Court also stated as follows:

> ... even when a court enforces civil and political rights such as equality, freedom of speech and the right to a fair trial, the order it makes will often have such implications. A court may require the provision of legal aid, or the extension of state benefits to a class of people who formerly were not beneficiaries of such benefits. In our view it cannot be said that by including socio-economic rights within a bill of rights, a task is conferred upon the courts so different from that ordinarily conferred upon them by a bill of rights that results in a breach of the separation of powers.[31]

In *Paschim Bangha Khet Samity v State of West Bengal*,[32] the Indian Supreme Court found that the state had failed to provide emergency medical treatment as required by the Constitution and held that:

29 *Vaccination* case (n 28 above) para 29.
30 Para 10 General Comment 9.
31 See *The Certification of the Constitution of the Republic of South Africa, 1996* 1996 (4) SA 744 (CC) para 77.
32 (1996) 4 SCC 37.

> [There] is no doubt that financial resources are needed for providing these facilities. But at the same time it cannot be ignored that it is the constitutional obligation of the State to provide adequate medical services to the people.[33]

In handling either category of rights, the court should aim at the attainment of justice for the parties involved. It is vital for the courts to focus on the underlying values and interests of the vulnerable and disadvantaged, which human rights seek to serve. Courts should not leave socio-economic questions to the legislature. As Pieterse has correctly observed, it is true,

> the legislature has a primary role to play in giving content to human rights through the development of legal and policy frameworks. However, legislatures are typically large bodies made up of popularly elected 'laymen' who often lack the technical expertise necessary for effective socio-economic policy making ... A popular mandate further does not guarantee a commitment to social justice. This is because majority demands are often inimical to the social welfare of minorities. There is also a danger that politicians will pander to the demands of powerful members of society (whose class interests are likely to correspond with those of politicians themselves) at the cost of the survival requirements of vulnerable or marginalized members of society.[34]

The courts should not rely on antiquated doctrines such as the political question doctrine, which clearly undermine the judiciary's constitutionally guaranteed independence. Judges should exercise their judicial mind with activism and creativity in order to give a voice to many Ugandans whose health rights are violated daily. It is no longer tenable to argue that the judiciary is ill-equipped to adjudicate matters of social policy decided by the political branches of the state. The decision by the Constitutional Court was really extreme deference to the political branches. An opportunity to clarify the scope and content of the right to health and the attendant state obligations was lost.[35] The petitioners did not ask the Court to 'determine, formulate and implement policies of government' as alleged but to do the following: examine the allegations that women's human rights were violated through actions and omissions of the state and its officials especially the health workers, which matters fall within the scope of article 137 of the Constitution.

I am not arguing that the judiciary should usurp the roles of the legislature and the executive but it should be assertive as the guarantor of

33 *Paschim Bangha Khet Samity* (n 32 above) 40.

34 M Pieterse 'Coming to terms with judicial enforcement of socio-economic rights' (2004) *South African Journal on Human Rights* 383 387. On the justiciability of socio-economic rights such as the right to health, see also D Brand 'Socio-economic rights and courts in South Africa: Justiciability on a sliding scale' in F Coomans (ed) *Justiciability of economic and social rights: Experiences from domestic systems* (2006).

35 The petitioners have appealed to the Supreme Court of Uganda.

human rights especially for the disadvantaged and vulnerable members of our society. Indeed, as Pieterse has further pointed out:

> [I]n technically specialist areas, the executive is the only branch of government that can regularly and credibly lay claim to the expertise necessary to give effect to rights ... However, executive members are usually only indirectly accountable to the citizenry ... There is accordingly a need to develop mechanisms according to which the [executive] may be held accountable to citizens, at least in so far as their actions affect basic human rights. Given the executive stronghold over the legislature, citizens increasingly look to the judiciary to ensure executive accountability and for protection of their basic interests ... The judiciary acts both as a watchdog over other branches' adherence to the doctrine of separation of powers as primary protectors of citizen's rights within its confines.[36]

The Court should have assessed the course of action taken by the state, which is the primary duty bearer. In determining whether the rights in question had been violated or not, the judges would not have involved themselves in policy design and implementation, which are largely the preserve of the political branches of the state. The judges would simply examine the effectiveness of the measures or means chosen by the state to fulfil the rights in question. Through judicial review, the Court would find out whether the government legislation or regulations or policies comply with legal standards set out in the Constitution and international human rights instruments to which Uganda is a party. In any case, as the South African Constitutional Court stated in *Minister of Health v Treatment Action Campaign (No 2)*,[37]

> The primary duty of courts it to the Constitution and the law ... Where state policy is challenged as inconsistent with the Constitution, courts have to consider whether in formulating and implementing such a policy the state has given effect to its constitutional obligations. If it should hold in any given case that the state has failed to do so, it is obliged by the Constitution to say so. In so far as this constitutes an intrusion into the domain of the executive, it is an intrusion mandated by the Constitution itself.[38]

The Court could ask: How 'reasonable', 'adequate' or appropriate' are the means chosen by the so-called political branches to meet the core goals or duties outlined in the legal and policy frameworks? Does the existing health policy comply with a required legal standard for example protecting constitutionally guaranteed women's human rights such as access to emergency obstetric care?[39]

36 Pieterse (n 34 above) 388.
37 2002 (5) SA 721 (CC).
38 *Treatment Action Campaign (No 2)* (n 37 above) para 113.
39 On judicial protection of the right of access to emergency obstetric care, see BK Twinomugisha 'Exploring judicial strategies to protect the right of access to emergency obstetric care in Uganda' (2007) 7 *African Human Rights Law Journal* 283.

For example, the South African Constitutional Court has employed the test of reasonableness in adjudicating socio-economic rights. This test is derived from the Constitution of the Republic of South Africa, 1996, which provides that everyone has the right to have access to health care services, including the right to reproductive health care and no one may be refused emergency medical treatment.[40] The Constitution obliges the state 'to take reasonable and other measures, within its available resources, to achieve the progressive realization' of the rights enunciated under section 27.[41] In *Soobramoney v Minister of Health, Kwazulu-Natal,*[42] the Court relied on reasonableness of the hospital's ethics committee and the provincial hospital's budget to deny Soobramoney's claim that he was entitled to kidney dialysis for renal failure. The court observed that provision of such care 'would make substantial inroads into the health budget ... [which] would have to be dramatically increased to the prejudice of other needs which the state had to meet'.[43] In *Minister of Health v Treatment Action Campaign (No 2),*[44] the Court also relied on the test of reasonableness in finding that the health department's refusal to roll out an antiretroviral drug, which would prevent mother-to-child transmission of HIV was a violation of the right of access to health care. The Court held that the government policy on obstructing the use of privately available medicines was unreasonable. In *Rail Commuters Action Group v Transnet Ltd t/a Metrorail,*[45] the Court stated that,

> [w]hat constitutes reasonable measures will depend on the circumstances of each case. Factors that would ordinarily be relevant would include the nature of the duty, the social and economic context in which it arises, the range of factors that are relevant to the performance of the duty, the extent to which the duty is closely related to the core activities of the duty-bearer – the closer they are the greater the obligation on the duty-bearer and the extent of any threat to fundamental rights should the duty not be met as well as the intensity of any harm that may result. The more grave is the threat to fundamental rights, the greater is the responsibility of the duty-bearer ... A final consideration will be the relevant human and financial resource constraints that may hamper the organ of state in meeting its obligation. This last criterion will require careful consideration when raised. In particular an organ of state will not be held to have reasonably performed a duty simply on a bold assertion of resource constraints. Details of the precise character of resource constraints, whether human or financial in the context of the overall resourcing of the organ of state will need to be provided. The standard of reasonableness so understood conforms to the constitutional principles of accountability, on the one hand, in that it requires decision-makers to disclose their reasons for their conduct, and the principle of effectiveness on the other, for it does not unduly hamper the decision-maker's authority to determine

40 Sec 27(1)(a)& (3).
41 Sec 27(2).
42 1998 (1) SA 765 (CC).
43 As above.
44 n 37 above.
45 2005 (2) SA 359 (CC).

> what are reasonable and appropriate measures in the overall context of their activities.[46]

Thus, judges can and should play a critical role in the enforcement of socio-economic rights such as the right to health. Otherwise, what would be the purpose of providing for such rights in human rights instruments if there is no remedy in case they are violated? Through the system of 'checks and balances', the judges have a vital role to play: to monitor the activities of the executive and the legislature regarding their compliance with the obligations imposed on them by law. As Gostin has correctly observed,

> [t]he judiciary may lack the legitimacy to make resource allocation decisions that undermine democratically determined priorities. But at some point, government failure to provide essential health services must be actionable if the right to health is to have meaning. The judiciary could push harder for the right to health without overreaching into the political realm in at least three ways. First, it could invoke an immediate state obligation to spend the maximum available resources. If the budget clearly underfunds health vis-à-vis competing expenditures, the courts could redress the imbalance. Second, the courts could insist on minimum core obligations, stressing the need for at least prevention, primary care, and essential needs. Thirdly, the courts could pay special attention to the needs of the most vulnerable. Thus, if budgets leave society's poorest people without care, courts would be well positioned to intervene.[47]

2.2 Criminalisation of sexual and reproductive health rights (SRHR)

2.2.1 What are SRHR?

SRHR are core components of the broader right to health. At the International Conference on Population and Development (ICPD), reproductive health was defined as a 'state of complete physical, mental and social well-being and not merely the absence of disease or infirmity, in all matters relating to the reproductive system and to its functions and processes'.[48] Reproductive health also implies 'that people are able to have a satisfying and safe sex life and they have the ability to reproduce and the freedom to decide if, when and how often to do so'.[49] Reproductive health 'also includes sexual health, the purpose of which is the enhancement of life and of personal relations, and not merely counselling and care related

46 Para 88.
47 LO Gostin *Global health law* (2014) 268.
48 United Nations (1994) 'Report of the international conference on population and development' Cairo, 5-13 September 1994. A/CONF.171/13. On the importance of the ICPD, see, JC Caldwell 'The international conference on population and development, Cairo 1994: Is it important, desirable and feasible?' (1996) 6 *Forum: Health Transition Review* 71.
49 As above.

to reproduction and sexually transmitted diseases'.[50] The World Health Organisation (WHO) has defined sexual health as:

> A state of physical, emotional, mental and social well-being related to sexuality; it is not merely the absence of disease, dysfunction or infirmity. Sexual health requires a positive and respectful approach to sexuality and sexual relationships, as well as the possibility of having pleasurable and safe sexual experiences, free of coercion, discrimination and violence. For sexual health to be maintained, the sexual health of all persons must be respected, protected and fulfilled.[51]

It should be noted that there is no universally recognised definition of sexual health rights. However, according to the WHO, sexuality 'is a central aspect of being human throughout life and encompasses sex, gender identities and roles, sexual orientation, eroticism, pleasure, intimacy and reproduction'[52] and 'is experienced and expressed in thoughts, fantasies, desires, beliefs, attitudes, values, behaviours, practices, roles and relationships'.[53] The WHO further observes that '[s]exuality is influenced by the interaction of biological, psychological, social, economic, political, cultural, ethical, legal, historical, religious and spiritual factors'.[54] Sexual rights 'include the right of all persons, free from coercion, discrimination and violence to the highest attainable standard of health in relation to sexuality'.[55] These rights include the right of access to sexual health, including reproductive health care services, sexuality education and information, respect for bodily integrity, choice of partner and the decision to be sexually active or not.[56] The rights also encompass consensual relations and the pursuit of a satisfying, safe and pleasurable sexual life.[57] It is important to point out that the right to bodily integrity is at the centre of sexual and reproductive health and freedom and is 'an affirmative right to enjoy the full potential of one's body, whether for health, procreation or sexuality'.[58]

From the above brief conceptualisation of SRHR, these rights can be summarised as follows:

- the right to decide and exercise control over one's body, including the right to choose who one has sex with, when and where, and whether one wants to have sex at all;

50 As above.
51 WHO *Defining Sexual Health* (2006) 5.
52 As above.
53 As above.
54 As above.
55 As above.
56 As above.
57 As above.
58 S Correa & R Petchesky 'Reproductive and sexual rights: A feminist perspective' in G Sen et al *Population policies reconsidered* (1994).

- the right of access to modern family planning methods, including emergency contraception;
- the right to maternal, new-born and child health services, including emergency obstetric care;
- the right to safe, legal and accessible abortion services;
- the right to freedom from sexual and gender based violence in all its forms and the right of access to appropriate medical, counselling and legal services; and
- the right of access to comprehensive sexual education and information.[59]

2.2.2 How are SRHR criminalised? The examples of sex work and abortion

Sex work

It should be noted from the outset that sexual activity is a critical aspect of SRHR. In Uganda, sex work or prostitution is criminalised. A prostitute is defined as 'a person who, in public or elsewhere, habitually or regularly holds himself or herself as available for sexual intercourse or other sexual gratification or for monetary or other material gain'.[60] Uganda follows the prohibition model: all activities relating to prostitution or sex work are considered socially and legally unacceptable. Thus, the Penal Code Act[61] makes almost every activity related to prostitution illegal, prohibits prostitution in every public or private place and provides that '[a]ny person who practices or engages in prostitution commits an offence and is liable to imprisonment for seven years'.[62]

The above provisions raise disturbing questions. Is there any compelling justification for criminalising sexual activity between consenting adults because they have chosen to turn it into a commercial transaction? Who is hurt in the process? In other words, who is the 'victim' that the law seeks to protect in such a case? By definition, commercial sex is the voluntary sale of a labour or sexual service. As long as the sexual transaction is voluntary between consenting adults, is there any

59 For an outline of SRHR, see art 14 of the Women's Protocol. The African Commission has issued General Comments on article 14(1)(d) & (e) of the Protocol to guide states in the development of legal and policy frameworks. See http://www.achpr.org/news/2012/11/d65/ (accessed 17 June 2013). Although these Comments focus mainly on HIV/AIDS, they cover other related SRHR issues in so far as they apply to women's health status in the context of HIV/AIDS. Other relevant documents include, the 2006 'Continental Policy Framework on Sexual and Reproductive Health Rights' http:www.pages.au/sites/default/files/SRHR.English_0.pdf (accessed 10 April 2015); and the 2006 'Maputo Plan of Action for the Operationalization of the Continental Framework for Sexual and Reproductive Health Rights' (Maputo Plan of Action) http://www.pdafrica.org/docs/policy/maputo-e.pdf (accessed 9 April 2015).

60 Sec 138.

61 Cap 120 Laws of Uganda.

62 Sec 39.

justification for state interference? Doesn't such interference constitute a violation of key SRHR such as privacy and the right to control one's body? If adults want to engage in, buy or sell sex that is their choice, which should be respected provided no one gets hurt or harmed or coerced. The state has no legitimate reason to criminalise that choice. What is not permissible whatsoever is sexual activity involving minors or incest or where it is not consensual. It should be noted that laws criminalising sex work are simply outdated and patriarchal. They are underpinned by outdated and repressive notions of sexuality and the general position of women in society.[63]

Criminalisation of sex work simply drives sex workers underground where they are exposed to all sorts of harassment and exploitation. Criminalisation reinforces the stigma associated with sex work and pushes sex workers to the margins of society, where they are exposed to greater risk of harm. When sex workers are driven underground, they may not be meaningfully engaged by health workers for purposes of HIV related services such as voluntary counselling and testing, care, treatment and support. Criminalisation worsens the working conditions of the majority of sex workers and increases their risk of violence and contracting HIV.

Criminalisation increases stigmatisation, which is antithetical to improving sex workers' health generally and the enjoyment of their SRHR in particular and 'is particularly detrimental to the successful model of HIV/STI prevention and care programmes based on principles of social solidarity and human rights'.[64] Those who are infected may end up spreading HIV and other STIs amongst the population in which they live. Criminalisation of sex work has serious ramifications for sex workers' human rights generally and SRHR in particular. Because of the criminalisation and stigma associated with sex work, some health workers may find it difficult to associate with sex workers and yet as UNAIDS has

63 See S Tamale 'Paradoxes of sex work and sexuality in modern-day Uganda' (2009) 15 *East African Journal of Peace and Human Rights* 69; BK Twinomugisha 'Beyond "malaya" or prostitute: Interrogating sexual and reproductive health rights of young commercial sex workers in the context of HIV/AIDS in Uganda' HURIPEC Working Paper (2012). The government seems obsessed with legislating morality. Recently, Parliament passed the Anti-homosexuality Act 2014, which inter alia criminalises homosexuality (sec 2), aggravated homosexuality (sec 4), attempted homosexuality (sec 4) and promotion of homosexuality (sec 13). There were concerns that implementation of the Act is likely to increase homophobic stigma and discrimination against LGBT people and drive them underground where they may not access health services. The Act has been successfully challenged in the Constitutional Court in *Oloka-Onyango & Others v Attorney-General* Constitutional Petition 8/2014 (Unreported) on technicalities as it was passed without quorum. For an analysis of the bill leading to this Act and its potential health and human rights consequences, see JC Mubangizi & BK Twinomugisha 'Protecting the right to freedom of sexual orientation: What can Uganda learn from South Africa?' (2011) 22 *Stellenbosch Law Review* 330. Parliament also passed the Anti-pornography Act, 2014, which provides that a person 'shall not produce, traffic in, publish, broadcast, procure, import, export, sell or abet any form of pornography' (sec 13 (1)).

64 L Murray et al 'She is a professional like anyone else: Social identity among Brazilian sex workers' (2010) 12 *Culture, Health and Sexuality* 306.

observed, sex workers have a great potential to contribute to national HIV responses.[65] In fact, states are enjoined to

> review and reform criminal laws and correction systems to ensure that they are consistent with international human rights obligations and are not misused in the context of HIV or targeted against vulnerable groups.[66]

The UN General Assembly in 2011 also recommended that states should review all laws that affect the 'effective and equitable delivery of HIV services'.[67]

In *Bedford v AG, Canada*[68] the court struck down three provisions of the Canadian Criminal Code outlawing prostitution on grounds that they violate the country's Charter of Rights since they 'force prostitutes to choose between the liberty interest and their right to security of the person'.[69] In *Kylie v Commission for Reconciliation, Mediation & Arbitration & 2 Others*,[70] the court observed that although prostitution is illegal, persons who practice it were entitled to be treated with dignity and be protected against unfair discrimination by employers. Although in *S v Jordan*,[71] the South African Constitutional Court unanimously held that the anti-prostitution provision does not violate human rights as such and is justifiable; justices O'Regan and Sachs held that the provision constituted unfair discrimination. That by making the prostitute the primary offender and treating the customer as an accomplice, the law reinforced double standards and perpetuated gender stereotypes in a manner impermissible in a society committed to advancing gender equality. The decision in Jordan has been sharply criticised as denying sex workers their rights. For example, Bonthuys[72] has argued that the decision,

> conflicts sharply with progressive discourses of sexuality. [It] resonates with certain Christian and Western views which permit limited sexual expression for women and which blame women for the spread of disease. As a consequence, the judgment fails to alleviate, and possibly even contributes to, these women's powerlessness within intimate relationships and, thereby their inability to protect themselves, their children and their partners from sexually transmitted diseases.[73]

65 UNAIDS *Guidance note on HIV and sex work* (2009) 7.
66 UNAIDS 'International guidelines on HIV/AIDS and human rights' (2006) http://www.data.unaids/publications/irc-pub07/jc1252-interguidelines_en.pdf (accessed 4 October 2013).
67 UNGA Resolution A/65/L (2011).
68 2010 ONCA 0814.
69 As above.
70 2010 ZALA C8.
71 2002 (6) SA 642 (CC).
72 E Bonthuys 'Women's sexuality in the South African Constitutional Court' (2006) 14 *Feminist Legal Studies* 391.
73 Bonthuys (n 72 above) 392.

Abortion

Another way in which SRHR are criminalised is through anti-abortion laws. The legal regime on abortion in Uganda is restrictive. Abortion remains prohibited in Uganda, except under certain circumstances. The Constitution provides that, '[n]o person has the right to terminate the life of an unborn child except as may be authorized by law'.[74] The Penal Code Act criminalises attempting to procure, or knowingly supplying things to procure an abortion or miscarriage. The relevant sections of the Act provide as follows:

> Any person who, with intent to procure the miscarriage of a woman whether she is or is not with child, unlawfully administers to her or causes her to take any poison or other noxious thing, or uses any force of any kind, or uses any other means, commits a felony and is liable to imprisonment for fourteen years.[75]
>
> Any woman who, being with child, with intent to procure her own miscarriage, unlawfully administers to herself any poison or other noxious thing, or uses any force of any kind, or uses any other means, or permits any such things or means to be administered to or used on her, commits a felony and is liable to imprisonment for seven years.[76]
>
> Any person who unlawfully supplies to or procures for any person anything, knowing that it is intended to be unlawfully used to procure the miscarriage of a woman, whether she is or not with child, commits a felony and is liable to imprisonment for three years.[77]

However, the Ugandan penal regime does not absolutely prohibit termination of pregnancy. The law, which follows the English case of *Rex v Bourne*,[78] only prohibits 'unlawful' acts; it permits abortion in order to preserve the life and health of the mother. In the *Bourne* case, in 1938, Mr Alex Bourne, a highly skilled surgeon, carried out an abortion on a 14 year old girl who had become pregnant as a result of rape. The abortion took place in one of the London hospitals and the operation was performed without a fee. The surgeon was charged under the Offences against the Person Act, with unlawfully performing an abortion. The relevant provision,[79] provided as follows:

> Every woman, being with child, who, with intent to procure her own miscarriage, shall unlawfully administer to herself any poison or other noxious thing, or shall unlawfully use any instrument or other means whatsoever with the like intent, and whosoever, with intent to procure a

74 Art 22(2) of the Constitution.
75 Sec 141 of the Penal Code Act, Cap 120.
76 Sec 142 of the Act.
77 Sec 143.
78 (1939) 1 KB 687.
79 Sec 58.

> miscarriage of any woman, whether she be or be not with child, shall unlawfully administer to her or cause to be taken by her any poison or other obnoxious thing, or shall unlawfully use any instrument or other means whatsoever with the like intent, shall be guilty of a felony, and being convicted shall be liable ... to be kept in penal servitude for life.[80]

The court observed that the word 'unlawfully' in the Offences against the Person Act, which is largely similar to the above sections of the Ugandan Penal Code, meant 'intentional'. The judge noted that there are circumstances under which abortion could be 'lawfully' procured especially for the preservation of a woman's life, physical and mental health. The Bourne case was applied in the East African case of *Mehar Singh Bansel v R*,[81] where the appellant appealed against a sentence of 30 months' imprisonment for manslaughter. The charge of manslaughter arose out of the death in his surgery of a young woman following an operation performed on her by the appellant for the termination of pregnancy. The court held that a lawful abortion is one that is performed for a good medical reason, which in the eyes of the law 'is the genuine belief that the operation is necessary for the purpose of saving the patient's life or preventing severe prejudice to her health'.[82] The Penal Code Act partially adopts this position and provides as follows:

> A person is not criminally responsible for performing in good faith and with reasonable care and skill a surgical operation upon a person for his or her benefit, or upon an unborn child for the preservation of the mother's life, if the performance of the operation is reasonable, having regard to the patient's state at the time, and to all the circumstances of the case.[83]

The above section provides a defence to a health worker, who in good faith and with reasonable care and skill performs a surgical abortion to preserve the life of a pregnant woman. In case the prosecution seeks to counter this defence, it must prove beyond reasonable doubt that in performing the surgical operation, the health worker had a criminal intention or did not act in good faith. What amounts to good faith is a question of fact based on the circumstances of each case and guided by professional skill, judgment and training. The health worker should have professionally assessed the woman's health situation and reached a conclusion that she qualifies for an abortion. The decision to perform the abortion should not have been influenced by ulterior motives such as a big financial or other reward but should have been based on contemporary acceptable medical practice and standards.

As pointed out in Chapter 2, the Women's Protocol also enjoins states to

80 As above.
81 (1959) EA 813.
82 *Mehar Singh Bansel* (n 81 above) 832.
83 Sec 224.

> protect the reproductive rights of women by authorizing medical abortion in cases of sexual assault, rape, incest, and where the continued pregnancy endangers the mental and physical health of the mother or the life of the mother or the foetus.[84]

The Committee on ESCR has also noted that the respect, protection and fulfilment of human rights require, amongst others, 'the amendment of laws that criminalize medical procedures only needed by women, and punish women who undergo these procedures'.[85] The CEDAW Committee has also stated as follows:

> Measures to eliminate discrimination against women are considered to be inappropriate if a health care system lacks services to prevent, detect, and treat illnesses specific to women. It is discriminatory for a state party to refuse to provide legally for the performance of certain reproductive health services for women. For instance, if health service providers refuse to perform such services based on conscientious objection, measures should be taken to ensure that women are referred to alternative health providers.[86]

The policy framework also permits a woman to abort under certain circumstances: in case of severe maternal illnesses threatening the health of a pregnant woman for example severe cardiac disease, renal disease, severe pre-eclampsia and eclampsia; severe foetal abnormalities, which are not compatible with extra-uterine life such as pregnancy anencephaly; cancer cervix; HIV-positive women requesting for termination; and rape, incest and defilement.[87] The policy framework also permits abortion in cases of sexual violence. For example, the National Training Curriculum for Health Workers provides that 'in case of rape [relevant service providers may] ... offer referral for abortion if appropriate and possible'.[88] The Trainee's Handbook on management of sexual violence also provides

84 Art 14(2)(c) of the Protocol. See also African Commission, General Comment 2. It should be noted that Uganda ratified the Protocol with a reservation to the effect that this provision shall not apply to the Republic of Uganda unless permitted by domestic legislation. In my view, the reservation does not affect the application of the exception discussed above, ie the need to preserve the mother's life, physical and mental health and the possibility of developing future legislation removing the legislative barriers to abortion. For a discussion of article 14(2) of the Protocol, see CG Ngwena 'Inscribing abortion as a human right: Significance of the Protocol on the rights of women in Africa' (2010) 32 *Human Rights Quarterly* 783.

85 Concluding observations of the Committee on Economic, Social and Cultural Rights. E/C.12/1 Add. 101, para 23.

86 UN Committee on Elimination of Discrimination against Women, General Recommendation 24 (article 12 of the Convention [Women and Health], 20th Sess, para 11, A54/38/Rev 1, chap 1 (5 February 1999).

87 Ministry of Health *The national policy guidelines and service standards for sexual and reproductive health and rights* (2006) 45. See also Ministry of Health *The national policy guidelines and service standards for sexual and reproductive health and rights* 2012. The Ministry of Health has revised the guidelines to provide practical and standard information and guidance to various stakeholders on managing abortion and related complications. See Ministry of Health *The national policy guidelines and service standards for sexual and reproductive health and rights* (2015).

88 Ministry of Health *National training curriculum for health workers on adolescent health and development: Trainee handbook* (2001).

for access to termination of pregnancy in cases of sexual violence.[89] Unfortunately, the dominant view is that policies are merely inspirational and are not legally binding.

It should be noted that women who become pregnant as a result of crimes such as rape, defilement and incest are victims of sexual violence may be further traumatised by health professionals, the police and religious leaders. As Mavundla and Ngwena have observed,

> a woman who becomes pregnant due to an act of rape is the victim of a violent and morally reprehensive crime. Yet, the issue of not providing safe abortion to victims of rape must be understood as a form of violence against women for the reason that it puts their health and lives in serious danger.[90]

The traumatising experience that women undergo in their struggle to access safe abortion services may be illustrated by the case of *P & S v Poland*,[91] where P, then 14 years old, was raped by a classmate. The next day, P and her mother S reported the matter to the police. Although P was referred to a health clinic for examination, she was not offered emergency contraception. Several weeks later, she found out she was pregnant and decided to terminate the pregnancy. Even though P was entitled to an abortion under Polish law, which allows an abortion in cases of rape, she was repeatedly and continuously denied timely and professional medical attention. After obtaining a certificate stating that her pregnancy was a result of a crime, which she needed to undergo an abortion, P contacted various hospitals seeking the service. However, none of the medical professionals who were qualified to give her the referral were willing to do so. One of the professionals even told her that she needed the services of a priest and not an abortion, and organised an unrequested meeting between P and a catholic priest. He also shared confidential information regarding P with the priest without her consent. Even after she was able to obtain a referral, the doctor who was willing to perform the abortion procedure expressed reservations when he was contacted by the priest and others who claimed that P was being coerced by her mother to have the abortion. P and S were also interrogated by the police and P was subsequently removed from her mother's custody. However, the Ministry of Health later intervened and P was able to get an abortion just a few days before the 12th week of gestation, which is the cut-off date of abortions of pregnancy as a result of rape.

Albeit the abortion was legal, the hospital refused to register P as a patient and it was done in a clandestine manner. In a complaint brought

89 As above.

90 S Muvundla & C Ngwena 'Access to legal abortion for rape as a reproductive health right: A commentary on the abortion regimes of Swaziland and Ethiopia' in C Ngwena & E Durojaye (eds) *Strengthening the protection of sexual and reproductive health and rights in the African region through human rights* (2014) 61 - 78 62.

91 App 57375/08 Eur Ct HR (30 October 2012).

before the European Court on Human Rights, P submitted that Poland violated her right to be free from torture, cruel, inhuman and degrading treatment; right to private life; right to an effective remedy; and the right to be free from discrimination. The Court held that although article 8 does not confer the right to abortion, prohibition of abortion in situations of health falls within the scope of the right to respect private life. The Court also held that the decision whether or not to have a child is a matter of private life and since Poland had adopted legislation permitting abortion on certain grounds, it must ensure that there is a procedural framework to enable women to access the service. The court stressed that the decision to terminate a pregnancy is time sensitive and any procedure put in place should take this into account. The court found that there was a violation of the rights to private life and privacy. The court also held that there was a breach of article 3, which prohibits torture as the applicant was treated by authorities in a deplorable manner and that her suffering reached a minimum threshold of severity.

In spite of the legal and policy frameworks that seem to permit women to abort, unsafe abortion is common in Uganda. The annual abortion rate in the country is 54 abortions per 1000 women of reproductive age, or one abortion for every 19 such women.[92] The 2003 national abortion incidence study indicates that 15 out of every 1000 Ugandan women of reproductive age were treated for abortion complications that year.[93] Although the high levels of unintended pregnancies may be attributed to the low use of modern contraceptives in the country,[94] criminalisation of abortion also has a significant contribution to make. Because of the restrictive legal provisions on abortion and the attendant sanctions, most health workers may be reluctant to assist women who are in need of abortion services.

The question is: What are the implications of criminalisation of abortion for SRHR? In the first place, because of fear of arrest and prosecution, health workers may clandestinely perform abortion at exorbitant prices thereby making abortion services economically inaccessible for the majority of rural and urban poor women. In any case, because of criminalisation of abortion, information about the discreet services provided by health workers may not be available. Poor rural women, whose access to modern health services is limited by financial constraints and geographical distance, often resort to abortions performed

92 WHO *Unsafe abortion: Global and regional estimates of the incidence of abortion and associated mortality in 2008* (2011).

93 S Singh et al 'The incidence of induced abortion in Uganda' (2005) 31 *International Family Planning Perspectives*183. On the difficulty of obtaining accurate data on unsafe abortion, the WHO has also noted that '[d]eaths and disability related to unsafe abortion are difficult to measure. Given that these deaths or complications occur following a clandestine or illegal procedure, stigma and fear of punishment deter reliable reporting of the incident. It is especially difficult to get reliable data on deaths from unsafe second-trimester abortions'. See WHO *Safe abortion: Technical and policy guidance for health systems* (2012) 19.

94 UBOS *Uganda demographic and health survey 2011* (2012).

by untrained and unskilled providers using unsafe instruments or may attempt to self-induce an abortion.[95] Abortion significantly contributes to maternal mortality and morbidity in Uganda. It has been estimated that in 2008, abortion related causes accounted for 26 per cent of all maternal mortality in the country with many more women suffering debilitating injuries from unsafe abortion procedures.[96] According to the WHO,

> complications of unsafe abortion include haemorrhage, sepsis, peritonitis, and trauma to the cervix, vagina, uterus and abdominal organs. About 20-30% of unsafe abortion cause reproductive tract infections and 20-40% of these result in infection of the upper genital tract. One in four women who undergo unsafe abortion is likely to develop temporary or lifelong disability requiring medical care. For every woman seeking post-abortion care at a hospital, there are several who have had an unsafe abortion but who do not seek medical care, because they consider the complication as not serious, or because they may not have the required financial means, or because they fear abuse, ill-treatment or legal appraisal.[97]

It should also be pointed out that abortion is not only a question of gender but also a class issue. In 2003, 68-75 per cent of rural poor women who had an abortion experienced complications, compared with 17 per cent of non-poor urban women who were handled by a doctor.[98] In any case, most urban women may afford the cost of safe termination of pregnancy.[99]

It is unfortunate that the law restricts an important aspect of women's SRHR: the right of access to safe abortion services. The law is discriminatory in that it criminalises health services – access to abortion – that only women need. Such law impairs women's right to reproductive choice – to make free and responsible decisions. In so doing, the state through law exercises a significant influence over a woman's bodily autonomy in general and over the construction of her sexuality in particular. A woman is compelled to be a mother, yet from a human rights perspective, motherhood should be a choice that is available to those who need it. Denying women the right of access to safe abortion makes them bear the hardship and blame for unwanted pregnancies, ignoring the fact that men bear the responsibility too, and that unwanted pregnancies may have resulted from unwanted intercourse such as rape. In such a case, the law violates women's rights to health, bodily integrity and at times life itself.[100] As the World Health Assembly (WHA) noted in 2004,

95 E Prada et al *Abortion and post abortion care in Uganda: A report from health care professionals and health facilities* (2005).

96 As above.

97 n 93 above, 19.

98 See 'Fact sheet: Abortion in Uganda' http://www.guttmacher.org/pubs/FB-Abor (accessed 17 June 12013).

99 As above.

100 In its Concluding Observations, the Human Rights Committee observed that women who are compelled to seek illegal abortions experience a violation of their right to life under article 6 of ICCPR. See Senegal, 61st Sess, para 12, UN Doc CCPR/C/79/Add 82 (1997); Tanzania, HRC 63rd Sess, 1697th mtg para 15, UN Doc ccpr/c/79/

as a preventable cause of maternal mortality and morbidity, unsafe abortion must be dealt with as part of the Millennium Development Goal on improving maternal health and other international development goals and targets.[101]

2.3 The intellectual property regime and access to medicines

> Viewing access to medications as a matter of *fundamental human rights* forces us to face the momentous suffering and loss of life that is occurring in developing countries due to HIV/AIDS, tuberculosis, malaria, and other diseases as not just a tragedy; it forces us to recognize it as a horrific injustice... Human rights set out an alternative paradigm to models based entirely on charity or cost-effectiveness, which among other things, demands meaningful popular consultation and participation in decisions affecting access to medications, including the adoption of trade and intellectual property regimes that could affect accessibility.[102]

Access to essential medicines is an essential component of the right to health. The WHO defines 'essential medicines' as those medicines that 'satisfy the priority health care needs of the population'.[103] The UN Assembly has explicitly recognised that access to safe, effective, affordable and good quality medicines in the context of epidemics such as HIV is fundamental to the full realisation of the right to health.[104] The UN Commission on Human Rights has also pointed out that

> access to medication in the context of pandemics such as HIV/AIDS is one fundamental element in achieving progressively the full realization of the right of everyone to the enjoyment of the highest attainable standard of physical and mental health.[105]

Using the language in General comment 14 on the right to the heath, the UN Commission has called upon states to promote the availability of medicines and medical technologies for the treatment of pandemics such as HIV/AIDS and opportunistic infections; the accessibility of such medicines to all without discrimination, and affordability for all; and that

100 Add 97 (1998). For the human rights implications of denial of safe abortion services, see also, CG Ngwena 'Using human rights to realize access to safe, legal abortion in Uganda' CEHURD Discussion Series (2014).

101 Resolution WHA 57.12. 'Reproductive health: Strategy to accelerate progress towards the attainment of international development goals and targets' in Fifty-seventh World Health Assembly, Geneva, 17-22 May 2004 Geneva: WHO, 2004 (WHA 47/2004/ REC/1).

102 A Yamin 'Not just a tragedy: Access to medication as a right under international law' (2000)21 *Boston University International Law Journal* 325 370

103 WHO *The selection of essential medicines: Policy perspectives on medicines*(2002) 4.

104 UN General Assembly, Resolution 58/179'Access to medication in the context of pandemics such as HIV/AIDS, Tuberculosis and Malaria' UN Doc A/RES/58/179; 2004.

105 UN Commission on Human Rights, Resolution 2001/33'Access to medication in the context of pandemics such as HIV/AIDS' UN Doc E/CN.4/RES/2001/33; 2001, para 1.

such medicines are scientifically and medically appropriate and of good quality.[106] The UN Human Rights Council has also urged states to 'ensure full and unimpeded access for all ... to HIV prevention, treatment, care and support, in a public health environment free form discrimination'.[107]

Lack of access to quality and cost-effective medicines is a major public health challenge in Africa generally and Uganda in particular where diseases such as HIV/AIDS, TB and malaria are leading causes of mortality and morbidity. The WHA has observed that lack of affordable medicines hinders effective response to HIV/AIDS in many countries, especially the poor.[108] There are many challenges that affect the availability and accessibility of quality medicines. These challenges include health infrastructures, budgetary allocations, procurement, distribution and use of medicines. However, in the majority of cases, high prices for medicines are a major challenge. Access to medicines is partly compromised by high prices charged by pharmaceutical corporations, which are facilitated by the protection afforded to pharmaceutical patents by the Agreement on Trade Related Aspects of Intellectual Property (TRIPS) Agreement.[109] As Musungu has observed,

> [t]he grant of a patent over processes for the manufacture of medicines or with respect to medicines themselves as products has the effect of giving the patent holder a monopoly over the use of the process and or the manufacture and sale of the medicines ... For medicines, the high prices of new medicines resulting from mandatory requirements for patent protection under TRIPS in developing countries have seriously compromised the ability of communities, governments and other players in the health sector effectively to manage infectious and other diseases.[110]

The TRIPS Agreement prescribes minimum standards that relate to the protection of intellectual property rights (IPRs) which include patents, trademarks, copyright, geographical indications and industrial designs. The minimum standards are binding on all the World Trade Organisation (WTO) members, including Uganda. The TRIPS Agreement protects 'process patents' which are concerned with the protection of methods of manufacturing, and 'product patents' which relate to the protection of

106 As above.

107 UN Human Rights Council Resolution 16/28 'The protection of human rights in the context of human immunodeficiency virus (HIV) and acquired immunodeficiency syndrome (AIDS)' UN Doc A/HRC/RES/16/28; 2011.

108 WHA 'Scaling up the response to HIV/AIDS' Fifty-Fourth World Health Assembly, WHA 54.10; 2001. See also JC Mubangizi & BK Twinomugisha 'The right to health care in the context of access to HIV/AIDS medicines: What can South Africa and Uganda learn from each other?' (2007) 10 *African Human Rights Law Journal* 105.

109 World Trade Organization (WTO) 'Agreement on trade related aspects of intellectual property rights' http://www.wto.org/english/docs_e/legal_e/27-trips.pdf (accessed 20 January 2014). For the provisions that protect patents, see arts 27-34 of the TRIPS Agreement.

110 SF Musungu 'The right to health, intellectual property, and competition principles' in T Cottier et al (eds) *Human Rights and International Trade* (2005) 305.

pharmaceutical products. A patent, which is part of a set of intellectual property rights (IPRs),

> is an exclusive right granted to an inventor to prevent third parties from making, selling, distributing, importing, or using their invention without authorisation for a set period of time. For an invention to be able to receive patent protection, it must fulfil three conditions: novelty, inventiveness and utility or industrial application. In return the right [patent] holder is obliged to disclose his invention to the public so as to increase the body of knowledge and further research.[111]

Patent protection has been justified on grounds that it acts as an incentive for drug innovation, research and technological development. It is argued that patents enhance access to medicines through the development of new drugs.[112] It is further argued that patent holders need to recover the time (usually 10-15 years) and financial resources (averagely US$ 500 million) invested in the research and development (R&D) of a drug.[113] However, developing countries and civil society organisations have argued that patents increase prices and limit access to medicines by placing them beyond the reach of poor people in developed and least developed countries (LDCs) such as Uganda.[114]

The tension between the intellectual property rights embodied in the TRIPS Agreement and human rights such as the right to health was hinted at by the UN Sub-Commission on the Promotion and Protection of Human Rights that:

> [S]ince the implementation of the TRIPS Agreement does not adequately reflect the fundamental nature and indivisibility of all human rights, including the right of everyone to enjoy the benefits of scientific progress and its applications, [and] the right to health ... there are apparent conflicts between the intellectual property rights regime embodied in the TRIPS Agreement, on the one hand, and international human rights law, on the other.[115]

The Committee on ESCR has also urged states to ensure that scientific and technological innovations and inventions do not jeopardise the full realisation of human rights such as the right to health through

111 J Sellin *Access to medicines: The interface between patents and human rights* (2014) 38.
112 C Correa *Intellectual property rights, the WTO and developing countries: The TRIPS agreement and policy options* (2002) 35.
113 As above.
114 Musungu (n 110 above) 306.
115 UN Sub-Commission on Human Rights 'Intellectual property and human rights' E/CN.4/Sub.2/2000/7 http://www.twnside.org.sg/title/subcom.htm (accessed 13 April 2013).

patentability.[116] In *Patricia Asero Ochieng,*[117] the High Court of Kenya also emphasised the need to ensure that the protection of IPRs does not compromise the right of access to medicines and other related rights and stated:

> Should the [Anti-counterfeit Act] be implemented as it is, the danger that it poses to the right of the petitioners to access essential medicines which they require on a daily basis in order to sustain life is far greater and more critical than the protection of the intellectual property rights that the Act seeks to protect. The right to life, dignity, and health of the petitioners must take precedence over the intellectual property rights of patent holders.[118]

There is no doubt that intellectual property – especially patents – play a crucial role in the development of new medicines.[119] However, patent monopolies have a deleterious impact on the price of medicines. In the Doha Declaration on the TRIPS Agreement and Public Health, the WTO trade ministers acknowledged that they 'recognize that intellectual property protection is important for the development of new medicines'[120] and also the concerns about its effects on prices'.[121] The impact of patents on prices of medicines has also been decried by the UN Human Rights Council.[122] Patentability creates a monopoly market in the product, which eliminates competition thereby maintaining high prices. With a monopoly situation, there is no competition to bring the prices of medicines down. Thus, patent protection hinders access to medicines in poor countries such as Uganda. Patentability excludes the poor and all those people with a weak purchasing power from accessing essential medicines for both communicable and non-communicable diseases (NCDs).

The TRIPS Agreement contains a number of provisions which can be utilised for the enhanced promotion of public health generally and access to medicines in particular. The TRIPS Agreement stresses that the protection of intellectual property

116 Committee on ESCR General Comment 17 'The right of everyone to benefit from the moral and material interests resulting from any scientific, literary or artistic production of which he or she is the author' (Article 15, Para 1(c) of the Covenant) 12 January 2006, E/C.12/GC/17 http://www.refworld.org/docil/441543594.html (accessed 8 March 2014).

117 Petition 409/2009.

118 Para 85.

119 See for example, 'Role of intellectual property in innovation and new product development' http://www.wipo.int/sme/en/documents/ip_innovation_dvelopment.htm (accessed 19 June 2013).

120 WTO Ministerial Conference 'Declaration on the TRIPS agreement and public health' (adopted 14 November 2001) Fourth Session, Doha, WTO/Min (01)/Dec/2 (20 November 2001) para 3.

121 As above. On the legal status of the Doha Declaration, see GT Thuo 'The Legal status of the Doha Declaration on TRIPS and public health under the Vienna Convention on the Law of Treaties' (2002) 15 *Harvard Journal of Law and Technology* 291.

122 See UN Human Rights Council 'Access to medicines in the context of the right of everyone to the enjoyment of the highest attainable standard of physical and mental health' A/HRC/RES/12/24, 12 October 2009, para 5.

> should contribute to the promotion of technological innovation and to the transfer and dissemination of technology, to the mutual advantage of producers and users of technical knowledge and in a manner conducive to social and economic welfare, and to a balance of rights and obligations.[123]

In this vein, the Agreement permits members to

> adopt measures necessary to protect public health and nutrition, and to promote the public interest in sectors of vital importance to their socio-economic development, provided that such measures are consistent with the provisions of this Agreement.[124]

The TRIPS Agreement also allows certain exceptions for patent protection, namely:

- when commercial exploitation of an invention must be prevented to protect human, animal or plant life or health;
- when diagnostic, therapeutic and surgical methods for treating human or animals are invented; and
- in case of certain plant and animal inventions.[125]

The Agreement permits states to make limited exceptions to patent rights if certain conditions are met for example where the exceptions do not unnecessarily conflict with the normal exercise of the patent.[126] For example, a researcher may use a patented invention for research in order to understand it more fully, or the patented invention may be used to obtain marketing approval from public health authorities.

The TRIPS Agreement also has built-in flexibilities such as compulsory licensing,[127] which is the granting of permission by a government to a party – the licensee – to produce a patented product or process without the consent of the patent owner.[128] A compulsory license can only be issued where

> the proposed user has made efforts to obtain authorization from the right [patent] holder on reasonable commercial terms and that such efforts have not been successful within a reasonable period of time.[129]

According to the TRIPS Agreement, the foregoing requirement may be waived in case of an unusual situation such as 'a national emergency or

123 Art 7.
124 Art 8.
125 Arts 27(2) & (3)(a) - (b).
126 Art 30.
127 Art 31.
128 D Murthy 'The Future of compulsory licensing: Deciphering the Doha Declaration on the TRIPS Agreement and public health' (2002) 17 *American University International Law Rev* 1307 http://www.auilr.org/pdf/17/17-6-4.pdf (accessed 19 June 2013).
129 Art 31(b).

other circumstances of extreme emergency'.[130] Another flexibility which is important for access to medicines is what is called parallel importation. This is the import and resale in a country, without the consent of the patent holder, of a patented product that has been legitimately put on the market of the exporting country under a parallel patent. Parallel importation occurs when prices of medicines are compared, and medicines are bought cheaply on the world market, and imported into a country in need. The imported products will have been produced pursuant to a compulsory license issued in the exporting country.[131]

The TRIPS Agreement recognises the special position of least developed country (LDC) members.[132] Due to 'the special needs and requirements of least developed country Members, their economic, financial and administrative constraints, and their need for flexibility to create a viable technological base', such members were allowed ten years to implement the TRIPS Agreement, except the national treatment and most favoured nation (MFN) obligations.[133] Thus, LDCs were in general supposed to comply with TRIPS obligations as of 1 January 2006. However, they were exempted through a WTO waiver from obligations to grant exclusive marketing rights for pharmaceutical products until 1 January 2016.[134] The TRIPS Council decided to implement paragraph 7 of the Doha Declaration whereby LDCs shall be free to disregard the TRIPS obligations on patents and undisclosed information with respect to pharmaceutical products until 1 January 2016.[135]

The Doha Declaration reaffirmed the flexibilities in the TRIPS Agreement and stated as follows:

> We agree that the TRIPS Agreement *does not* and *should not* prevent Members from taking measures to protect public health. Accordingly, while reiterating our commitment to the TRIPS Agreement, we affirm that the Agreement *can* and *should be* interpreted in a manner supportive of WTO Members' right to protect public health and, in particular, to promote access to medicines for all [emphasis mine].[136]

130 As above.
131 See BK Twinomugisha 'Implications of the TRIPS Agreement for the protection of the right of access to medicines in Uganda' (2008) 2 *Malawi Law Journal* 253.
132 Art 66.
133 Art 66(1).
134 WTO 'Extension of the transition period under article 66.1 of the TRIPS Agreement for least developed country members for certain obligations with respect to pharmaceutical products' Decision of the Council of TRIPS of June 2002, IP/C/25.
135 As above.
136 Para 4 of the Doha Declaration. The use of flexibilities has also been emphasised by the African Commission on Human and Peoples' Rights 'Resolution on access to health and needed medicines in Africa' ACHPR/Res.141 (XXX1III) 08, ACHPR meeting at its 44th Ordinary Session held in Abuja, Nigeria, 10-24 November 2008 http://www.achpr.org/sessions/44th/resolutios/141 (accessed 20 April 2013).

The language used in the above text acknowledges the unmitigated right of countries to take measures to protect public health in spite of the patent monopoly created by the intellectual property regime. Thus, where patent rules are an obstacle to access to medicines, countries are permitted to override the patent regime. The Doha Declaration affirms 'the right of WTO Members to use the provisions of the TRIPS Agreement, which provide flexibility for this purpose'.[137] The flexibilities include 'the right to grant compulsory licenses and the freedom to determine the grounds upon which such licenses are granted'.[138]

It is also important to note that in the Doha Declaration, members recognised the question of limited pharmaceutical production capacities of developing countries and LDCs and thus the fact that they could 'face difficulties in making effective use of compulsory licensing under the TRIPS Agreement'.[139] Members were concerned about the requirement that production should be 'predominantly for the supply of the domestic market'.[140] This provision effectively limited the ability of countries that cannot manufacture pharmaceutical products from importing cheaper generics from countries where pharmaceuticals are patented. In response to this challenge, the WTO on 30 August 2003 gave an interim waiver to an exporting country from having to comply with the article 31(f) restriction, if it is exporting to countries with no or insufficient manufacturing capacity.[141] The August 30 decision allows any member country to export pharmaceutical products made under compulsory licenses provided that the country of export and the country of import have issued such licenses and notified the TRIPS Council of such importation or exportation. The decision covers patented products or products using patented processes in the pharmaceutical sector, including active ingredients and diagnostic kits.[142]

The August 30 decision led to the amendment of the TRIPS Agreement in December 2005 with an inclusion of article 31 *bis*, which solves the problem of economies of scale arising from the necessity to predominantly supply to the domestic market. It allows re-exportation of pharmaceutical products into another system. If a developing or LDC Member is a current member of a regional trade agreement where at least half of which are LDCs on the UN list of LDCs, the obligation of that member under the original article 31(f) to predominantly supply the domestic market with locally manufactured or imported products under the compulsory license does not apply if the other LDCs of the regional

137 Para 3.
138 Para 5(b).
139 Para 6.
140 Art 31(f) of the TRIPS Agreement.
141 WTO General Council Decision of 30 August 2003 'Implementation of paragraph 6 of the Doha Declaration on the TRIPS Agreement and public health' WT/L/540 and Corr 1, 1 September 2003, para 6.
142 M Khor *Patents and access to medicines: What can be done at the national level?* (2004).

agreement share the same national health problem that requires the drug. The major advantage of the TRIPS amendment (article 31 *bis*) is that an exporting member country can grant a compulsory license that is predominantly for the supply of the export market. This flexibility ensures access to pharmaceutical products in member countries, which have limited or no manufacturing capacity in the manufacturing sector.

2.4 Commercialisation of health related services

In the 1960s and early 1970s, in pursuance of its obligations, the government heavily invested in the provision of social services such as education and health care. These were viewed as public goods relatively accessible by everybody, including the poor. The role of the market in the provision of social services was not pronounced like it is today. In any case, most of the private facilities were owned by faith based organisations, which offered relatively cheap services. The poor were largely serviced by public facilities. Health was taken as a major priority for human survival. The state saw it as an obligation to invest in human development, including essential sectors such as health. It built hospitals and other health facilities and ensured that they were equipped with medicines and other health care related products. Health workers were well remunerated and highly motivated in order to professionally carry out their work. Agricultural services were extended to the people to ensure self-sufficiency in food, which is an essential component for health and well-being. For example, as I was growing up in Rukiga, Kabale, South Western Uganda, it was common to see agricultural extension workers moving in rural areas educating people about how to cultivate and care for their crops. Even during the military dictatorship of Idi Amin (1971-1979), which was generally a period of scarcity, every home was obliged to have a granary, which would periodically be inspected by a chief to ensure that the family is well-guarded against hunger and famine.

In the 1980s, the state adopted World Bank and International Monetary Fund (IMF)-inspired Structural Adjustment Programmes (SAPs), which dictated the supremacy of the market in the provision of socio-economic services. SAPs included privatisation, cutbacks in public spending, dismantling of social welfare, retrenchment of the formal labour force and deregulation of labour markets. According to the World Bank and IMF, the state had to withdraw from the provision of these services and concentrate on creating the so-called enabling environment so that people could provide for themselves. Consequently, like a magic wand, SAPs would spur growth, whose benefits would trickle down to the poor thereby leading to development. This view was of course wrong. There is a world of difference between growth and development. Growth is quantitative and generally refers to the Gross Domestic Product (GDP), whose yardstick is per capita income, which takes the total income of the rich or wealthy and divides it amongst the population. On the other hand, development is qualitative and generally refers to the quality of life of the people. It is therefore highly possible to have high figures of growth with many poor people lacking access to basic services such as health care.

Following pressure from civil society and the realisation by the World Bank and IMF that SAPs had simply caused artificial growth and miserably failed to enhance development and had in fact plunged poor countries into further debt and poverty, these financial institutions introduced the so-called Poverty Reduction Strategy Papers (PRSPs), which were a precondition for qualification for debt-relief. Since 1997, Uganda has embraced these PRSPs, the recent being the Poverty Eradication Action Plan (PEAP), which has been replaced by the National Development Plan (NDP).[143] The NDP does not seriously question the neo-liberal macro-economic framework that guided the imposition of SAPs on the country and the eventual development of the PEAP.

I have argued elsewhere that like the PEAP, PRSPs are simply a reincarnation of the discredited SAPs, which negatively impacted on the realisation of socio-economic rights such as the right to health.[144] In fact, a careful reading of the NDP shows that the private sector – the market – is still viewed as the engine of growth, including the provision of socio-economic services. Like the Plan for Modernisation of Agriculture (PMA), the NDP promotes the so-called modernisation or commercialisation of agriculture, instead of self-sufficiency in food, which ensures proper nutrition –an essential requirement for good health.[145] Although the NDP recognises health and agriculture as priorities for the development of the country, they attract limited funding from the state. For example, health attracts only about 9 per cent as against the agreed upon Abuja target of 15 per cent.[146] Neo-liberal economists who advocate for privatisation of social services argue that increasing funding for socio-economic services like health has inflationary tendencies, which are likely to disturb the economy.[147] This is of course wrong given that a healthy population is a pre-requisite for growth and development of the economy. SAPs simply breed state patronage and corruption and thus have deleterious consequences for the right to health by diverting public resources to private use.

143 Republic of Uganda *National development plan 2010/11-2014/15* (2010) http://www.opm.go.ug/assets/media/resources/30/NationalDevelopmentPlan201:112014:15.pdf (accessed 20 March 2013).

144 BK Twinomugisha 'A critique of Uganda's PEAP' in K Matlosa et al (eds) *The state, democracy and poverty eradication in Africa* (2008) 298.

145 As above.

146 The heads of state of the African Union met and pledged to set a target of at least 15 per cent of their annual budget to improve the health sector. See, para 26 of the 'Abuja declaration on HIV/AIDS, tuberculosis and other related infectious diseases' http://www.un.org/ga/aids/pdf/abuja_declaration.pdf (accessed 20 March 2013). See also WHO 'The Abuja Declaration: Ten years on' http://www.who.int/healthsystems/publications/Abuja.pdf (accessed 24 March 2013).

147 See for example, B Marc 'Privatizing the delivery of social welfare services: An idea to be taken seriously' *Privatization and the Welfare State* (1989) 179.

The question is: what does the above narrative mean for the right to health? Privatisation, or simply put, having the market play a dominant role in the provision of social services, has negative consequences for the right to health. By definition, the poor lack the necessary income for purchasing health care goods and services. Because they cannot afford, they are denied access to safe, appropriate high quality preventive and curative care which is provided by private persons. As the Committee on ESCR has observed, a poor person's situation may result in discrimination and the denial of crucial services such as health care.[148] It should be pointed out that even public referral institutions such as Mulago hospital in Kampala, have both the so-called private and public sections of health care provision. The private wing has the best consultants and doctors who attend to private patients. Patients in this section are provided with all types of care including relatively good food. Indeed, there are two worlds in Mulago hospital: one for the rich and the other for the poor. In the general wards, the situation is pathetic and disturbing. The services are poor, the drugs are generally not available and patients are asked to purchase them elsewhere. The workers are also of course overworked and poorly remunerated.

It is entirely wrong to treat health care as a commodity to be regulated by the forces of demand and supply. Reliance on market forces by privatising health care ignores the reality that the poor lack sufficient income, and thus access to the market where health care is bought and sold is restricted. It is a fallacy to assume the neutrality of the market. In any case, without a welfare-oriented state, market relationships tend to favour those already richer and better endowed. Promoting privatisation or commercialisation of health-related services as a substitute for provision of public services, which have been eroded by the neo-liberal economic framework, is illusory. Health related services are not like ordinary commercial goods or commodities which can be left to the control of market forces. The market, its imperfections notwithstanding, is left to dictate the prices of health care goods and services without state intervention. You simply need to walk into a pharmacy or drug shop in Kampala or any town in Uganda. The price of ACTs for the treatment of malaria ranges between 12 000 and 20 000 Uganda shillings.[149] This is far above what the majority of the population can afford, given that they have to spend on other social services such as education, whose provision has been abdicated by the state.

148 Committee on ESCR, General Comment 20 'Non-discrimination in economic, social and cultural rights' (art 2, para 2, of the International Covenant on Economic, Social and Cultural Rights) Forty-Second Session, Geneva, 4-22 May 2009, E/C.12/GC/20 para 35.

149 On how access to anti-malaria treatment is adversely affected by high prices of ACTs, see Twinomugisha (n 4 above).

Unfortunately, the above sad state of affairs is backed by the law. For example, the Medical and Dental Practitioners' Act[150] and the Nurses and Midwives Act[151] empower private health care providers who are regulated by these laws to levy reasonable charges for services rendered including the sale of drugs and enforce recovery of the same in courts of law. However, there is neither a legal instrument nor yardstick to determine the reasonableness of the charges. Yet, the state has an obligation to protect the right to health, which requires it to take steps to ensure that the activities of private actors do not violate this right. For example, Tanzania has passed a legislation, which empowers the minister to regulate the prices charged by private providers of health care goods and services.[152] Unlike LDCs such as Rwanda where health insurance has been implemented and is reported to be functioning properly, free of corruption,[153] in Uganda, those unable to pay for health services in the market have to accept their fate and die or suffer debilitating injuries. The Rwanda government has ensured that about 98 per cent of Rwandans have health insurance and the premiums are small and affordable.[154]

In addition to the bad economic policies considered above, there is naked corruption in government in general and the health sector in particular. Funds meant for health services are diverted and in fact there is a debilitating lack of accountability in the health sector. In one of the scandals in the health sector, funds under the Global Fund to fight HIV/AIDS, Tuberculosis and Malaria were misappropriated. In public health facilities where services are ostensibly supposed to be free, patients are asked to pay for the services. A patient may have to pay a bribe to have a doctor or nurse attend to him or her, and sometimes patients are asked to buy the medication prescribed. Corruption in the health sector can thus lead to death or injury, thereby preventing a person from enjoying his or her right to health.

2.5 Inequitable gender relations

The concept of gender refers to the distinctive qualities of women and men that are constructed by society. Gender relations refer to the relations

150 Cap 272 Laws of Uganda, sec 42.

151 Cap 274 Laws of Uganda, sec 49.

152 The Private Hospitals (Regulation) Act, Cap 151. The Act inter alia, provides for the control of fees and other charges payable in respect of medical treatment and other services rendered by private hospitals. The Act applies to all private hospitals, which are defined to include 'a dispensary, maternity home, clinic and also any place or premises used for purposes of medical treatment, whether regularly or periodically' (sec 3).

153 DG. Mc Neil Jr 'Rwanda's health care success story' *New York Times* http://www.nytimes.com/2013/02/05/science/rwanda-health-care-success-story.html (accessed 4 May 2015).

154 See M Nyandekwe et al 'Universal health coverage in Rwanda: Dream or reality?' (2014) 17 *Pan African Medical Journal* 232.

between men and women that are socially, economically, politically and culturally constructed. Meena defines gender as

> [s]ocially constructed and culturally variable roles that women and men play in their daily lives. It refers to a structural relationship of inequality between men and women as manifested in labour markets and in political structures, as well as in the household. It is reinforced by custom, law and specific development policies. Whereas sex is biological, gender is acquired and constructed by society.[155]

Inequitable gender relations are a key challenge to the realisation of women's right to health and all its components.[156] Inequality of these relations is perpetuated by the state and private actors, including the family and the community. Most women are continuously kept under time pressures because of the triple gender roles they play. Traditional division of labour assigns women the responsibility of domestic work and care of adults in addition to their child bearing and rearing roles. Men are often assigned productive work which generates income.

Some women work in agricultural plantations and fields where they are exposed to all sorts of pesticides, which may be harmful to their health. Rural women use firewood to prepare food and are exposed to smoke, which may harm their lungs. Women who work in the agricultural and manufacturing sectors may not have protective gear and may be exposed to occupational accidents, hazards and injuries.[157] Women in the agricultural sector are required to perform labour intensive tasks such as weeding, transplanting and harvesting irrespective of whether a woman is pregnant or lactating. Because of their triple gender roles, women hardly get time to effectively utilise health care services. This strenuous work has deleterious consequences for women's health. While men's work is valued, either directly through paid remuneration or indirectly through status and power, women's work is often not recognised. Women's work is vital to the country's economy, but remains unrecognised and or unpaid. Perhaps, if women's work was recognised and paid, they would have money to purchase health care and other socio-economic services.

3 Conclusion

The main objective of the chapter was to map out major challenges to the realisation of the right to health. The discussion revealed that like other

155 R Meena (ed) *Gender in southern Africa: Conceptual and theoretical issues* (1992) 102.

156 On the interface between gender inequality and the right to health, see BK Twinomugisha 'Beyond juridical approaches: What role can the gender perspective play in interrogating the right to health in Africa?' in F Viljoen (ed) *Beyond the law: Multidisciplinary perspectives on human rights* (2012) 41.

157 See International Labour Organization (ILO) 'Safety and health in agriculture' http://www.ilo.org/wcmsp5/groups/---ed_protect---protrav/---safework/documents/publication/wcms_110193.pdf (accessed 15 March 2014).

human rights, realising the right to health is not easy. The realisation of the right is affected by a number of multidisciplinary and multifaceted challenges: juridical, economic, social and political. Because of the broad and complex nature of the right to health, it was not possible to examine all the challenges affecting the realisation of the right. However, some of the major challenges, that were considered, namely, muted recognition of the right and a reluctant judiciary, criminalisation of SRHR, the intellectual property regime, commercialisation of health related services, and inequitable gender relations, affect most of the components of the right to health. Given the importance of realisation of the right to health to the dignity and life of everyone, especially the marginalised and vulnerable members of our society, the state and other actors must devise deliberate interventions to overcome these challenges. These challenges are not insurmountable. Consequently, in the next chapter, I examine possible juridical and other strategies that may assist in the struggle to realise this right.

4

RIGHT TO HEALTH: SOLUTION TO CHALLENGES

1 Introduction

In the previous chapter, we saw that like other human rights, the realisation of the right to health and all its components is affected by a number of challenges: juridical, economic, social and political. The struggle to realise human rights, including the right to health, has historically never been easy. Although it may be a struggle to have a right declared in a human rights instrument, it is a daunting task to have that right realised. It takes courage, resilience and determination to have the state implement the obligations it has assumed in the Constitution and various human rights instruments it has ratified. Human rights advocates have to deal with socio-political structures, which are deeply rooted in the family, culture, and religion. Consequently, this chapter explores possible strategies that may be employed to overcome or mitigate challenges to realisation of the right.

2 Mapping out the strategies

2.1 Lobbying for legislative measures

2.1.1 Lifting restrictions on abortion

Matters concerning health should not be left to the policy framework, which may not create legally binding obligations. There is a need for CSOs engaged in health and human rights to lobby Parliament for the amendment of the Constitution so that socio-economic rights such as the right to health are explicitly recognised in the Bill of Rights of the Constitution. Like with the Kenyan and South African Constitutions, a provision should be introduced in the Constitution allowing the direct application of international law in Uganda. The 1996 South African Constitution enjoins courts and other legal bodies to consider international law when interpreting the Constitution.[1] According to the Constitution, a treaty binds South Africa after approval by the National Assembly and the National Council of Provinces, unless it is self-executing, or of a technical, administrative or executive nature.[2] Customary international law forms part of the law of South Africa unless it is inconsistent with the Constitution or legislation.[3] In *The Government of the Republic of South Africa v Grootboom & Others*,[4] Justice Yacoob stated as follows:

> The relevant international law can be a guide to interpretation but the weight attached to any particular principle or rule of international law will vary. However, where the relevant principle of international law binds South Africa, it may be directly applicable.[5]

The 2010 Kenyan Constitution also provides that the general rules of international law shall form part of the laws of Kenya.[6] According to the Constitution, 'any treaty or convention ratified by Kenya shall form part of the law of Kenya under this Constitution'.[7]

There is also a need for Parliament to give effect to article 8A of the Constitution especially in regard to NODPSP XX on provision of medical services and NODPSP XIV on access to health services, clean and safe water and food security, in order to clear any questions about their justiciability. This can be achieved through a framework legislation that reiterates the right to health and the state's obligations to respect, protect, promote and fulfil the right to health.

The framework legislation operationalises 'the right to health national strategy'[8] and lays down major standards and benchmarks in the area of prevention and curative health care and leaves details to subsidiary legislation. The legislation should also provide for duties of private actors, including families and communities in the protection and promotion of health. The framework legislation may also domesticate the health related provisions in the international and regional human rights instruments,

1 Sec 39.
2 Sec 231.
3 Sec 232.
4 2000 (11) BCLR 1169.
5 As above.
6 Art 2(5).
7 For a discussion of the scope of application of international law in Kenya, see T Kabau & C Njoroge 'The application of international law in Kenya under the 2010 Constitution: Critical issues in the harmonization of the legal system' (2011) 44 *Comparative and International Law Journal of Southern Africa* 3.
8 Committee on ESCR General Comment 14 para 56.

which Uganda has ratified.[9] There is also a need for reviewing the laws on sex work with the view of legalising and eventually decriminalising prostitution.

There is also an urgent need for reviewing the restrictive abortion laws to conform to the existing policy framework and give effect to article 22(2) of the Constitution. Uganda should lift the reservation to article 14 of the Women's Protocol on access to abortion related services. Lessons can also be drawn from legislative frameworks of other jurisdictions in order to ensure safe termination of pregnancy. Parliament can amend the Constitution to include the circumstances under which termination of pregnancy may be permitted. For example, although the 2010 Kenyan Constitution provides for the right to life for every person, including the unborn,[10] it permits abortion where 'in the opinion of a trained health professional, there is need for emergency treatment, or the life or health of the mother is in danger or it is permitted by any other written law'.[11] The 2005 Constitution of Swaziland[12] also permits abortion on medical or therapeutic grounds, including where the doctor certifies that the pregnancy threatens the life of the woman or when it constitutes a serious threat to the physical or mental health of the pregnant woman,[13] or where 'there is a serious risk that the child will suffer from [a] physical or mental defect of such nature that the child will be irreparably seriously handicapped'.[14] Abortion is also allowed where the 'pregnancy resulted from rape, incest or unlawful sexual intercourse with mentally retarded female'.[15]

Apart from Kenya and Swaziland, in most jurisdictions, the question of abortion is handled by other legislation rather than the Constitution. Thus, Parliament may enact a standalone termination of pregnancy law or amend the Penal Code to provide for circumstances under which abortion may be permitted. For example, in South Africa, termination of pregnancy is a woman's choice and is allowed 'upon the request of a woman during the first 12 weeks of the gestation period of her pregnancy'.[16] Under the

9 The framework legislation model has been applied in Uganda. For example, in the field of environmental law, sec 106 of the National Environment Act, cap 153, which is a framework legislation, empowers the minister by statutory order and with the approval of Parliament by resolution to: '(a) set out the provisions of the convention or treaty; (b) give the force of law in Uganda to the convention or treaty or any part of the Convention or treaty required to be given the force of law in Uganda; (c) amend any enactment other than the Constitution for the purpose of giving effect to the convention or the treaty; (d) make such other provision as may be necessary for giving effect to the convention or treaty in Uganda or for enabling Uganda to perform its obligations or exercise its rights under the convention or treaty'.

10 Art 26(1) & (2).

11 Art 26(4).

12 The Constitution of the Kingdom of Swaziland Act 1, 2005.

13 Sec 15(5)(a)(i) & (ii).

14 Sec 15(5)(iii).

15 Sec 15(5)(b).

16 Sec 2(1) of the Choice of Termination of Pregnancy Act 92 of 1996.

Ethiopian Criminal Code, although abortion is criminalised,[17] termination of pregnancy by a recognised medical institution is allowed where the pregnancy is a result of rape or incest; or 'the continuation of the pregnancy endangers the life of the mother or the child or the health of the mother or where the birth of the child is a risk to the life or health of the mother'; or 'where the pregnant woman, owing to a physical or mental deficiency she suffers from or her minority, is physically as well as mentally unfit to bring up the child'.[18]

In Ghana, albeit abortion or miscarriage is criminalised,[19] it is permitted,

> where the pregnancy is the result of rape, defilement of a female idiot or incest and the abortion or miscarriage is requested by the victim or her next of kin or the person in loco parentis, if she lacks the capacity to make such a request;

or

> where the continuance of the pregnancy would involve risk to the life of the pregnant woman or injury to her physical or mental health and such woman consents to it or if she lacks the capacity to give such consent it is given on her behalf by her next of kin or the person in loco parentis;

or 'where there is substantial risk that if the child were born, it may suffer from, or later develop, a serious physical abnormality or disease'.[20]

In Rwanda, the Penal Code provides for the crime of abortion[21] and criminalises self-induced abortion,[22] causing a woman to abort with or without the consent of the husband,[23] and abortion resulting in death.[24]According to the Rwandan Penal Code, no crime is committed when a woman has become pregnant as a result of rape, forced marriage, incest, or 'when the continuation of the pregnancy jeopardizes the health of the unborn baby or that of the pregnant woman'.[25] However, the woman must first procure a court order recognising one of these exceptions. This requirement is problematic given that court proceedings are usually cumbersome and lengthy and by the time a judgment is granted, the woman may have already given birth! In any case, most women in poor countries such as Rwanda may not afford the costs and expenses for the court and the lawyer handling the case. In Tunisia, a predominantly Muslim and a developing country, abortion was legalised

17 On crimes against abortion, see arts 545-552 of The Criminal Code of the Federal Republic of Ethiopia, Proclamation No 414/2004.
18 Art 551(1)(a)-(d) of the Criminal Code.
19 Sec 58(1) of the Criminal Code (Amendment) Act 2003 of Ghana, Act 646.
20 Sec 58(2)(a)-(c) of the Criminal Code.
21 Sec 5 of the Organic Law Instituting the Penal Code (01/2012/02).
22 Art 162.
23 Art 163.
24 Art 164.
25 Art 165.

and safe abortion services are fully incorporated into other reproductive health services.[26]

2.1.2 Balancing the rights of a fetus and a woman's rights

It is important to note that some individuals or groups may object to legalising termination of pregnancy on grounds that it amounts to murder of a fetus or unborn child. In a number of jurisdictions, courts have handled the protection of the so-called life of a fetus *vis-à-vis* women's human rights in the context of abortion. In the South African case of *Christian Lawyers' Association of South Africa & Others v Minister of Health & Others*,[27] the plaintiff challenged the constitutionality of the Choice of Termination of Pregnancy Act on grounds that section 11 of the South African Constitution protects the life of everyone, and the terms 'everyone' and 'every person' include a fetus from the moment of conception. The defendants responded that a fetus was not legally recognised under the Constitution and that a woman's right to decide whether to terminate a pregnancy or carry it to term is constitutionally protected. The court held that section 11 of the Constitution does not explicitly protect the right to life of a fetus. The court also pointed out that section 12(2) of the Constitution provides that everyone has the right to security and autonomy over their reproduction, which provision does not contain any exception for the protection of the fetus. The court noted that section 28, which protects the rights of the child, expressly defines a child as a person who is under the age of 18 years. The court observed that since 'age' begins at birth, a fetus is not recognised as a child. The court held that given the fact that section 28 neither expressly nor impliedly applies to a fetus, section 11 could not have been intended to protect a fetus and to hold otherwise would violate women's constitutional rights.[28]

In the Brazilian case of *National Confederation of Health Workers (CNTS) v Courts of Justice of the States*,[29] whereas Brazil's abortion laws are very restrictive, the Supreme Court of Brazil held that women have a right of access to abortion if they are carrying pregnancies suffering from anencephaly, and the state is obliged to provide them with medical care. The majority of the Court was of the view that criminalising the abortion of anencephalic fetuses with no possibility of long-term survival could not prevail over the woman's constitutional rights of dignity, autonomy,

26 See I Nazer 'The Tunisian experience in legal abortion' (1980) 17 *International Journal of Gynecology & Obstetrics* 488.
27 1998 (11) BCLR 1434 (T).
28 See C Ngwena 'The history and transformation of abortion laws in South Africa' (1998) 30 *Acta Academia* 32 50-60; C Ngwena *Using human rights to realize access to safe, legal abortion in Uganda* (2014).
29 ADPF 54 (Supreme Court) 12 April 2012.

privacy, and physical, psychological, and moral integrity. In *Re Abortion Law Challenge in Colombia,*[30] a citizen filed a petition in the Colombian Constitutional Court challenging the constitutionality of Colombia's abortion law, which prohibits abortion. In the petition, she argued that the Constitution of Columbia requires exceptions to the prohibition of abortion to protect a woman's fundamental rights to life, health, privacy, and dignity. The Court held that the prohibition of abortion in all circumstances violates women's fundamental rights. The court observed that the absolute ban of abortion in order to protect foetal interests places a disproportionate burden on women's exercise of their human rights. The court held that abortion must be permitted when a pregnancy threatens a woman's life or health, in cases where the fetus has malformations incompatible with life outside the womb, and in cases of rape and incest.

It should be noted that article 34 of the Ugandan Constitution, which protects children's rights, neither explicitly nor impliedly applies to a fetus. In fact, according to the Children's Act, a child is a person under the age of 18 years. It may thus be argued that the *Christian Lawyers' Association* case[31] is a persuasive authority for the view that interpreting article 34 to include protection of a fetus would be a violation of women's reproductive rights, which are guaranteed under article 33 of the Constitution and international and regional human rights instruments. It is also important to point out that in respect of the offences of murder and manslaughter, the Penal Code Act[32] provides that a child 'becomes a person capable of being killed when it has completely proceeded in a living state from the body of its mother, whether it has breathed or not, and whether it has an independent circulation or not and whether the navel string is severed or not'.[33] It is therefore necessary that any legislation on termination of pregnancy should give precedence to a woman's reproductive rights over those of a fetus.

30 Decision C-355/2006 (10 May 2006)

31 *Christian Lawyers' Association of South Africa* (n 27 above). See also the case of *The State v Mashumpa* 2008 (1) SACR 126 (E), where the court held that the killing of a fetus does not amount to the crime of murder. The court also alluded to the difficulty of determining the precise time when a fetus would be considered a 'person' within the scope of the law.

32 Cap 120 Laws of Uganda. See also the Kenyan case of *Republic of Kenya v Nyamu & Others* Case 81/2004 (High Court of Kenya), where the court held that fetuses were not persons capable of being killed. See Sec 214 of the Kenyan Penal Code, which is similar to sec 197 of the Ugandan Penal Code Act.

33 Sec 197. However, this section seems to be in conflict with sec 212 on 'killing an unborn child', which provides as follows: 'Any person who, when a woman is about to be delivered of a child, prevents the child from being born alive by any act or omission of such a nature that if the child had been born alive and had died, he or she would be deemed to have unlawfully killed the child, commits a felony and is liable to imprisonment for life'. It may be argued that the phrase 'when a woman is about to be delivered of a child' only applies to 'late' pregnancies and does not apply eg to the first trimester – 12 weeks – where termination of pregnancy should be provided on demand like under the South African law.

2.1.3 The right to freedom of conscience in the context of abortion

It is important for any proposed legislation on abortion to clearly indicate under what circumstances the right to refuse to terminate a pregnancy on grounds of conscience may be exercised. Some health providers and even judicial officers may refuse to handle abortion related cases on grounds that doing so would deny them their right to 'conscientious objection'. They may argue that carrying out an abortion violates their freedom of thought, conscience, belief and religion, which is guaranteed by the Constitution.[34] However, it should be made clear: the right to conscientious objection is not absolute. It should not be used to infringe a woman's exercise of her rights, including access to safe and legal abortion. According to the ICCPR,

> freedom to manifest one's religion or beliefs may be subject to such limitations as are prescribed by law and are necessary to protect public safety, order, health, or morals or the fundamental rights and freedoms of others.[35]

The Ugandan legal framework does not specifically address the right to conscientious objection. However, a few countries in Africa have abortion laws that provide for this right. For example, the 1977 Zimbabwean Termination of Pregnancy Act provides as follows:

> Notwithstanding any law or agreements to the contrary, no medical practitioner or nurse or person employed in that capacity at a designated institution shall be obliged to participate or assist in the termination of a pregnancy.[36]

The Zimbabwean law is retrogressive in the sense that it permits health providers to rely on conscientious objection without balancing it with the right to health and life of the women seeking abortion. The law certainly disproportionately limits women's reproductive rights. The 1972 Zambian Termination of Pregnancy Act provides that,

> no person shall be under any duty, whether by contract or any statutory or other requirements, to participate in any treatment authorized by this Act to which he has a conscientious objection.[37]

However, the enjoyment of the right to conscientious objection

> shall not affect any duty to participate in treatment which is necessary to save the life or to prevent grave permanent injury to the physical or mental health of the pregnant woman.[38]

34 Art 29(1)(b)&(c).
35 Art 18(3). See also art 43 of the Ugandan Constitution.
36 Ch 15, 10, as amended by the Criminal Law (Codification and Reform Act) of 2004, chap 9, 23 (Zim).
37 Sec 4(1).
38 Sec 4(2).

There are no East African cases where the right to conscientious objection has been considered. However, the scope of conscientious objection has been considered elsewhere. For example, in *Decision T-388/09*,[39] the Colombian Constitutional Court illustrated how a health care professional's or other public officer's conscientious objection to participate in an abortion procedure should be balanced with a woman's conscientious claim of access to safe abortion care. In this case, a *tutela* action was filed on behalf of a pregnant woman whose fetus had serious deformities incompatible with life outside the womb. A *tutela* action is a quick and simple procedure to protect fundamental rights under the Colombian Constitution. Regarding the *tutela*, the Constitution provides as follows:

> Every person has the right to file a *tutela* action before a judge, at any time or place, through a preferential and summary proceeding, for himself/herself or by whomsoever acts in his or her name for the immediate protection of his/her fundamental constitutional rights when that person fears they may be violated by the action or omission of any public authority…In no case more than ten days shall elapse between filing the *tutela* action and its resolution. The law will establish the cases in which the *tutela* action may be filed against private individuals entrusted with providing a public service or whose conduct may affect seriously and directly the collective interest or in respect of whom the applicant may find himself/herself in a position of subordination or vulnerability.[40]

Albeit the woman's case in *Decision T-388/2009* fell under the circumstances in which abortion is legal in Colombia, the doctor she was referred to for the procedure demanded a court order before performing the abortion. The trial judge also refused to hear the case and grant relief for reasons of conscience. On appeal, the case was decided in the woman's favour, and the abortion was performed.

The Constitutional Court developed case law on the scope of conscientious objection in the context of abortion. The court held that the right to conscientious objection is legitimately available where two conditions are met: first, when the objector is legally obliged to participate directly in the abortion procedure; and second, when the woman seeking the abortion has a feasible alternative for accessing a timely procedure. The objecting health professional is obliged to refer the woman denied abortion to another professional obliged to provide it. The court noted that the referral should be expeditious and the health provider willing to perform the abortion must be available. This standard is important since abortions are usually safer in the first trimester. Any delay results into denial of

39 Constitutional Court (CC), 28 May 2009, Decision T-388/09, Gaceta de la Corte Constitucional (GCC). For a detailed discussion of this case, see O'Neill Institute *T-388/2009 Conscientious objection and abortion: A global perspective on the Colombian experience* (2014) 26-57.

40 Art 86.

women's right to timely, safe legal abortion and may force poor women to utilise the services of unskilled and unqualified people leading to maternal deaths or injuries. The court further stated as follows:

> [H]ealth care professionals can object to terminating a pregnancy for reasons of conscience if and only if there is a guarantee that a pregnant woman will have access to the procedure in conditions of quality and safety, that she will face no additional barriers that interfere with her ability to access necessary health care services and that her fundamental constitutional rights to life, sexual and reproductive health, personal integrity and human dignity will be respected.[41]

Thus, conscience cannot be invoked to deny abortion care when continuation of pregnancy would endanger a woman's life or her health. The court noted that only providers such as doctors, nurses, midwives and anaesthetics directly participating in the abortion procedure are entitled to claim a right to conscientious objection. Thus, a hospital or other institution cannot rely on this right. The employees of a hospital or institution should be free to exercise their freedom to assist women who need safe and legal abortion services. On this point, the court stated:

> Highlighting the inability of legal persons [such as hospitals and other institutions] to exercise the right to conscientious objection, in addition to fully addressing the essence of the right, is an effective mechanism for preventing legal persons that provide health care services from limiting the freedom of their individual employees who might be coerced by the restrictive positions imposed on them by these institutions' managerial staff.[42]

The court also held that although as private individuals, judges enjoy freedom of thought, conscience and religion in their personal or private lives, like health-care professionals, they should not use their religion and beliefs to deny others their fundamental rights or freedoms. In any case, by their judicial oath, judicial officials undertake to administer justice without fear or favour. The court observed as follows:

> Individuals who voluntarily serve as judicial authorities cannot conscientiously object in an attempt to avoid complying with a regulation that has been adopted in accordance with [the Constitution] ... Claiming conscientious objection is thus inadmissible under these circumstances, as it would translate into an unjustified hindrance in the administration of justice and linked to a serious arbitrary and disproportionate restriction on constitutional rights, even more, where many of these rights developed out of struggles led by sectors of the society that have historically been discriminated against and whose successes have generally not been well-received by many sectors of society that, shielded by their conscientious objections, try to project their private convictions in the public sphere, using a domineering and exclusionary rationale that is entirely contrary to the mandate of protecting

41 Para 4.6.
42 Para 5.2.

and stimulating cultural diversity as specifically established in the Constitution.[43]

2.2 Claiming health rights through the courts

The Constitution allows any person who claims that his or her right has been violated to seek redress from court, including compensation.[44] The Committee on ESCR has also stressed that,

> [a]ny person or group victim of a violation of the right to health should have access to effective judicial or other appropriate remedies at both national and the international levels. All victims of such violations should be entitled to adequate reparation, which may take the form of restitution, compensation, satisfaction or guarantees of non-repetition.[45]

Thus, courts and other quasi-judicial bodies can be utilised to challenge violations of the right to health. Courts can play a significant role in the struggle to realise the right. Courts can clarify on the nature, scope and content of human rights such as the right to health, thereby enriching the jurisprudence in the area. Litigation can be used to catalyse policy reform and give greater clarity and meaning to the right to health. By framing poverty issues in the language of rights and constitutional obligations, the litigation process assists in placing issues on the agenda, both before the judge and the court of public opinion, especially through media reporting. Litigation is an important tool for demanding accountability from the state and non-state actors. It can be used to challenge inappropriate state action and address state inaction. Through litigation, the court may act as a 'voice for the poor'.[46]

The Constitution provides for the concept of public interest litigation (PIL), whereby 'any person or organization may bring an action against the violation of another person's or group's human rights'.[47] PIL seeks to precipitate social change through court action and as Scott Cummings and Deborah Rhode have observed, PIL

> is a key strategy for protecting the rights and enlarging the power of subordinate groups, particularly when other channels of influence are

43 Para 5.4(vii).
44 Art 50(1) of the Constitution.
45 Committee on ESCR 'The Maastricht guidelines on violations of economic, social and cultural rights' para 22-23, Committee on ESCR, General Comment 14 (UN Doc E/C 12/2000/4) para 59.
46 J Dugard & R Theunis 'The record of the South African Constitutional Court in providing an institutional voice for the poor: 1995-2004' in R Gargarelle et al (eds) *Courts and social transformation in new democracies: An institutional voice for the poor?* (2006).
47 Art 50(2) of the Constitution.

> unavailable. Groups hobbled by discrimination or collective action problems may turn to courts as allies in the struggle for social justice.[48]

PIL is an important mechanism for enforcing human rights and recognises the vulnerability of disadvantaged persons or groups such as the indigent who, owing to their poverty, may not be in a position to file actions in their own names. Thus, PIL affords juridical space to previously ignored or excluded groups who lack formal access to power; they are able to enter into contested policy issues and participate in the broader social agenda.[49]

A person is not required to have a personal interest or injury before lodging an action alleging a violation of another person's or groups' human rights. Individuals or CSOs working for the public good can bring the violation or threatened violation of specific rights to the attention of the court. Thus, the state can be challenged in court to show what steps it has taken to realise the right to health. Lawyers engaged in PIL must be ready to confront objections from the state against the justiciability of socio-economic rights such as the right to health. As in the CEHURD case above, the state is likely to argue that judges are not particularly well equipped to deal with issues involving economic, social and other questions, which have budgetary implications. It should be emphasised to the court that both civil and political and socio-economic rights involve expenditure and thus have resource implications. The lawyers can cite examples of funding of elections, financial support to the judiciary, the construction of courts, and prisons. Drawing on judicial precedent from other jurisdictions, it should be impressed upon the judges that the Constitution mandates them to adjudicate all categories of rights without discrimination.[50] Public interest lawyers can also rely on civil and political rights such as the right to life to argue the case for socio-economic rights such as the right to health.

The Constitution is clear: judicial power 'is derived from the people and shall be exercised by the courts ... in the name of the people'[51] in accordance with their 'values, norms and aspirations'.[52] The courts have the legitimacy and competence to adjudicate socio-economic rights. The poor, who are of course people, from whom judicial power is derived, also aspire to live a healthy and dignified life. The courts have to exercise their constitutionally guaranteed independence: to administer political and

48 LC Scott & LR Deborah 'Public interest litigation: Insights from theory and practice' (2009) *Fordham Urban Law Journal* 606.

49 On the value of litigation, see also AE Yamin & S Gloppen (eds) *Litigating health rights: Can courts bring justice to health?* (2001).

50 For an elaborate discussion of the legal enforcement of socio-economic rights, see C Mbazira 'The legal nature of socio-economic rights: Are they capable of judicial enforcement?' in C Mbazira *Litigating socio-economic rights in South Africa: A choice between corrective and distributive justice* (2009) 15.

51 Art 126(1) of the Constitution.

52 As above.

socio-economic justice without 'control or direction of any person or authority'.[53]

In order to succeed in its objectives, PIL should be buttressed by research, organisation and lobbying. CSOs and lawyers engaged in PIL must form important alliances with the major constituent groups and relevant stakeholders. There is need for public education and sensitisation of these groups and stakeholders, including legislators, judges, human rights commissioners, and health workers about the need to protect the right to health and the implications of neglecting the right. Mbazira has outlined some of the strategies that can be employed to make PIL successful:

- Selection of the right case, one in which the violation has caused, and continues to cause, significant harm. The facts of the case must be appropriate and the case must have potential for wide impact, while the targeted relief should have the prospects of benefiting a wide section of disadvantaged persons;
- The decision to take on the case and the manner in which it is pursued must be influenced by the resources at the disposal of the petitioners. Where resources are limited, it may be necessary to mobilize more resources with organizations interested in pursuing the same cause. Alliances may provide both material and technical support;
- Successful PIL must be pursued concurrently with social mobilization and the mounting of political pressure for reform. The litigation must be publicized in the media in order to instigate public debate and maximize the social impact. When the social impact is significant, the case may lead to positive reforms. Even when litigation is lost - the case may be lost but the cause has been won;
- Rather than seek to redress past violations, PIL should aim at preventing future violations and [focus on] those violations of a continuous nature and those with a potential of recurrence if not proscribed;
- Litigation must be accompanied by consultation with [and involvement and participation of] the relevant stakeholders in order to garner support and appreciate the social facts. This is in addition to consultation with experts in the litigated field in order to build a good legal case; and
- There is need to appreciate the social, political and legal context in which PIL is pursued. The context may dictate the kinds of cases that may be litigated and the approaches to be adopted in pursuing the case.[54]

Although litigation may not be a panacea to the challenges resulting from criminalisation of abortion, and 'might even engender a backlash from patriarchal authorities and constituencies',[55] it sensitises civil society and raises 'public consciousness about how national authorities deny human

53 Art 128(2) of the Constitution.
54 C Mbazira *Public interest litigation and judicial activism in Uganda: Improving the enforcement of economic, social and cultural rights* (2008) iii-iv.
55 C Ngwena *Using human rights to realize access to safe, legal abortion in Uganda* (2014) 50.

rights through failure to implement rights already guaranteed and, in the process foreground or reinforce transformative strategies'.[56]

Public spirited CSOs and lawyers can for example challenge the constitutionality of the restrictive abortion laws on grounds that they violate fundamental human rights such as equality and non-discrimination, freedom from cruel, inhuman and degrading treatment, the right to privacy and above all the right to life. For example, in *KL v Peru*,[57] KL a 17 year old adolescent was pregnant with a fetus with anencephaly, a severe fatal anomaly causing the fetus to lack parts of the brain and to have no chance of survival after birth, was denied a therapeutic abortion by Peruvian health authorities in spite of the fact that Peruvian law permits termination of pregnancy for health reasons, including mental health. She was compelled to carry the pregnancy to term, and gave birth and was forced to breastfeed a baby who died a few days later. The Human Rights Committee ruled that compelling a woman to continue a pregnancy that posed risks to her physical and mental health violated article 17 on the right to privacy and article 7 on right to be free from cruel, inhuman, and degrading treatment of the ICCPR. The Committee ordered the Peru government to provide KL with reparations, and to adopt the necessary regulations to guarantee access to safe abortion. In *Roe v Wade*,[58] the Supreme Court of the United States of America also held that the right to privacy encompassed a woman's right to decide whether to terminate her pregnancy.

2.3 Using the Uganda Human Rights Commission

Another avenue that may be utilised by public interest lawyers is the Uganda Human Rights Commission (UHRC), which is empowered by the Constitution to 'investigate, at its own initiative or on a complaint made by a person or group of persons against the violation of any human rights'.[59] It also has powers to recommend effective measures to protect human rights.[60] Additionally, the UHRC is enjoined to monitor the government's compliance with international treaty obligations.[61] The UHRC has powers of the High Court, and can summon witnesses and issue relevant orders against the state, its agencies and private persons in matters involving violations or threatened violations of human rights. The UHRC has a wide mandate which can be effectively used to enhance the protection of all categories of human rights, including the right to health. The Right to Health Unit of the UHRC can monitor discrimination in the provision of health services. It should follow up the international trade

56 As above.
57 UN Doc CCPR/C/85/d/1153/2003 (22 November 2005).
58 410 US 113 (1973).
59 Art 52(a) of the Constitution.
60 Art 52(c) of the Constitution.
61 Art 52(h) of the Constitution.

negotiations entered into by Uganda to ensure that they do not inhibit access to medicines in the country. It should also follow up the extent to which the state has fulfilled its reporting obligations under treaties with a bearing on the right to health.

2.4 Utilising mechanisms at the regional level

Individuals and CSOs may file communications or complaints with the African Commission alleging violations of the right to health, which as illustrated in chapter two is recognised under article 16 of the ACHPR. The complainant need not be related to the victim(s) of the violation although the victims must be mentioned. Where the alleged violation relates to a large number of people, or a specific category of people, an individual or CSO can file a class or representative action.[62] The communication to the African Commission must satisfy the admissions criteria outlined in the ACHPR.[63] The communication must be compatible with the Constitutive Act of the African Union (AU) or with the ACHPR and it must specifically address violations of human rights.[64] The communication must not be written in disparaging or insulting language directed against the state concerned and its institutions or to the AU.[65] The communication must not be based exclusively on news disseminated through the mass media.[66] The author of the communication must have exhausted local remedies, if any, unless it is obvious that this procedure is unduly prolonged.[67] In *Article 19 v Eritrea*,[68] the African Commission stated:

> The exhaustion of local remedies rule is a principle under international law of permitting states to solve their internal problems in accordance with their own constitutional procedures before accepted international mechanisms can be invoked. The particular state is thus enabled to have an opportunity to redress the wrong that has occurred within its own legal order. It is a well established rule of customary international law that before international proceedings are instituted, the various remedies provided by the state should have been exhausted.[69]

The remedies must be available, effective and adequate and the complainant has the burden to prove that local remedies exist and have been exhausted. In *Article 19* above, the African Commission stated:

62 See *Zimbabwe Lawyers for Human Rights & Another v The Government of Zimbabwe* (2008) AHRLR (ACHPR 2008).
63 Art 56.
64 Art 56(2).
65 Art 56(3).
66 Art 56(4).
67 Art 56(5).
68 (2007) AHRLR 73 (ACHPR 2007).
69 Para 45.

> Whenever a State alleges the failure by the complainant to exhaust domestic remedies, it has the burden of proving that the remedies that have not been exhausted are available and sufficient to cure the violation alleged ie that the function of those remedies within the domestic legal system is suitable to address an infringement of a legal right and are effective. When a state does this, the burden of responsibility shifts to the complainant who must demonstrate that the remedies in question were exhausted or that the exception provided for in article 56(5) of the African Charter is applicable.[70]

Another mechanism at the regional level is the filing of cases concerning violation of health- related rights with the African Court on Human and Peoples' Rights, which was established by the Protocol to the African Charter on Human and Peoples' Rights on the Establishment of an African Court on Human and Peoples Rights.[71] The Court shall complement the protective jurisdiction of the African Commission.[72] The jurisdiction of the Court extends

> to all cases and disputes submitted to it concerning the interpretation and application of the Charter, this Protocol and any other relevant human rights instrument ratified by the States concerned.[73]

The Court can make an appropriate order to remedy violations of human rights, including compensation and reparation. The Court may also adopt provisional or interim measures to maintain the status quo until it makes a final judgment on the matter in question. The Court may also encourage the parties to reach an amicable settlement.[74]

In order for an individual or NGO with observer status before the African Commission to bring an action before the Court, the offending state party must have made a declaration permitting individuals and NGOs to directly access the Court.[75] However, the African Commission may bring a case before the Court involving violation of human rights by a state party to the ACHPR. Given that Uganda has not yet signed a declaration permitting individuals and NGOs to have direct access to the court, these may engage the African Commission to file cases on health rights issues. CSOs should also launch campaigns to exert pressure on the state to lodge the declaration with the Secretary General.[76]

Individuals or CSOs alleging violations of health rights may also institute cases in the East African Court of Justice (EACJ). Although there is no instrument explicitly granting the Court jurisdiction over human rights, the Court has previously found that certain human rights violations

70 Para 51.
71 Art 1. Uganda ratified the Protocol on 16 February 2001.
72 Art 2.
73 Art 3.
74 Art. 9.
75 Art 34(6).
76 Art 34(7).

are contrary to the principles of good governance and the rule of law under the EAC treaty.[77] It may be argued that violations of the right to health, which as illustrated in chapter two, implicates all categories of human rights, contravene the principles of good governance and the rule of law.

2.5 Utilising TRIPS flexibilities

As earlier pointed out, being a LDC, Uganda is currently not obliged to become TRIPS compliant.[78] However, in order to take advantage of the TRIPS flexibilities, CSOs engaged in the struggle for enhanced access to medicines have urged the government to amend its patent legal regime. Indeed, the Industrial Property Act,[79] which repealed the Patents Act,[80] and attracted great input from CSOs, contains flexibilities that could be utilised to promote public health. For example, the Act excludes from patentability, 'diagnostic, therapeutic and surgical methods for the treatment of humans'[81] and

> pharmaceutical products and test data until 1st January 2016 or such other period as may be granted to Uganda or least developed countries by the Council responsible for administering the Agreement on trade related aspects of intellectual property under the World Trade Organization.[82]

The rights of the patent holder also 'extend only to acts which are done for industrial or commercial purposes but do not extend to acts which are done for scientific research'.[83]

77 Arts 6(d), 7(2) & 27(1). See the cases of *James Katabazi v Secretary General of the EAC* 20 November 2007, EACJ First Instance Division, Ref 1/2007; *Plaxeda Rugumba v Secretary General of the EAC and Attorney General of Rwanda* 1 December 2011, EACJ First Instance Division, Ref 8/2010; *Samuel Mukira Mohochi v Attorney General of Uganda* 17 May 2013, EACJ First instance Division, Ref 5/2011; and *Independent Medico Legal Unit v Attorney General of Kenya* 29 June 2011, EACJ First Instance Division, Ref 3/2010.

78 On 5 November 2005, LDCs made a request to the Council for TRIPS for an extension of the transition period under art 66(1) in which to comply with the relevant provisions of the TRIPS Agreement. On 11 June 2013, the Council noted 'the special needs and requirements of least developed country members and the economic, financial and administrative constraints they continue to face, and their need for flexibility to create a viable technological base' and decided to extend the transition period. The Council decided as follows: 'Least developed country members shall not be required to apply the provisions of the Agreement, other than articles 3, 4 and 5, until 1 July 2021, or until such a date on which they cease to be least developed country members, whichever date is earlier (para 1). The Council also reiterated the right of LDCs to make full use of the flexibilities provided by the Agreement to address their needs (para 2). See, WTO Council for TRIPS, 'Extension of the transition period under article 66.1 for least developed country members' 11 June 2013, IPC/C/64. On the rationale for extending the transition period for LDCs, see UNAIDS, 'TRIPS transition period extensions for least developed countries' http://www.unaids/contentassets/documents/unaids/unaidspublication/2013/JC2474_TRIPS-transition-period-extensions_en.pdf (accessed 8 March 2013).

79 Act Supplement 2/2014.

80 Cap 216.

81 Sec 8(3)(c).

82 Sec 8(3)(f).

83 Sec 43(1).

A patent holder also exhausts his rights in the patent once articles 'have been put on the market in Uganda or in any other country or imported into Uganda by the owner of the patent or with his or her consent'.[84] Thus, exhaustion is one of the limits to intellectual property rights (IPRs). After a product protected by an intellectual property right has been sold with the consent of an intellectual property holder, the rights of commercial exploitation over this particular product can no longer be exercised by the owner, since they are exhausted. Exhaustion is at times referred to as the first sale doctrine as the rights of commercial exploitation for the product end with its first sale. Subsequent acts of resale or other forms of commercial use can no longer be opposed or controlled by the IP holder. There are three types of exhaustion: national, regional and international. Regarding national exhaustion, the IP owner is not allowed to control the commercial exploitation of goods put on the domestic market by the owner or with his or her consent. With regional exhaustion, the first sale of the product by the IP owner or with his or her consent exhausts any IP rights over this particular product not only domestically, but within the whole region. This means that parallel imports within the region may no longer be opposed or controlled based on the IP right. In case of international exhaustion, the IP rights are exhausted the moment the product has been sold by the IP owner or with his or her consent in any part of the world.

Another limitation to IP rights is where a person uses 'the patented invention in relation to the preparation for individual cases, in a pharmacy or by a medical doctor, of a medicine in accordance with a medical prescription'.[85] It is also not an infringement of a patent where a person manufactures and exports 'to another country a patented health care invention where the export of the invention addresses a health need identified by the other country'.[86] The Act also provides for compulsory licenses[87] and exploitation of patented inventions by the government or by persons authorised by the government on grounds of public interest, including nutrition or health, national emergency or 'the development of other vital sectors of the economy'.[88]

The question is: to what extent can Uganda effectively utilise the TRIPs flexibilities to enhance public health, including access to medicines, given that it has insufficient technical expertise and infrastructural capacities? It may be necessary for Uganda to adopt a regional approach to the use of flexibilities. Uganda may take advantage of the EAC, which comprises of Uganda, Kenya, Tanzania, Rwanda and Burundi. Of all the EAC countries, only Kenya is classified by the UN as a developing

84 Sec 43(2).
85 Sec 44(d).
86 Sec 44(e).
87 Secs 58 - 65.
88 Sec 66(a).

country. Regional economic blocs such as the EAC that have LDCs forming at least half of their membership are eligible to be treated as a 'domestic market' regarding the supply of generic medicines under compulsory licensing. For example, Kenya as a developing country can export a pharmaceutical product produced or imported under a compulsory license to other EAC countries that share a public health problem. A number of commentators have argued that a regional approach to the use of flexibilities will enable similarly situated countries to address their constraints jointly by drawing on each other's expertise and experience by pooling and sharing resources and information.[89] The EAC countries must individually and collectively build their capacity by prioritising investment in health-related research and development of relevant medicines.

2.6 Claiming the right to health through participation

The concept of participation is enshrined in both legal and policy frameworks. According to the Constitution, the state 'shall involve the people in the formulation and implementation of development plans and programmes which affect them'.[90] The Constitution further provides that the state 'shall be based on democratic principles which empower and encourage the active participation of all citizens at all levels in their own governance'.[91] At the policy level, the Alma-Ata Declaration,[92] which has influenced public health policy frameworks in most countries including Uganda, calls for the provision of essential health care to individuals and families through their full participation. The Declaration provides that the people have a right and duty to participate individually and collectively in the planning and implementation of their health care.

Participation is both a human right in itself[93] and an instrumental tool to the realisation of all human rights generally and the right to health in

89 See for example, S Musungu et al *Utilizing TRIPS flexibilities for public health protection through South-South co-operation* (2004).
90 NODPSP X.
91 NODPSP II.
92 Declaration of Ama-Ata 'International conference on primary health care' Alma-Ata, USSR, 6-12 September 1978 http://who/int/publications/almaata_declaration_en.pdf (accessed 21 April 2014).
93 See for example art 25 of ICCPR, which guarantees the right to participation in the conduct of public affairs. In General Comment 25, the Human Rights Committee (HRC) stated as follows: 'The conduct of public affairs referred to in paragraph (a) [of article 25], is a broad concept which relates to the exercise of political power, in particular the exercise of legislative, executive and administrative powers. It covers all aspects of public administration, and the formulation and implementation of policy at international, national, regional and local levels ...' See HRC, General Comment 25(57), The right to participate in public affairs, voting rights and the right of equal access to public service (Article 25) UN Doc. CCPR/C/21/Rev.1/Add.7 (1996) http://www.umn.edu/humanrts/gencomment/hrcom25.htm (accessed 10 March 2014).

particular.[94] Community participation in decision making is crucial to realising a rights-based approach to health. Participation leads to an increased sense of ownership and improves the relationship between health providers and the community. Through participation, communities get informed of health issues, including their heath rights and this may serve to hold health service providers and government officials accountable. Participation must be genuine, active and meaningful taking into account the views, concerns and voices of the affected people. Participation should ensure that the rights and responsibilities of marginalised and vulnerable groups are respected. Community participation should not be tokenistic or manipulative. As Gostin has aptly pointed out,

> Free flows of information are necessary to support public [community] participation. Listening to citizens' concerns is an expression of a government's commitment to fairness and justice. Civic participation also gives communities a stake in their own health – it provides a feedback mechanism for informing policy and arriving at more considered judgments. Deliberative decision making requires genuine listening, as well as attention to the views of relevant constituencies – the public, stakeholders, and the disadvantaged, who might not be heard if their input is not actively sought.[95]

Through genuine, active and meaningful participation, communities may be able to question the neo-liberal top-down market oriented policies discussed above, which deprive them of their health related entitlements. Through participation, they may also demand an increased budgetary expenditure on health. They may also minimise corruption in the health sector by following up the health goods that have been allocated to the health centres in their area.

Participation should not be only for the elite and the rich. Indigent people may be illiterate, but they are certainly not ignorant individuals who need enlightenment on all their problems. They are acutely aware of the issues that affect them and thus must be afforded an opportunity to actively participate in the design, implementation, monitoring and evaluation of all health-related policies intended for their benefit. Policies and programmes that do not solicit their input are antithetical to the right of participation and are bound to fail. They should be sensitised on how to demand accountability from health providers and government officials. In other words, they should be sensitised about their health-related rights and how to claim them.

94 See, H Potts 'Participation and the right to the highest attainable standard of health' http://www.essex.ac.uk/human_rights_centre/reserach/rth/projects.aspx (accessed 13 May 2013); AE Yamin 'Suffering and powerlessness: The significance of promoting participation in rights based approaches to health' (2009) 11 *Health & Human Rights* 5.

95 LO Gostin *Global health law* (2014) 264.

2.7 Tackling inequitable gender relations

A gender perspective should be incorporated in all policies, programmes and practices, and in all spheres of life including family and community life. The policy frameworks must take into account women's special health needs by providing free health care services near their work place to enable them access and utilise such services. Gender relations must become an integral part of all health-related issues. Tackling inequitable gender relations may not be easy because they involve entrenched and deeply embedded norms of behaviour and traditional beliefs about gender roles in society. There is a need for strong political will to tackle the challenge. The state should recognise the economic value of women's work because of its vital contribution to families, communities and the state. There is need for aggressive education and sensitisation programmes to tackle or mitigate negative cultural practices that discriminate against women.

It should be noted that men are marginalised by most sexual and reproductive health frameworks, yet they play a critical role in women's lives. Men should be encouraged to participate in sexual and reproductive health (SRH) interventions meant for their women's benefit. They should also be educated and sensitised about their SRH rights and responsibilities.

2.8 Providing free health care to those unable to afford

As illustrated in chapter two, state parties to the CESCR are obliged to fulfil the right to health, which includes providing health care goods and services to those who are unable, by the means at their disposal to provide for themselves. The state is therefore obliged to provide essential health-care services such as malaria treatment, ARTs and emergency obstetric care free of charge to its people.

The state can also learn from countries such as Rwanda by designing and implementing a community health insurance scheme. People can contribute small affordable premiums to the insurance fund. In the short and medium terms, this can be supplemented by funds from the donors. However, in order to make the scheme sustainable, the state must contribute funds to it. The funds can be obtained through indirect taxation of the wealthy. For example 2 per cent tax can be levied on the sale of luxury goods such as fuel, beer or cigarettes.

3 Conclusion

The right to health has a firm foundation in international and regional instruments, which Uganda has signed and ratified. However, one major challenge for the realisation of the right to health in Uganda is that the constitutional foundation for the right is not strong enough. There are other juridical challenges such as a judiciary that lacks sufficient creativity. However, these challenges are surmountable through well thought out strategies such as lobbying Parliament for the amendment of the Constitution and other relevant legislation to take into account the standards set forth in international and regional instruments on the right to health.

The concept of PIL has taken shape in the country and lawyers should be encouraged to embrace it in respect to the right to health. Judges should also be sensitised on the fact that they have the mandate and competence to listen to the poor whose right to health is under constant threat.

There is also need to revisit the restrictive laws on abortion to ensure that women may access safe termination of pregnancy. However, given the emotive nature of abortion, there is need for aggressive sensitisation of key stake holders such as legislators, the executive, judicial officers, religious and cultural leaders. CSOs should mobilise experts to explain to these stakeholders the benefits of legalising abortion. The experts should be equipped with data on the contribution of unsafe abortion to maternal morbidity and mortality in the country. Evidence from other jurisdictions where unsafe abortion has reduced as a result of changes in the law should be adduced. The experts should emphasise the health and human rights consequences of unsafe abortion.

The government should also take advantage of TRIPS flexibilities in order to enhance access to medicines. The government should also review its health policies to ensure that special attention is paid to those who are unable to provide for themselves. The government should provide free services such as emergency obstetric care where necessary. The poor, marginalised and vulnerable members of society should actively participate in the design, implementation, monitoring and evaluation of policies and programmes intended for their benefit. They should be sensitised about their health rights and how to demand them. In short, their voices must be heard and answered.

5

LAWS REGARDING PUBLIC HEALTH AND HEALTH RIGHTS

> *[Public] [h]ealth legislation can be an important vehicle towards ensuring the promotion and protection of the right to health. In the design and review of health legislation, human rights provide a useful tool to determine its effectiveness and appropriateness in line with human rights and public health goals.*[1]

1 Introduction

The World Health Organisation (WHO) fulfils its mandate of promoting the health of communities and populations through the provision of leadership on matters critical to health. It plays an essential role in the global governance of health and disease.[2] It spearheads the generation, translation and dissemination of knowledge on health, assesses health trends, sets norms and standards and monitors and evaluates their implementation.[3] One of the ways through which it achieves the objectives of promotion and protection of public health is through legislation. The WHO has observed that appropriate legislation is fundamental to the promotion and protection of public health.[4] Legislation is necessary to

> protect and promote the health of populations; sustain health policies and programmes; fight new and re-emerging communicable diseases; support the development of health systems; and combat continuing poverty, inequalities in health and discrimination.[5]

As noted in the previous chapters, one of the ways in which the right to health may be realised is through juridical measures, which include

1 WHO *25 questions on health and human rights* (2002) 23.
2 See JP Ruger & D Yach (2008) 'The global role of the World Health Organisation' Global Health Governance vol II, No 2, 1-11.
3 Ruger & Yach (n 2 above) 1.
4 WHO 'Health and human rights' http://who.int/hhr/health_law/health (accessed 20 June 2013).
5 As above.

legislation and case law. The government has an obligation to develop laws that enhance the promotion and protection of this right.

Uganda has many laws with a bearing on public health.[6] However, most of them are antiquated and outmoded in ways that curtail their effectiveness and conformity with modern standards in the area of public health. The laws are mostly disease specific and do not adequately address the underlying conditions of health and the relevant public health infrastructure. They do not reflect the contemporary understanding of disease and injury. In fact, public health law in Uganda generally lags behind the public health policy framework, which attempts to address the different health risks that affect the population. Most of public health legislation in Uganda is piece-meal and multi-layered and contains weak enforcement mechanisms, all of which may undermine its effectiveness in the protection of public health. Against this backdrop, this chapter uses the framework of public health and human rights, to examine some of the public health legislation with a view of finding out the extent to which they balance the goals of promoting public health without unduly undermining internationally and constitutionally recognised human rights and freedoms.

2 What is public health law?

Before mapping out the meaning of public health law, it is necessary to understand the concept of public health. In the first part of the 20th century, Winslow defined public health as,

> the science and art of preventing disease, prolonging life and promoting physical health and efficiency through organized community efforts for the sanitation of the environments, the control of community infections, the education of the individual in the principles of personal hygiene, the organization of medical and nursing service for the early diagnosis and preventative treatment of disease, and the development of social machinery which will ensure to every individual in the community a standard of living adequate for the maintenance of health.[7]

The Institute of Medicine defines public health as 'what we as a society do collectively to assure the conditions in which people can be healthy'.[8] Acheson also defines public health as 'the science and art of preventing disease, prolonging life and promoting, protecting and improving health through the organized efforts of society'.[9] Turnock defines public health as

6 See for example the Public Health Act, the Venereal Diseases Act, the National Drug Policy and Authority Act, the Water Act, the Food and Drugs Act, and the HIV/AIDS Prevention and Control Act.

7 CEA Winslow 'The united fields of public health' (1920) 51 *Science* (1306) 30.

8 Institute of Medicine *The future of public health* (1988) 19.

9 D Acheson *Committee of inquiry into the future development of the public health function* (1998) 50.

a 'collective effort to identify and address the unacceptable realities that result in preventable and avoidable health outcomes, and it is the composite of efforts and activities carried out by people committed to these ends'.[10]

The above definitions illustrate the point that public health is multi-faceted and is at times a contested concept.[11] It covers many factors that affect health, including the natural and built environment, sanitation, smoking, pollution, and hygiene. It also covers key factors that affect the quality of life such as preventive and curative health care, income, societal inequalities, availability of employment, nutrition, education, domestic violence and general socio-economic well-being of the people. Public health concerns the health of populations or at least larger groups of persons rather than the clinical improvement of individual patients.[12] The major objective of public health interventions is to prevent and manage diseases, injuries and other health conditions.[13] Novick and Morrow also observe that public health aims at ensuring conditions that promote health and 'consists of organized efforts to improve the health of communities. The operative components of this definition are that efforts are organized and directed to communities rather than to individuals'.[14] Rothstein also observes that a key element in public health is the role and power of the government to apply mandatory or coercive measures to tackle a threat to the public's health.[15]

The question now is: what is public health law? According to Tobey, public health law may be defined as 'that branch of jurisprudence which treats the relation and application of the common and statutory law to the principles and procedures of hygiene, sanitary science, and public health administration'.[16] Gostin aptly defines public health law as,

> the study of the legal powers and duties of the state, in collaboration with its partners (e.g. health care, business, the community, the media, and academic), to ensure the conditions for people to be healthy (to identify, prevent, and ameliorate risks to health in the population), and of the limitations on the powers of the state to constrain for the common good the autonomy, privacy, liberty, proprietary, and other legally protected interests of individuals. The primary objective of public health law is to pursue the highest possible level of

10 BJ Turnock *Public health: What it is and how it works* (2001) 19.
11 On the contested nature of the concept of public health, see, M Verweij & A Dawson 'The meaning of "public" in public health' http://fds.oup.com/www.oup.co.uk/pdf/o-19-9 (accessed 4 July 2013).
12 LO Gostin 'Public health law: Power, duty and restraint: A resource guide' (1999) http://www.turningpointprogram.org (accessed 3 July 2013).
13 Verweij & Dawson (n 11 above) 21.
14 LF Novick & CB Morrow 'Historical and contemporary developments' http://www.jblearning.com/samples/076373842 (accessed 4 July 2013).
15 MA Rothstein 'Rethinking the meaning of public health' (2002) 20 *The Journal of Law, Medicine and Ethics* 144.
16 AJ Tobey *Public health law* (1947) 4.

physical and mental health in the population, consistent with the values of social justice'.[17]

Thus, public health law can be defined as that branch of health law that empowers the government to discharge its obligations to promote and protect the health and safety of the population. It delimits the functions and powers of government agencies and specifies the ways in which they may exercise their authority for the purposes of assuring the conditions for the public's health. In the exercise of its powers, the government must ensure that the rights and freedoms of individuals and groups in society may be restricted or limited only in circumstances permitted by the law.

3 Public health and human rights

Human rights are the basic rights and freedoms to which all human beings are entitled basically because they are human. Human rights treat all people as equal and are universal, interdependent, indivisible and interrelated.[18] They cover all categories of civil, economic, political, social and cultural rights and include: human dignity, the right to life, the right to health, the right to property, access to food and water, liberty, non-discrimination and equality, privacy, autonomy and integrity, freedom of movement, freedom of expression and assembly and the right to work.

It is increasingly recognised that the fields of public health and human rights complement each other and share the same goal: the advancement of human well-being.[19] Public health 'is concerned with promoting and protecting health – in other words, physical, mental, and social well-being – and with preventing or reducing morbidity (illness, disability, or suffering) and premature mortality'.[20] Human rights such as the right to health are also concerned with promoting the health and well-being of individuals and populations. Human rights violations such as torture, degrading and inhuman treatment or denial of health care may have serious health impacts, including loss of life. Progress in tackling public health challenges will most likely contribute to improvement in the realisation of the right to health. Thus, each is dependent on the other to improve the human condition. However, it cannot be denied that public health and human rights may conflict in approach. Whereas the human rights based approach (HRBA) emphasises respect for individual rights and freedoms such as liberty, privacy and autonomy, public health may employ mandatory and coercive measures, such as compulsory

17 Gostin (n 12 above).
18 United Nations Human Rights (UNHR) 'Vienna declaration and programme of action' Adopted by the World Conference on Human Rights in Vienna 25 June 1993 http://www.ohchr/enprofessionalinterest/pages/vienna.aspx (accessed 13 October 2013).
19 JA Mann et al *Health and human rights: A reader* (1999) 11
20 Mann et al (n 19 above) 46.

examination, compulsory quarantine, compulsory isolation and detention of infected persons. These measures may have serious implications for individual rights and freedoms.

A HRBA to health specifically aims at realising the right to health and other related human rights. The approach should aim at developing the capacity of duty bearers to meet their obligations and empowering rights holders, especially marginalised groups, to effectively understand and claim their health rights.[21] The HRBA also aims at developing the capacity of duty bearers to meet their obligations and empowering rights holders to effectively claim their health rights.[22] Elimination of all forms of discrimination and achieving equality is at the heart of a HRBA. The Committee on ESCR[23] has stressed that discrimination, which is an immediate and cross-cutting obligation in the CESCR, undermines the fulfilment of economic, social and cultural rights.[24] Thus, states parties should eliminate all forms of discrimination in the realisation of economic, social and cultural rights such as the right to health.[25] The state should ensure that any public health legislation does not discriminate on prohibited grounds, including health status and sexual orientation.[26] States parties should ensure that a person's sexual orientation or actual and perceived health status are not barriers to realising the rights in the CESCR.[27] The Committee on ESCR has further noted that although the protection of public health is often cited by states as a basis for restricting human rights in the context of a person's health status, many such restrictions are discriminatory.[28] Thus, states parties should adopt measures to address widespread discrimination of persons on the basis of their health status in respect for example of mental illness, women who have suffered obstetric fistula, tuberculosis (TB), leprosy and HIV/AIDS.[29]

It should be noted that the limitation of human rights for protection of public interest, which includes public health, is permitted by the human rights framework, in very narrow circumstances. According to the Universal Declaration,

> In the exercise of his rights and freedoms, everyone shall be subject only to such limitations as are determined by law solely for the purpose of seeking

21 OHCHR 'A human rights-based approach' http://www.ohchr.org/Documents/Issues/Escr (accessed 1 July 2013).
22 As above.
23 General Comment 20 'Non discrimination in economic, social and cultural rights (art 2, para 2 of the International Covenant on Economic, Social and Cultural Rights) Forty-Second Session, Geneva, 4-22 May 2009, Agenda item 3, E/C.12/GC/20.
24 Para 1.
25 Para 7.
26 Paras 8, 32 & 33.
27 Paras 32 & 33.
28 As above.
29 As above.

> due recognition and respect for the rights and freedoms of others and of meeting the just requirements of morality, public opinion and the general welfare in a democratic society.[30]

According to the ICCPR, '[n]o one shall be subjected to arbitrary arrest or detention'[31] and '[n]o one shall be deprived of his liberty except on such grounds and in accordance with such procedure as are established by law'.[32] Coercive measures should be used sparingly and as a last resort. The CESCR also provides that,

> [t]he States Parties to the present Covenant recognize that, in the enjoyment of those rights provided by the State in conformity with the present Covenant, the State may subject such rights only to such limitations as are determined by law only in so far as this may be compatible with the nature of those rights and solely for the purpose of promoting the general welfare in a democratic society.[33]

The Siracusa Principles have elaborated on the scope of limitation of human rights and freedoms.[34] According to these principles, the limitation or restriction must meet the following conditions:

- The limitation must be justified by the protection of a legitimate goal such as ... protection of public health ...;
- Limitations can be allowed only in a democratic society which presumes a participatory process and capacity of redress;
- A right may be limited only if the limitation is provided by law;
- The limitation of rights must be strictly necessary in order to achieve the public good, which must be carefully assessed on a case-by-case basis;
- The limitation of individual rights must be proportional to the public interest and its objective;
- The limitation must be the least intrusive and least restrictive measure available which will accomplish the public health goal; [and]
- The limitation of rights must be applied in a non-discriminatory manner.[35]

As pointed out above, public health law can provide a legal mandate for action by government and its agencies in their quest to promote and protect public health. However, in the enforcement of public health measures, the right to health and related human rights may be burdened by such measures. Thus, in the context public health legislation, the Siracusa Principles provide a normative framework for mediating between a state's

30 Art 29(2).
31 Art 9(1).
32 Art 9(1).
33 Art 4.
34 The Siracusa Principles on the limitation of and derogation provisions in the international covenant on civil and political rights, E/CN.4/A985/4.
35 The Siracusa Principles have been summarised by J Mann et al (n 19 above) 47 - 48.

powers to protect public health, and the human rights and freedoms of individuals. The principles were drafted in response to concerns about the violation of individual human rights that may occur when a state acts to protect the public good by limiting the rights of an individual. The Siracusa Principles aim at balancing the rights of the individual versus the state's interest in ensuring the well-being of the larger population. The Siracusa Principles have been applied in a number of cases. For example, in *Sunday Times v United Kingdom (No 1)*,[36] a case concerning freedom of expression, the European Court of Human Rights, interpreted the phrase 'prescribed by law' requirement as follows:

> First, the law must be adequately accessible: the citizen must be able to have an indication that is adequate in the circumstances of the legal rules applicable to a given case. Secondly, a norm cannot be regarded as 'law' unless it is formulated with sufficient precision to enable the citizen to regulate his conduct: he must be able – if need be with appropriate advice – to foresee, to a degree that is reasonable in the circumstances, the consequences which a given action may entail.[37]

On the main purpose of a limitation clause, the Supreme Court of Ghana, in *Republic v Thompson Books Ltd & Others*,[38] stated as follows:

> In other words the primary purpose of a constitutional limitation clause is to limit the governmental restrictions themselves. And the clause does so by indicating the limited ends that the restriction must serve as well as the limited means that it may employ. Thus, in a case involving a claim of right vis-à-vis a governmental restriction of that right, what should be on trial is the governmental restriction, not the constitutional right. The effect of a restriction on the essence of the right is a primary factor in determining constitutionality. The evolving comparative jurisprudence emphasizes the principles of necessity, reasonableness, and proportionality (least restrictive means) as benchmarks that reviewing courts must apply in evaluating the constitutionality of a particular statutory restriction.[39]

In *Media Rights Agenda & Others v Nigeria*[40] the African Commission also observed that the limitation must be necessary or acceptable in a democratic society and not render the right illusory. The Commission held that the onus is on the state to prove that the limitation is justified. In *Article 19 v Eritrea*,[41] it was held that the limitation of rights must be consistent with international law and that '... only restrictions which are consistent with the Charter and with the states parties' international obligations should be enacted by the relevant national authorities'.[42] The African Commission further stated as follows:

36 (1979-1980) EHRR 245.
37 Para 49.
38 (1996-7) SGGLR 484.
39 *Thompson Books Ltd* (n 38 above) 489.
40 (2000) AHRLR 191 (ACHPR 1998).
41 (2007) AHRLR 73 (AHRLR 2007).
42 Para 82.

> To allow national law to have precedence over the international law of the Charter would defeat the purpose of the rights and freedoms enshrined in the Charter. International human rights standards must always prevail over contradictory national law. Any limitation on the rights of the Charter must be in conformity with the provisions of the Charter.[43]

It should be noted that that case law that discusses limitation of rights and freedoms on ground of public health powers is limited. However, according to jurisprudence of the European Court of Human Rights, any detention imposed to protect public health must comply with the principle of proportionality, demonstrate a lack of arbitrariness, be the measure of last resort, and have its objective of not only protecting the healthy but also care for the ill. For example, in *Enhorn v Sweden*,[44] a HIV positive man detained by Swedish public health authorities on public health grounds successfully challenged his detention on the grounds that it violated the Convention. In *Kiyutin v Russia*,[45] the applicant, a national of Uzbekistan with a Russian spouse, was asked to undergo a medical examination in conjunction with his application for a resident permit in Russia. He was refused a permit because he tested HIV positive. Given that he had been subjected to differential treatment on account of his health status, the European Court of Human Rights examined whether the state's justification was reasonable. The court rejected Russia's public health rationale for excluding PLHA as residents, and observed that,

> [t]he mere presence of a HIV positive individual in a country is not in itself a threat to public health: HIV is not transmitted casually but through specific behaviours that include sexual intercourse and sharing syringes as the main routes of transmission.[46]

According to the Ugandan Constitution, derogation of human rights is prohibited only in respect of: (a) freedom from torture and cruel, inhuman or degrading treatment or punishment; (b) freedom from slavery or servitude; (c) the right to a fair hearing; and (d) the right to an order of habeas corpus.[47]Albeit the Constitution guarantees personal liberty, a person may also be deprived of this right: 'for the purpose of preventing the spread of an infectious or contagious disease'[48] and this may involve solitary confinement, quarantining, destruction of property, and other mandatory and coercive measures. A person may also be deprived of liberty if he or she 'is, or is reasonably suspected to be, of unsound mind or addicted to drugs or alcohol, for the purpose of the care or treatment of that person or the protection of the community'.[49] However, derogation or limitation of any right must not be 'beyond what is acceptable and

43 Para 105.
44 ECHR 5652/00 (2005).
45 ECHR 2011/14 (10 March 2011), app 2700/10.
46 Para 68.
47 Art 44(a) - (d) of the Constitution.
48 Art 23(1)(d) of the Constitution.
49 Art23(1)(f) of the Constitution.

demonstrably justifiable in a free and democratic society'.[50] In *Charles Onyango Obbo & Another v AG*,[51] a case concerning freedom of expression, the Supreme Court of Uganda stated as follows:

> Protection of the guaranteed rights is a primary objective of the Constitution. Limiting their enjoyment is an exception to their protection, and is therefore a secondary objective. Although the Constitution provides for both, it is obvious that the primary objective must be dominant. It can be overridden only in the exceptional circumstances that give rise to that second objective. In that eventuality, only minimal impairment of enjoyment of the right, strictly warranted by the circumstance is permissible.[52]

On the standard of limitation of rights, the Court observed that under article 43(2) of the Constitution, 'democratic values and principles are the criteria on which any limitation on the enjoyment of rights and freedoms guaranteed under the Constitution has to be justified'.[53] On the meaning of the phrase 'free and democratic society', Mulenga JSC cited the Canadian case of *R v Oakes*,[54] where the Supreme Court of Canada, in interpreting the limitation clause in the Canadian Charter on Rights and freedoms, which is similar to that in the Ugandan Constitution, stated as follows:

> Inclusion of these words ('free and democratic society') as the final standard of justification for limits on rights and freedoms refers the court to the very purpose for which the Charter was originally entrenched in the Constitution: Canadian society is to be free and democratic. The court must be guided by the values and principles essential to a free and democratic society, which I believe embody, to name but a few, respect for the inherent dignity of the human person, commitment to social justice and equality ... The underlying values and principles of a free and democratic society are the genesis of the rights and freedoms guaranteed by the Charter and the ultimate standard against which a limit on a right or freedom must be shown ... to be reasonable and demonstrably justified ... The onus of proving that a limit on a right or freedom is reasonable and demonstrably justified in a free and democratic society rests upon the party seeking to uphold the limitation.[55]

It can be seen from the above discussion that any legislation that seeks to promote and protect public health may limit rights and freedoms only in exceptional circumstances. As Mulenga JSC observed in *Onyango Obbo* case above, the test of what is acceptable and demonstrably justifiable for the purposes of limitation is objective and not subjective. The test must conform to what is universally accepted to be a free and democratic society since there can be no varying degrees of democratic societies.

50 Art 43(2)(c) of the Constitution.
51 (2004) AHRLR 256.
52 Para 30.
53 Para 49.
54 (1986) 1 SCR 103.
55 *R v Oakes* (n 54 above) para 48.

There is no doubt that Uganda is obliged to protect public health, including preventing the spread of infectious diseases. In fact, one of the steps to be taken by states towards the realisation of the right to health is '[t]he prevention, treatment and control of epidemic, endemic, occupational and other diseases'.[56] According to the Committee on ESCR, the state is obliged to establish

> prevention and education programmes for behaviour-related health concerns such as sexually transmitted diseases, in particular HIV/AIDS, and those adversely affecting sexual and reproductive health, and the promotion of social determinants of good health ...[57]

In doing so, the state must ensure that any public health legislation or other prevention programmes or interventions purporting to limit human rights and freedoms do not exceed the criteria laid down in international and regional human rights instruments and the Constitution. In this vein, I consider in the next section the extent to which relevant provisions of three pieces of legislation – the Public Health Act, the Venereal Diseases Act, and the HIV and AIDS Prevention and Control Act – meet the criteria on limitation of human rights and freedoms while dealing with infectious or communicable diseases.

4 Public health legislation and infectious or communicable diseases

4.1 General public health

The main legislation regulating public health in Uganda generally and infectious or communicable diseases in particular is the Public Health Act,[58] which seeks to 'consolidate the law regarding the preservation of public health'.[59] Under the Act, the Minister may by statutory order declare any infectious disease a notifiable disease for the purpose of the Act.[60] An infectious disease is defined as 'any disease which can be communicated directly or indirectly by any person suffering from it to any other person'.[61] The Minister may make rules in respect of the notification of the disease as to, inter alia, duties of medical practitioners, heads of families, head teachers, and local authorities in handling the disease.[62] The Act further provides that a medical officer of health is empowered to inspect premises where he has reasonable grounds to believe that any

56 Art 12(2)(c).
57 Para 16.
58 Cap 281 Laws of Uganda
59 Long title to the Act.
60 Sec10(a).
61 Sec 1(u).
62 Sec 10(a) - (j).

person(s) suffering from an infectious disease has or have resided on the premises.[63] Such person(s) may be compulsorily medically examined by the medical officer who may order the destruction of buildings and articles therein provided that the local authority shall provide reasonable compensation.[64] The medical officer may also recover the expenses incurred from the owner or occupier as a civil debt.[65]

Part V of the Act deals with certain epidemic or endemic diseases, which include

> smallpox, plague, Asiatic cholera, yellow fever, cerebrospinal meningitis, typhus, sleeping sickness or human trypanosomiasis and any other disease which the Minister may by statutory order declare to be a formidable epidemic disease for the purpose of the Part of this Act.[66]

The Minister may make rules for inter alia, the speedy interment of the dead; house to house visitation; provision of medical aid and accommodation; preventing a person from leaving any infected area; destruction of rats and mosquitoes; and the destruction of infected property.[67] From a public health point of view, some of these measures are critical in enabling the Minister to quickly act in case of an outbreak of a disease in a specific area. It may be argued that compulsory measures for patients suffering from some communicable diseases such as TB, typhoid, yellow fever or cholera may be aimed at a legitimate objective: to protect the community from infection. The measures may thus be relevant to the general interest and well-being of the entire population.

However, implementation of the above measures may have serious implications for human rights. The measures may adversely affect a number of human rights, including freedom from torture, cruel, inhuman and degrading treatment, privacy, confidentiality, the right to refuse medical treatment and bodily integrity. The measures taken may even increase stigma and discrimination against a person(s) suffering from such a disease. Since the rules made by the minister may be hurriedly made due to the urgency of the matter, it is even not clear whether they would meet the necessary procedural safeguards for limitation of rights as discussed above. It is necessary to ensure that the rules describe the individuals to be subject to any compulsory examination and treatment measures. The rules should also contain mechanisms to monitor confinement or treatment to ensure that it was carried out safely and humanely. It is also vital that the rules provide patients, who have been deprived of their liberty, with the opportunity, including legal representation to challenge the legality of their detention.

63 Sec12.
64 See secs 12 - 27 of the Act.
65 Sec 13(2).
66 Sec 28 of the Act.
67 Sec 29(a) - (u).

Part VIII of the Act deals with venereal diseases, which include

> primary or secondary syphilis in its contagious forms, acute and chronic gonorrhoeal opthalmia, soft chancre, lympho granuloma inguinale, granulaoma venereum and any other disease that may be declared by the Minister by statutory instrument as a venereal disease.[68]

The Act also bars the employment of a person suffering from a venereal disease and provides as follows:

> Every person who, while suffering from any venereal disease in a communicable form, accepts or continues in employment either as an employee or on his or her own account in or about any factory, shop, hotel, restaurant, house, or any place in any capacity entailing the care of children, or the handling of food intended for consumption, or food utensils for use by any other person, commits an offence, unless he or she proves that he or she did not know or suspect, and had no reasonable means of knowing or suspecting, that he or she was so suffering.[69]

A person who employs a person suffering from a venereal disease in the circumstances outlined above also commits an offence and is supposed to summarily dismiss the employee with payment of wages up to the date of dismissal.[70] These draconian and obnoxious provisions violate the right of every person to work[71] and 'to practice his or her profession and to carry out any lawful occupation, trade or businesses'.[72] The provisions also violate the principles of equality and non-discrimination on grounds of health status. They contravene employment laws which prohibit discrimination and stigma in the work place. The provisions may be abused by an overzealous minister who may declare HIV/AIDS a venereal disease, and subject its prevention and management to these onerous provisions since it is also largely spread through sexual contact. This may exacerbate HIV/AIDS related stigmatisation and discrimination contrary to the advice by UNAIDS that states should ensure that public health law provisions 'applicable to sexually transmitted diseases are not inappropriately applied to HIV and that they are consistent with international human rights obligations'.[73] The Employment Act also calls for promotion of 'equality of opportunity, with a view to eliminating discrimination in employment'[74] and expressly outlaws discrimination on grounds of HIV status.[75]

68 Sec 49.
69 Sec 50(1).
70 Sec 50(2) &(3).
71 Art 40 of the Constitution; Art 6 of the CESCR.
72 Art 40(2) of the Constitution.
73 Guideline 3.
74 Sec 6(1) of the Employment Act, 2006.
75 Sec 6(3).

The question of discrimination of PLHA in the work place was considered in the South African case of *Hoffman v South African Airways*,[76] where the appellant challenged the constitutionality of the South African Airways (SAA) practice of refusing to employ PLHA as cabin attendants. The appellant, living with HIV was refused employment by SAA as a cabin attendant because of his HIV positive status. The question before the court was whether such practice was consistent with the Bill of Rights of the South African Constitution. SAA argued that exclusion of the appellant from employment was dictated by its employment practice, which required exclusion from employment as cabin attendants of all PLHA. SAA justified the practice on safety, medical and operational grounds. It argued that in addition to being unfit to fly, people who are HIV positive are prone to contracting opportunistic diseases such as diarrhoea and TB and may transmit the diseases to others.[77] The High Court agreed with SAA that the practice was justified and did not unfairly discriminate against PLHA.

When evidence on the nature of the disease, its progression, prevention and treatment was presented on appeal, SAA conceded that: (a) the employment practice in question cannot be justified on medical grounds; and (b) its refusal to consider employing the appellant because he was HIV positive was unfair. In spite of this concession, court went ahead to determine whether any constitutional rights of the appellant were violated by SAA, and if so, the appropriate relief to which he is entitled. The court observed that as an organ of the state, SAA was expressly prohibited from discriminating against others by the Constitution.[78] The court cited the case of *President of the Republic of South Africa v Hugo*[79] where it was held that, '[a]t the heart of the prohibition of unfair discrimination is the recognition that under our constitution all human beings regardless of their position, must be accorded equal dignity'.[80] Albeit the court took cognisance of the fact that the commercial interests of SAA had to be taken into account in determining whether it was justified in refusing the appellant employment, Ngcobo J stated that,

> we must guard against allowing stereotyping and prejudice to creep in under the guise of commercial interests. The greater interests of society require the recognition of the inherent dignity of every human being and the elimination of all forms of discrimination. Our Constitution protects the weak, the marginalised, the socially outcast, and the victims of prejudice and stereotyping. It is only when these groups are protected that we can be secure that our own rights are protected.[81]

76 2001 (1) SA 1 (CC).
77 Para 7.
78 Sec 9.
79 1997 (4) SA 1 (CC) para 41.
80 Para 27. For a comment on the constitutional values espoused by the *Hoffman* case, see C Ngwena 'Constitutional values and HIV/AIDS in the workplace: *Hoffman v South African Airways*' (2001) 1 *Developing World Bioethics* 42.
81 Para 34.

The court noted that discrimination against a PLHA is an assault on their dignity and held that SAA discriminated against the appellant because of his HV status and there was no justification for such discrimination. The court pointed out that PLHA enjoy special protection under the South African Employment Equity Act. The court noted that SAA should not be permitted to condemn the appellant to 'certain economic death' and granted an order of instatement which

> requires an employer to employ an employee, [and] is a basic element of the appropriate relief in the case of a prospective employee who is denied employment for reasons declared impermissible by the Constitution. It strikes effectively at the source of unfair discrimination. It is an expression of the general rule that where a wrong has been committed, the aggrieved person, should as a general matter and as far as possible, be placed in the same position the person would have been but for the wrong suffered. In proscribing unfair discrimination, the Constitution not only seeks to prevent unfair discrimination but also eliminate the effects thereof. In the context of employment, the attainment of that objective rests not only upon the elimination of the discriminatory practice but also requires that the person who suffered a wrong as a result of unlawful discrimination be, as far as possible, restored to the position in which he or she would have been but for the unfair discrimination.[82]

One of the cases cited by the court in *Hoffman* case is the Indian case of *MX v ZY*[83] where MX, a casual labourer with a public sector corporation was denied permanent employment after testing HIV positive. The Court rejected the company's argument that it was legitimate to insist that candidates meet medical requirements in order be eligible for employment and to refuse candidates whose medical examinations showed them to be suffering from a serious disease. The court emphatically stated that the state should not condemn HIV positive people to economic death[84] and stated as follows:

> The impugned rule which denies employment to the HIV-infected person merely on ground of his HIV status irrespective of his ability to perform the job requirements and irrespective of the fact that he does not pose any threat to others at the workplace is clearly arbitrary and unreasonable and infringes the wholesome requirement of Article 14 [equality before the law] as well as Article 21 [protection of life and personal liberty] of the Constitution of India. Accordingly we hold that the [employer's policy] in so far as it directs that if the employee is found to be HIV-positive by ELISA test, his services will be terminated is unconstitutional, illegal and invalid and therefore is quashed.[85]

Part VIII of the Act contains a provision which could be used by the Ministry of Health or the National Drug Authority (NDA) to deal with

82 Para 50.
83 AIR 1997 Bom 406 (High Court of Bombay).
84 Para 56.
85 Para 54.

misleading and deceptive advertisements, which are likely to endanger public health. The Act provides as follows:

> No person shall publish, exhibit or circulate any advertisement or statement intended to promote the sale of medicine, appliance or article for the alleviation or cure of any venereal disease or disease affecting the generative organs or functions, or of sexual impotence, or for any complaint or infirmity arising from or relating to sexual intercourse.[86]

It should be noted that a number of advertisements in some tabloids in the country such as *Red Pepper*[87] for example, claim to administer 'concoctions' for manhood enlargement, treatment of premature ejaculation, gonorrhoea, syphilis, tightening women's private parts, and manpower boosting. Such concoctions may be injurious or dangerous to health since there is no scientific evidence to show that they work as alleged.

The Act has a number of weaknesses, which may render it ineffective in the protection of the public health. In the first place, the Act is generally obsolete having not kept pace with rapid and extensive changes in science and technology in the areas of prevention, treatment and care. For example, it only focuses on infectious or communicable diseases, yet non-communicable diseases (NCDs) are a public health concern. NCDs include hypertension, cardiovascular diseases, diabetes, chronic respiratory diseases, mental illness, cancer conditions, injuries, and oral diseases.[88] In respect of child health, the Act provides for immunisation against small pox, which was eradicated from the country, but does not address other child killer diseases such as measles, tetanus, diarrhoea and pneumonia.

Another major weakness of the Act is the over reliance on criminal sanctions as an enforcement mechanism. It cannot be denied that criminal law is a powerful tool that may serve various societal interests and may express a collective social view that a particular behaviour is wrong. Criminal law may also be a means through which a social group validates its views. One of the functions of punishment is to make criminals internalise the social and economic cost of their action. Penal sanctions are

86 Sec 51(1).
87 See eg *Red Pepper* 3 February 2014.
88 Ministry of Health *Health sector strategic plan 2010/11-14* (2010) 16 - 17. The World Health Assembly (WHA) has passed a number of resolutions to reduce the major NCD factors responsible for cardiovascular disease, cancer and diabetes. See for example WHA, Resolution WHA 55.23 'Global strategy on diet, physical activity and health' 18 May 2002; WHA, Resolution WHA 57.17 'Global strategy on diet, physical activity and health' 22 May 2004. See also WHO *Action plan for the global strategy for the prevention and control of non-communicable Diseases* (2009).

supposed to deter the criminal and others from committing similar crimes.[89] However, as Gostin has aptly noted,

> [p]robably the most important goal of the criminal law in the context of a disease epidemic is deterrence. The best that can be hoped for is that the threat of criminal sanctions will prevent people from taking unreasonable risks that could transmit the virus. The criminal law is not a likely vehicle for deterring such behaviour. In most cases where the criminal law has been used ... there was no motive or advance planning. Spontaneous behaviour driven by human anguish, despair or passion is difficult to prevent.[90]

Apprehending criminals is very costly: it requires manpower, considerable time and other resources. Thus, a sentence or fine imposed on the criminal should be punitive enough: equivalent to the social cost of the crime. However, the penalties under the Act are not punitive enough to achieve their intended purpose. The fines under the Act range from 80 Uganda shillings to 2000 Uganda shillings. Although these amounts may have been reasonable when the Act was enacted, they are now worthless and are certainly not equivalent to the injury or damage to public health. In any case, enforcement of certain penal provisions may threaten some human rights. For example, penalising a person who has refused or failed to disclose to an employer that he or she has a venereal disease threatens the right to privacy and the right to health. Such persons who are mandatorily required to disclose their health status may be driven underground and not access health care services. Legislative approaches to a public health challenge must ensure that they respect individual human rights and freedoms and any restriction should be a last resort.

4.2 Venereal diseases

It is necessary to read Part VIII of the Public Health Act together with the Venereal Diseases Act,[91] which provides for the examination and treatment of persons infected with venereal diseases. The Act provides for compulsory medical examination: it empowers any medical officer of health to require 'any person whom he or she knows or reasonably suspects to be infected with [a] venereal disease to submit himself or herself to medical examination'.[92] The medical officer may enter a person's premises for purposes of requiring such a person to undergo medical examination.[93] If the person is found to be positive, he or she is put on treatment and may be detained for such a time as the medical officer may

89 Some commentators have questioned whether punishment achieves the deterrence purpose. On this view see, N Walker *Why punish?* (1991); G Tullock 'Does punishment deter crime?' (1974) 36 *The Public Interest* 103.
90 L Gostin 'The Politics of AIDS' (1989) 49 *Ohio State Law Journal* 1019 1017.
91 Cap 284 Laws of Uganda.
92 Sec 2 of the Venereal Diseases Act.
93 Sec 3(1).

determine.[94] The person may appeal to the chief medical officer, whose decision shall be final.[95] This provision is wrong because it seeks to oust the jurisdiction of the courts by denying the aggrieved person a remedy granted by the court.

The Act requires a person who in the opinion of a medical officer or health inspector is suffering or has recently suffered from or is a carrier of a venereal disease to name the person who infected him or her.[96] Failure to comply with this requirement amounts to an offence, attracting a penalty of a fine not exceeding 2000 shillings or imprisonment for a period not exceeding six months or both.[97] A person who has been treated of a venereal disease may also be required to undergo periodic medical tests for purposes of ascertaining whether he or she is free from the disease.[98] Failure to undergo such tests amounts to an offence and attracts a fine of not more than 2000 shillings or imprisonment not exceeding six months or both.[99] Any person who 'unlawfully or negligently does any act which is and which he or she knows or has reason to believe to be likely to spread the infection of a venereal disease'; or knowingly harbours that disease; or maliciously reports a person as having infected him or her, commits an offence and shall be liable to the foregoing punishment.[100]

The provisions of the Act are counterproductive both from public health and human rights perspectives. From a public health perspective, the provisions may divert attention from more feasible measures to combat the spread of STIs by scaring away people from voluntary testing, counselling and treatment. It is necessary to encourage people to voluntarily seek testing services, disclose their status and practice safer sex without fear of stigma and discrimination. Disclosure can reveal intimate or private details about an individual's health status, which may lead to negative consequences such as stigma and discrimination, violence, sexual exclusion and isolation. The Act does not contain any safeguards ensuring that the medical officer does not disclose a person's health status to his or her partner. Disclosure to a person that his or her spouse or partner has a venereal disease may lead to violence. There is even no scientific evidence to show that criminalisation of STIs has ever rehabilitated or deterred offenders. Coercive approaches are counterproductive especially when dealing with STIs whose prevention, management and control largely involve the modification of behaviour. As Holland has correctly noted,

> [w]e cannot be very sanguine about the use of criminal law to compel changes in human behaviour. Realistically, criminal law is likely to be of minimal

94 Sec 3(2).
95 Sec 3(4).
96 Sec 4(1).
97 Sec 4(2).
98 Sec 5(d).
99 Sec 8(1).
100 As above.

> significance in influencing conduct: other factors, such as fear of infection are likely to be of greater effect in influencing sexual practices.[101]

The Act violates many rights such as privacy and confidentiality, security of the person, the right to health and freedom from cruel, inhuman and degrading treatment. More progressive enforcement mechanisms such as public awareness may be more productive than criminal sanctions. People need to be educated about the benefits of practicing safer sex through for example the use of condoms in order not to spread the so-called venereal diseases. Good public health legislation to tackle STIs necessitates use of the best available evidence as a basis of its enactment. Prevention of the STI should be the primary objective of the legislation, which must respect human rights. Any infringement of human rights of persons suffering from STIs must be sufficiently justified.

4.3 HIV and AIDS

HIV/AIDS remains a significant public health challenge for Uganda. In spite of years of success in tackling the HIV/AIDS epidemic, HIV prevalence has increased from 6,4 per cent in 2005 to 7,3 per cent in 2011.[102] There is no doubt that law plays an important role in HIV prevention work. Legislative approaches to prevention of HIV transmission have been used in a number of jurisdictions since the emergency of the HIV epidemic in the 1980s.The strategies employed to tackle HIV have been both protective and punitive towards PLHA. Against this backdrop, the HIV and AIDS Prevention and Control Act, 2014, which was introduced in 2010 as a private member's bill,[103] aims at providing for a legal framework that attempts to achieve the objectives of public health. The Act is geared towards the prevention and control of HIV and reducing its transmission. However, the question is whether this law is likely to facilitate or may be a barrier to effective HIV prevention efforts.

4.3.1 Giving credit where it is due: Does the Act meet public health and human rights goals?

There is no doubt that the Act contains a number of progressive provisions, which can be justified from public health and human rights perspectives. The Act provides for pre and post HIV testing and counselling services,[104] which is an entry point to treatment, care and support of PLHA. In some jurisdictions, testing and counselling have been said to be essential

101 W Holland 'HIV/AIDS and the criminal law' (1994) 36 *Criminal Law Quarterly* 279 316.
102 Ministry of Health *Sero-Behavioural Survey* (2011) 9.
103 Bills Supplement 4, 30 April 2010. The Bill was passed by parliament on 13 May 2014 and assented to by the President on 31 July 2014.
104 Secs 3 - 23, part III of the Act.

ingredients of informed consent. For example, in the South African case of *C v Minister of Correctional Services*,[105] the High Court found that the Johannesburg prison did not comply with the national strategy regulating HIV and AIDS in prisons. The plaintiff was awarded damages because the prison deviated from the norm of informed consent and the lack of pre-test counselling. It was held that the norm of informed consent contains a requirement of pre and post testing counselling.

The Act creates government obligations towards HIV management,[106] and makes provision for the protection of rights of PLHA. It obliges the state to formulate and implement a national public health strategy and plan of action for HIV and to provide treatment, care and support to all persons on a non-discriminatory basis.[107] The Act also prohibits discrimination in the workplace and in schools on grounds of health status.[108] It provides guidelines within which bio-medical research on HIV should be conducted without violating the rights of the subjects participating in the research.[109] The Act establishes a HIV and AIDS Trust Fund,[110] in order 'to secure a predictable and sustainable means of procuring goods and services for HIV and AIDS counselling, testing and treatment'.[111] The Act guarantees confidentiality of HIV results, which shall 'only be disclosed or released by a medical practitioner or other qualified officer to the person tested'.[112] The Act also creates offences such as breach of medical confidentiality,[113] wilful and unlawful breach of provisions relating to safe procedures and practices,[114] and misleading information or statement on the cure of HIV/AIDS.[115]

4.3.2 HIV and AIDS control strategy: The use of criminal law

The Act contains a number of draconian provisions, which are likely to worsen the HIV prevalence in the country generally and undermine the human rights of PLHA in particular. Unlike the 2012 East African Community HIV/AIDS Prevention and Management Act, which adopts a management approach, the Act employs a control strategy and has the potential to increase stigma and discrimination against PLHA.

105 1996 (4) SA 292 (T).
106 Sec 24.
107 As above.
108 Secs 32 & 33.
109 Secs 29 & 30.
110 Sec 25.
111 Sec 26.
112 Sec 18(1).
113 Sec 40.
114 Sec 42(1) & (2).
115 Sec 45.

Attempted transmission of HIV

The Act criminalises attempted transmission of HIV to another person but does not define the offence.[116] This contravenes the Constitution, which provides that '[e]xcept for contempt of court, no person shall be convicted of a criminal offence unless the offence is defined'.[117] In any case, how does the state prove 'attempted transmission'? The prosecution will certainly find it difficult, if not impossible to obtain evidence that a person attempted to transmit HIV in order to secure a conviction. This overly broad provision is vague and may lead to arbitrary application and misuse. For example, a parent or guardian could simply call the police upon seeing his or her adult daughter or son in a conversation with a PLHA or suspected of being HIV positive.

It is extremely necessary for legal provisions that create offences to be well defined and unequivocal in accordance with the principle of legality, which amongst other things requires that a law should be clear and precise enough to be understood. In the Kenyan case of *AIDS Law Project v Attorney-General & Others,*[118] the petitioner challenged the constitutionality of section 24 of the HIV/AIDS Prevention and Control Act 14 of 2006 on grounds that it is vague and extreme and thus offends the constitutionally protected principle of legality. The relevant section requires a person infected with HIV/AIDS to reveal his or her status to his or her sexual contact and where that person fails to do so, a medical practitioner may disclose such information to the contact. The petitioner argued that the law is vague and extreme because words such as 'sexual contact' are not defined. That the law does not provide what is contained in 'sexual contact'; whether it includes kissing, holding hands, exploratory contact or penetrative intercourse. That the provision discriminates against PLHA and violates article 27(1) and (4) of the Constitution, which guarantees that every person is equal before the law and has the right to equal protection and the benefit of the law. The court also observed that the section is likely to undermine the already existing HIV prevention methods because it will discourage people from finding out their status. The court also observed that although human rights are not absolute, they can be derogated from only in limits provided in constitutional and international law. The court cited the case of *Onyango Obbo* above to the effect that for a limitation to be justified, it must satisfy the criteria that it is reasonable and justifiable in an open and democratic society based on human dignity, equality and freedom.[119]

The court held that section 24 does not meet the principle of legality which is a component of the rule of law. That the said section is vague and

116 Sec 41.
117 Art 28(1) of the Constitution.
118 Petition 97 of 2010 (High Court of Kenya).
119 n 51 above.

overboard and lacks certainty especially with respect to the term 'sexual contact'. It fails to meet the legal requirement that an offence must be clearly defined in law as one cannot know from the wording of the section what acts or omissions will make him or her liable. That to retain that provision in the statute books would lead to an undesirable situation of the retention of legislation that provides for vague criminal offences which leave it to the court's subjective assessment whether a defendant is to be convicted or acquitted.[120] Consequently, the court declared section 24 unconstitutional because of its vagueness and uncertainty. The court advised the state to 'take a serious look at the Act with a view to avoiding further litigation surrounding the said piece of legislation'.[121]

Intentional transmission of HIV

The Act also criminalises wilful or intentional transmission of HIV.[122] It is certainly not good to intentionally infect a person with HIV or any other disease. Where an individual maliciously and intentionally transmits or exposes another to HIV infection with the express purpose of causing harm to that person, the perpetrator should face the wrath of the law. However, the provision is not necessary since the Penal Code Act already contains sufficient provisions on assault, homicide and causing bodily harm to address criminal acts. The provision contravenes the UN International Guidelines on HIV/AIDS and Human rights, which urge states to ensure that 'criminal and or public health legislation should not include specific offences against the deliberate and intentional transmission of HIV but rather should apply general criminal offences to these exceptional circumstances'.[123] From an evidential point of view, it may be difficult, if not impossible, for the prosecution to prove who between the two partners was infected first or who caused the transmission. Thus, how do you determine who infected another? Are there modalities of determining how long a person would have lived with the virus? The state must prove that HIV was transmitted by the accused in order to secure a conviction. Proving that the accused knew that they had HIV and that they understood how it is transmitted is critical to the determination of legal culpability. The provision may deflect attention from measures that are more urgently needed to combat the HIV epidemic. The provision demonises and stigmatises individuals living with HIV. One may ask: why criminalise HIV and not any other equally dangerous disease such as hepatitis? Doesn't this tantamount to discrimination on grounds of HIV status, which the Act ostensibly seeks to combat?

120 Para 88.
121 Para 90.
122 Sec 43.
123 Guideline 21(a).

The extent to which criminalisation can make a significant contribution to preventing HIV prevention is not clear. Criminalising HIV transmission may reduce the number of people seeking to know their HIV status, thus undermining HIV/AIDS prevention, treatment, care and support programmes. Criminalisation may also increase stigma and discrimination against PLHA. This does not advance the primary objective of preventing HIV transmission and may actually undermine HIV prevention efforts. Discrimination against PLHA certainly contravenes international human rights law and the Constitution[124] and has been condemned in many jurisdictions. For example, in *XX v Gun Club Corporation & Others*,[125] the court held that discrimination against PLHA is not permissible mainly because

> discrimination is an unjust act *perse* and the rule of law is founded in justice, the basis of social order [and] because the right to equality, in accordance to article 13 [of the Constitution of Colombia], places an obligation on the state to specifically protect those who are in a position of manifest weakness.[126]

In *Cortez & Others v El Salvador*[127] it was observed that the stigmatisation of, or discrimination against, a person who is HIV positive can lead to reluctance to go for medical controls, which creates difficulties for preventing infection. In any case, does imprisoning a PLHA prevent him or her from spreading the virus? What about through high-risk behaviour with other prisoners?

In my view, what is required to tackle HIV is not criminalisation but effective prevention, protection against discrimination, reduced stigma and greater access to testing and treatment. The success Uganda had attained in combating HIV was not through criminalisation but aggressive information, education and communication (IEC) strategies through the 'abstinence, be faithful and use a condom' (ABC) approach. There is even new evidence that antiretroviral therapy reduces HIV transmission risk. As the Global Commission on HIV[128] has cautioned,

> [p]roponents of criminalisation often claim that they are promoting public health or morality … but criminalisation guarantees no one's well-being. There is no evidence that laws regulating the sexual conduct of PLHIV change their behaviour in a positive way. Nor do such laws take into account the success of ART in significantly reducing transmission risk and improving the quality of life and longevity of PLHIV … The threat of prosecution

124 CESCR Gen Comment 20'Non-discrimination in economic, social and cultural rights' (art 2, para 2 of the International Covenant on Economic, Social and Cultural Rights) E/C 1/GC/20, 2 July 2009, para 33; UNGA 'Declaration of Commitment on HIV/AIDS' UNGA Res/S-26/2, 27 June 2001, para 37 & 58; 'Political Declaration on HIV/AIDS' UNGA A/RES/60/262, 15 June 2006; and 'Political Declaration on HIV/AIDS: Intensifying our Efforts to eliminate HIV/AIDS' a/65/1.77 8 July 2011.

125 Constitutional Court Judgment SU-256/96 (1996).

126 As above.

127 Case 12.249 20 March 2009 Report 27/09.

128 UNDP *Global commission on HIV and the Law: Risks, rights and health* (2012).

> neither empowers PLHIV to avoid transmission nor motivates them to protect themselves. Indeed, the fear of prosecution isolates them and discourages them from getting tested, participating in prevention treatment programmes or disclosing their status to partners …[129]

It should be noted that the accused person may raise defences to the offence of intentional transmission. He or she may aver that 'the person was aware of the HIIV status of the accused and the risk of the infection and he or she voluntarily accepted the risk'.[130] The accused may also argue that 'the alleged transmission was through sexual intercourse and protective measures were used during penetration'.[131] In *R v Dica*[132] the appellant was diagnosed with HIV in 1995 and began treatment. He had unprotected sex with two women, allegedly without disclosing his HIV-positive status. He was convicted of two counts of causing grievous bodily harm under section 20 of the Offences against the Person's Act, 1871 and subsequently appealed the conviction. The accused averred that the women knew his status but agreed to have sexual intercourse with him. Later both women tested HIV positive. The court observed that the ultimate question is not knowledge but consent and that in every case where the issue arises, the question whether the complainant did or did not consent to the risk of a STI depends on the facts of each case. The appeal was allowed and the court ordered a retrial. It is unfortunate that the Act does not include fear of violence, abandonment or abuse as a defence, especially for women in abusive relationships.

4.3.3 Disclosure and mandatory testing

Although the Act guarantees confidentiality of HIV results, it has a number of exceptions, which have adverse implications for the rights of PLHA. For example, the Act empowers medical workers to disclose a person's HIV status,

> where any other person with whom an HIV infected person is in close or continuous contact including but not limited to a sexual partner, if the nature of contact, in the opinion of the medical practitioner, poses a clear and present danger of HIV transmission to that person.[133]

Disclosure of a person's HIV status without his her consent is a clear violation of human rights such as privacy and confidentiality and may also be abused by medical workers. The rationale for confidentiality in the context of HIV was aptly expressed in the South African case of *Van Vuuren & Another v Kruger*[134] where the court stated that,

129 At 20.
130 Sec 43(2)(a).
131 Sec 43(2)(b).
132 (2004) EWCA Crim 1103, Court of Appeal (England and Wales).
133 Sec 18(2)(e).
134 1993 (4) SA 842 (A).

> [t]he serious personal and social consequences of the virus for the infected person justifies the protection of confidentiality. Such circumstances include isolation and rejection which may lead to increased anxiety, depression and psychological conditions that tend to hasten the onset of so-called full-blown AIDS.[135]

Disclosure by medical workers of a person's HIV status based purely on an individual opinion represents an institutionalised form of stigma and discrimination and may increase violence against women. Take the hypothetical case of Jane, a resident of a remote rural village in Kabale district. She tests HIV positive but does not inform her husband out of fear that he may beat her. Without Jane's knowledge, the medical worker who carried out the test informs the husband of the result. How may the husband react? There is likelihood that Jane may be subjected to violence. It should even be noted that HIV is increasingly feminised as women and girls are more vulnerable to infection and bear the burden for the care of the infected in addition to their multiple gender roles.[136] The feminisation of HIV/AIDS not only reflects women's greater vulnerability to infection, but also their social and psychological vulnerability caused by interrelated economic, social, legal and other factors. Thus, a law that subjects Jane to violence exacerbates her vulnerability. In any case, what type of 'close and continuous contact' is criminalised? Would the medical practitioner disclose a person's HIV status if he or she found two people hugging, kissing or holding hands? It can be argued that *AIDS Law Project v Attorney General & 3 Others*[137] is a persuasive authority for the view that the provision above[138] may be declared unconstitutional on the ground that it is vague and overly broad and thus offends the principle of legality.

The Act also provides that a pregnant woman and her partner shall be subjected to routine HIV testing for purposes of prevention of HIV transmission.[139] How will this provision be enforced? It may be easy to test a pregnant woman who reports for ANC. But how will her husband or partner be reached? How will the pregnant woman ensure that her partner accompanies her for testing? It may be difficult for a sex worker, who may have multiple partners, to determine who is responsible for the pregnancy and convince him to go for testing. In my view, it is better to sensitise and educated men about their sexual and reproductive health responsibilities than coercing them into compliance.

According to the Act, a person 'who is apprehended for a sexual offence shall be subjected to HIV testing for purposes of criminal

135 Para 10.
136 See eg S Harman 'The dual feminisation of HIV/AIDS' (2011) 8 *Gender, Governance and Power* 213.
137 n 118 above.
138 Sec 18(2)(e).
139 Sec 13(b) & (c).

proceedings and investigations'.[140] This provision may be understandable where the persons apprehended are alleged to have committed for example rape, defilement or incest.[141] However, these offences are already catered for in the Penal Code. There is also a possibility that this provision is targeted at female sex workers, who are alleged to have contravened the provisions against prostitution and whose bodies are viewed by many people as disgusting, dangerous and hazardous and likely to spread HIV and other STIs in a manner that does not apply to their male clients. The provision in question reinforces the stigma associated with prostitution or sex work and pushes sex workers to the margins of society. It is unfortunate that sex workers are perceived by legislators, as carriers of disease, including HIV and other STIs. They are addressed as law breakers instead of treating them as crucial stakeholders in the struggle to combat the spread of HIV. Sex workers are experts on their lives. They are acutely aware of their situation and should be involved in the development of HIV prevention strategies instead of subjecting them to inhuman and degrading treatment.

In a study of how female sex workers negotiate their SRHRs, I found that some of them educate their sexual partners about the benefits of safe sex.[142] I also found that criminalisation of sex work drives sex workers underground and prevents them from seeking sexual and reproductive health services or other help that they may need as they fear arrest, prosecution and at times persecution by the police.[143] Instead of criminalising sex workers' sexuality, they should be meaningfully engaged by policy makers as transformative agents in the area of HIV/AIDS. They should be provided with the necessary HIV/AIDS related information, goods and services to ensure that they and their clients live healthier and responsible lives.

It should be noted that the provision may also be used to subject men who have sex with men (MSM) to an HIV test against their consent when they are alleged to have engaged in the so-called unnatural offence of sodomy.[144] It can be seen that the law dehumanises those most at risk such as sex workers and MSM. Rather than providing protection, the law targets these key populations, who are more vulnerable to HIV.

140 Sec 12.
141 Sec 1.
142 BK Twinomugisha 'Beyond "malaya" or prostitute: Interrogating the sexual and reproductive health rights of young female sex workers in the context of HIV/AIDS in Uganda' HURIPEC Working Paper 37.
143 As above.
144 Secs 145 & 146 of the Penal Code Act.

5 Conclusion

Public health law can play a critical role in the promotion and protection of public health. The state has an obligation to develop laws that enhance the promotion and protection of public health without unduly undermining human rights generally and the right to health in particular. The state is legally mandated to apply mandatory or coercive measures for the protection of public health. However, it must respect individual rights and freedoms. Any restriction of human rights or freedoms must be within the limits prescribed by law. It is clear that the laws on public health examined in this chapter suffer from a number of weaknesses. In the first place, the Public Health Act and Venereal Diseases Act are outdated and outmoded and cry out for repeal or reform. They have not kept pace with changes in science and technology in the area of prevention, treatment and care. Secondly, they do not conform to standards of human rights in general and those of the right to health in particular. Thirdly, they largely rely on criminal law as an enforcement mechanism and do not explore other modalities to ensure compliance. The HIV and AIDS Prevention and Control Act contains some progressive provisions, which can be used to promote and protect public health and human rights of PLHA. However, the success of these provisions may be curtailed by the retrogressive provisions on attempted transmission, intentional transmission, disclosure and mandatory testing. These provisions defeat the primary objectives of the Act: prevention of HIV and protection of the rights of PLHA.

The question is: what should be done? Given the piece meal nature of Uganda's public health legislation, the state should adopt framework health legislation.[145] The advantage of this type of legislation is that it lays down the main standards in the area of public health and leaves details to be handled through subsidiary legislation such as regulations and guidelines. The legislation should create an optimum balance between the promotion and protection of public health and human rights. The legislation should also take into account the health related obligations imposed by the Constitution and relevant international human rights instruments. The legislation should operationalise the main standards in the national health policies, plans, strategies and other interventions. It should be guided by technological and scientific developments in the field of prevention, treatment and care. In addition to criminal sanctions, which should be commensurate with the offences committed, the legislation should explore other enforcement mechanisms such as public awareness and education, incentives for observing the law and disincentives for breaking it. It should be guided by human rights based principles of non-

145 See para 56, General Comment 14.

discrimination, gender, equity, proportionality, participation, accountability, transparency, sustainability, prevention, and partnership.

As the Global Commission on HIV has advised, there is a need to repeal punitive laws and enact laws that facilitate and enable effective responses to HIV prevention, care and treatment for all who need them. Laws that criminalise HIV transmission, exposure or non-disclosure of HIV status are counterproductive and should be repealed.[146] There is also a need to decriminalise private and consensual adult sexual acts and voluntary sex work. The state can suspend the HIV and AIDS Prevention and Control Act and consider revising some of the negative provisions based on new scientific evidence. However, in my view, we do not need a law specifically targeting a disease such as HIV/AIDS. Why target HIV/AIDS? It is dangerous to have piecemeal legislation. Are we going to have separate legislation to tackle TB, hepatitis, typhoid and other communicable diseases? What about non-communicable diseases? As pointed out in chapter four, good framework legislation can cover most public health challenges, including HIV/AIDS. In order for the framework legislation to be effective, health care workers, legal professionals, judges, employers and trade unionists, and the academia should be sensitised about their legal responsibilities to protect the rights of PLHA. The latter should also be informed of their rights.

The advantages of public interest litigation were considered in Chapter 4. Thus, there is a need for public spirited individuals or organisations to challenge the unconstitutionality of draconian health laws considered above on grounds that they violate the human rights and freedoms guaranteed in the Constitution and international human rights instruments, which Uganda has ratified.

146 n 128 above, 9.

6

LAWS REGARDING MENTAL HEALTH

1 Introduction

Mental health is a critical component of the right to health. The need to promote mental health is recognised in legal and policy frameworks. All the key international and regional human rights instruments, which Uganda has signed such as: the International Covenant on Civil and Political Rights (ICCPR); the International Covenant on Economic, Social and Cultural Rights (CESCR); the Convention on the Rights of the Child (CRC); the African Charter on Human and Peoples' Rights (ACHPR); and the Women's Protocol to the ACHPR, contain human rights provisions applicable to persons with disabilities (PWDs) generally and persons with mental disabilities (PWMDs) in particular. Uganda is also a party to the Convention on the Rights of Persons with disabilities (CRPD), which specifically provides for rights of PWDs. There are also various soft law instruments which apply to PWMDs as illustrated in this chapter. The Constitution also recognises the rights of PWDs. There are also the 2006 Persons with Disabilities Act and the 2003 National Council for Disability Act, which are intended to enhance the protection of rights of PWDs. Uganda also has a Mental Health Policy (MHP),[1] which is part of the National Health Policy[2] that recognises mental health as a key component to be delivered at all levels of health care. The MHP emphasises decentralisation, integration, evidence-based services, strong partnerships and collaboration.

In spite of the above fairly elaborate legal and policy frameworks that seek to promote mental health rights, PWMDs are some of the most

1 On analysis of the MHP, see E Fayd et al 'An assessment of mental health policy in Ghana, South Africa, Uganda and Zambia' (2011) 9 *Health Research Systems* 17 http://www.health-policy-systems.com/content/9/1/17 (accessed 8 December 2014); F Kigozi 'Integrating mental health into primary health care: Uganda's experience' (2007) 10 *South African Psychiatry Review* 1.

2 Ministry of Health *National health policy* (2010).

vulnerable people in society[3] that 'have been largely overlooked as a target of development programmes'.[4] They are often subject to discrimination, social isolation and exclusion; they are stigmatised and disenfranchised and suffer all kinds of human rights violations. They are subject to violence and abuse. They are confined, against their will, in institutions such as hospitals and deprived of their freedom, human dignity and other basic human rights. The situation of PWMDs is exacerbated by the negative attitudes of society in general towards disability[5] and an outdated Mental Treatment Act,[6] which marginalises PWMDs and excludes them from participating in the affairs of mainstream society.

Against this background, I examine in this chapter the mental health legal framework at the international and regional levels with the view of finding out the extent to which it may inform legal reform at the domestic level and thus contribute to the protection of mental health rights in the country. It should be pointed out from the outset that mental health disabilities (MHDs) are caused by a complex mix of biological, psychological, cultural, socio-political and juridical factors. Thus, combating stigma and discrimination against PWMDs requires a holistic, multi-disciplinary approach. However it may not be possible to examine all the factors that affect mental health; they are out of the scope of this chapter. Thus, this chapter focuses on juridical interventions given the critical role played by law in the promotion of mental health especially in outlawing disability based discrimination and the promotion of human rights of PWMDs.

2 Mental health situation

Mental health is a major public health and development concern. Globally, mental and neurological disorders are responsible for approximately 14 per cent of the global burden of disease.[7] A large proportion of global health burden is due to mental health disorders. Mental health conditions account for 13 per cent of the total burden of disease, and 31 per cent of all years lived with disability.[8] By 2030, depression is likely to be the highest contributor to the global burden of disease than heart disease, stroke, road traffic accidents and HIV/AIDS.[9] In Africa, it is estimated that between 76 per cent and 99 per cent of people

3 Kigozi (n 1 above) 2.
4 As above.
5 FT Abbey 'An assessment of the legal securities and uncertainties of persons with disabilities in Eritrea' (2013) 19 *East African Journal of Peace and Human Rights* 60.
6 WHO 'Guidelines for the promotion of human rights of persons with mental disorders' http://www.who,int/mental_health/policy/legislation/guidelines_promotion.pdf?ua=1 (accessed 24 November 2014).
7 WHO *Mental health and development: Targeting people with mental health disabilities as a vulnerable group* (2010) 30.
8 As above.
9 As above.

with serious mental disorders do not have access to the treatment they need for their mental health problems.[10] In Uganda, about 6.8 million out of a population of 34 million people have some degree of mental illness or mental disorder, ranging from anxiety and depression to severe madness.[11] Mental health contributes 13 per cent of the national disease burden. Mental disorders are responsible for increased mortality due to suicide and reduced life expectancy. Mental health challenges are increasing, with depression at 12-68 per cent, anxiety disorders at 20-62 per cent and alcohol dependency at 14 per cent of the general population.[12] About 75 per cent of attendances at mental health clinics have some form of neurological problems such as epilepsy, with cases of dementia on the increase especially amongst persons living with HIV/AIDS (PLHA).[13]

Albeit mental health is one of the 12 components of the National Minimum Health Care package to be provided at all levels of health care,[14] mental health care in Uganda receives inadequate attention compared to other areas of health care especially communicable diseases.[15] The burden of caring for the mentally ill is largely left to families, especially women who are already burdened by their multiple gender roles.[16] Although there are six regional mental hospitals and one referral mental hospital, the human resource situation for mental health is alarming. For example, the total number of mental health professionals per 100000 is 1.13.[17] There are only 0.08 psychiatrists, 0.04 medical doctors, 0.78 nurses, 0.01 psychologists, 0.01 social workers, 0.01 occupational therapists, and 0.2 psychiatric clinical officers.[18] Only 1 per cent of the medical doctors and 4 per cent of the nurses are specialised in psychiatry.[19]

3 Understanding mental health disabilities

Mental health, which is a key component of the right to health, is a broad, multifaceted and complex subject. It is more than mere absence of mental illness and is vital to individuals, families and society. Mental health relates to a positive state: it looks at mental well-being, which is affected by

10 As above.
11 F Kagolo '32 psychiatrists for 34 million Ugandans' *The New Vision* 12 May 2012 4; Ministry of Health *Health Sector Strategic Plan* (2011) 16; J Ssebunya et al 'Integration of mental health care into primary health care in a rural district in Uganda' (2010) 13 *African Journal of Psychiatry* 128.
12 As above.
13 Kigozi (n 1 above) 3.
14 E Fayd (n 5 above) 16; F Kigozi et al 'An overview of Uganda's mental health care system: Results from an assessment using the world health organization's assessment instrument for mental health systems (WHO-AIMS)' (2010) 4 *International Journal of Mental Health Systems* 1.
15 As above.
16 On how women with disabilities experience double discrimination, see A Ndeezi *The Disability Movement in Uganda* (2004) 37.
17 WHO *Report on the mental health systems in Uganda* (2006) 6.
18 As above.
19 As above.

legal, political, social, economic and environmental factors. The World Health Organisation (WHO) defines mental health as

> a state of well-being in which every individual realizes his or her own potential, can cope with normal stresses of life, can work productively and fruitfully, and is able to make a contribution to her or his community.[20]

Mental health includes 'analysis and diagnosis of a person's mental condition, and treatment, care and rehabilitation for a mental illness or suspected mental illness'.[21]

In order to understand mental health disabilities, it is necessary to map out the meaning of disability through the various models on disability, which have been developed over the years. The discourse on disability has been dominated by the medical and social models. The medical model views disability as a physical or mental impairment or biological condition of the individual that must be corrected through medical or surgical intervention.[22] The model regards disability as a deficiency that must be fixed by a rehabilitation or medical professional. It regards the limitations faced by people with disabilities as resulting primarily, or solely, from their impairments.[23]

In contrast to the medical model, the social model views disability as a product of social exclusionary practices. Advocates of the social model attribute disability to economic, environmental or cultural barriers, which are imposed on PWDs by society. For example, the Union of the Physically Impaired against Segregation (UPIAS), a disabilities movement, has observed as follows:

> In our view, it is society which disables physically impaired people. Disability is something imposed on top of our impairments by the way we are unnecessarily isolated and excluded from full participation of society. To understand this, it is necessary to grasp the distinction between the physical impairment and the social situation, called 'disability', of people with such impairment. Thus, we define impairment as lacking all or part of a limb, or having a defective limb, organism or mechanism of the body and disability as the disadvantage or restriction of activity caused by a contemporary social organization which takes little or no account of people who have physical impairments and thus excludes them from participation in the mainstream of social activities.[24]

20 WHO 'Mental health: A state of well-being' http://www.who.int/features/factfile/mental_health/an (accessed 1 December 2014).
21 As above.
22 For an elaborate discussion of the medical and social models, see Stanford Encyclopedia of Philosophy *Disability: Definitions, Models, Experience* (2011).
23 As above.
24 UPIAS *Fundamental principles of disability* (1976) 22

It is true that the social model provides a convincing approach to the understanding of disability. However, what is clear is that both individual impairment and the social environment play a critical role in defining disability. Although the CRPD does not explicitly define disability, it defines PWDs as including

> those who have long-term physical, mental, intellectual or sensory impairments which in interaction with various barriers may hinder their full and effective participation in society on an equal basis with others.[25]

The 2006 Persons with Disabilities Act also defines disability as 'a substantial functional limitation of daily life activities caused by physical, mental or sensory impairment and environment barriers resulting in limited participation'.[26]

It has been correctly pointed out that there is need to look at disability as 'an interaction between biological and social causes, denying causal priority to either'.[27] The WHO has also pointed out that,

> [d]isability is thus not just a health problem. It is a complex phenomenon, reflecting the interaction of features of a person's body and features of the society in which he or she lives. Overcoming the difficulties faced by people with disabilities requires interventions to remove environmental and social barriers.[28]

The WHO has also noted that

> [m]ental health intervention, including psychosocial, care management, and pharmacological strategies, have proved effective. Interventions reduce severity of symptoms and improve daily functioning in work, social, and community life.[29]

Ngwena has also noted that both models should be juxtaposed in order to respond adequately to disability related discrimination.[30]He has correctly observed as follows:

> [A] social construction of disability provides a meaningful paradigm in which to understand the definition of disability...disability is a fluid and highly contested construct. The medical model, with its focus on intrinsic pathology, is a limited, though not dispensable, paradigm for transacting disability. Disability is more than just the sum total of individual pathology and consequent mental and physical limitations. Extrinsic factors are extremely

25 Art 8.
26 Sec 2.
27 n 22 above, 18.
28 WHO 'Disabilities' http://www.who.int/topics/disabilties/en/ (accessed 2 November 2014).
29 WHO (n 20 above) 35.
30 C Ngwena 'Deconstructing the definition of disability under the Employment Equity Act: Legal deconstruction' (2007) *South African Journal of Human Rights* 116.

> relevant to a meaningful interpretation of disability. The social model, with its overt political nuances, provides invaluable insights into the epistemology of disability and the formulation of normative responses that would otherwise be lost to the medical model operating on its own.[31]

What emerges from the literature on the subject points to one fact: disability is a fluid, complex and contested concept. Tackling disability related stigma and discrimination requires a multi-faceted strategy involving bio-medical, political and socio-economic interventions.

The question is: what are mental health disabilities? These may be taken to refer to those impairments or conditions that have a long term effect on a person's mental well-being. When these impairments or conditions are combined with environmental and social factors such as stigma and discrimination, they deny that person the enjoyment of his or her rights. Mental health disabilities include schizophrenia, bipolar disorder, depression, epilepsy, alcohol and drug use disorders, and intellectual impairments.[32] It should be noted that mental disability poses a distinct set of human rights challenges when compared with other types of disability. This is largely because this type of disability is stereotypically considered to diminish the autonomy of the person and thereby undermine the position of that person as an active bearer of human rights.[33]

4 The normative framework for realisation of mental health at the international level

4.1 The mainstream international human rights instruments

It should be pointed out from the outset that until recently, international human rights law ignored PWDs. Apart from the CRPD which covers questions of disability at a general level, there is no international treaty specifically dealing with mental health disabilities. However, the mainstream international human rights instruments such as the Universal Declaration, ICCPR, CRC and ICESCR, apply to PWMDs just in the same way that they do to everyone else.

Albeit a detailed analysis of all the international human rights instruments is beyond the scope of this chapter, suffice to say that most of the rights contained therein are critical for the promotion of mental health. According to the UDHR, international human rights are applicable to all persons [including PWMDs] since '[a]ll human beings are born free and equal in dignity and rights'.[34] The rights and freedoms, which are directly

31 Ngwena (n 30 above) 117.
32 Kigozi (n 1 above).
33 A Dimopoulous *Issues in human rights of intellectually disabled persons* (2010).
34 Art 1 of the Universal Declaration.

applicable to PWDs generally and PWMDs in particular, include, the right to life, liberty and security of person;[35] freedom from torture, cruel, inhuman or degrading treatment or punishment;[36] equal protection of the law;[37] protection from arbitrary arrest or detention;[38] privacy;[39] freedom of movement and residence;[40] family rights;[41] participation in the cultural life of the community;[42] and a right to a standard of living adequate for health and well-being.[43] It should be noted that the Universal Declaration recognises the indivisibility and interdependence of civil, political, economic, social and cultural rights. In this vein, the Declaration provides that economic, social and cultural rights are indispensable for a person's 'dignity and the free development of his [her] personality'.[44]

The rights and freedoms, which are guaranteed by the ICCPR and are relevant for promotion of mental health include, self-determination;[45] life;[46] liberty and security of the person;[47] freedom from arbitrary arrest or detention;[48] fair hearing;[49] privacy;[50] family rights;[51]and equality before the law.[52] According to the ICCPR, '[a]ll persons deprived of their liberty shall be treated with humanity and with respect for the inherent dignity of the human person'[53] and no person 'shall be subjected to torture, cruel, inhuman or degrading treatment or punishment'.[54] In *Price v United Kingdom,*[55] the European Court on Human Rights considered whether the treatment of the applicant contravened article 3 of the European Convention, which like article 7 of the ICCPR prohibits torture, cruel, inhuman and degrading treatment. The applicant who had a physical disability and moved in a wheel chair was jailed for contempt of court. Her cell was not adopted for PWDs and she was forced to sleep in a wheel chair. She had difficulty accessing her toilet. In order to access the toilet, she had to undress in front of male guards. It was held that her treatment constituted degrading treatment under the Convention. The court noted that in order to fall within the ambit of the Convention, the ill-treatment

35 Art 3.
36 Art 5.
37 Art 7.
38 Art 9.
39 Art 12.
40 Art 13.
41 Art 18.
42 Art 27(1).
43 Art 25.
44 Art 22.
45 Art 1 of the ICCPR.
46 Art 6(1).
47 Art 9.
48 As above.
49 Art 14.
50 Art 17.
51 Art 23.
52 Art 26.
53 Art 10.
54 Art 7.
55 (2001) EHRR 1285.

must attain the minimum level of severity. That in determining whether treatment is 'degrading' within the meaning of the Convention,

> one of the factors the court will take into account is the question whether its object was to humiliate the person concerned although the absence of any such purpose cannot conclusively rule out a finding of violation ...[56]

In *Ireland v United Kingdom*,[57] the court also held that the treatment will be inhuman only if it reaches a level of gravity involving considerable mental or physical suffering, and degrading if the person has undergone humiliation or debasement involving a minimum level of severity.[58] The court noted that inhuman and degrading treatment depends on all the circumstances of the case, including the nature and context of the treatment, the manner and the method of its execution, its duration, 'its physical or mental effects and, in some cases, the [victim's] sex, age, and state of health'.[59]

The CESCR provides that the rights in the covenant 'derive from the inherent dignity of the human person'.[60] It guarantees such rights as self-determination,[61] work,[62] enjoyment of just and favourable conditions of work,[63] protection of the family,[64] adequate standard of living,[65] highest attainable standard of physical and mental health,[66] education[67] and participation in cultural life,[68] all of which are critical for the promotion of mental health.

On their face, the international human rights instruments outlined above protect all people, including PWMDs. However, it cannot be denied that the instruments marginalise disability rights. Though they are certainly relevant for the promotion of mental health, the instruments do not explicitly prohibit discrimination on disability grounds. Consequently, over the years, the disability movement has fought for social construction of disability and rights based approaches to disability. In order to tackle the stigma and discrimination associated with disability, the movement correctly argued that there was need for a specialised human rights instrument to fight discrimination and monitor human rights of PWDs.[69]

56 Para 24.
57 (1978) 2 EHRR 162.
58 Para 65.
59 As above.
60 Preamble to the CESCR.
61 Art 1.
62 Art 6.
63 As above.
64 Art 10.
65 Art 11.
66 Art 12.
67 Art 13.
68 Art 15.
69 JE Lord 'Disability rights and the human rights mainstream: Reluctant gate-crasher' in C Bob (ed) *The international struggle for new human rights* (2010) 82 - 83.

4.2 The pre-CRPD situation: Soft law instruments recognising disability as a human rights issue

In early 1970s, the UN developed various soft law instruments to protect PWDs. For example, the UN adopted the Declaration on the Rights of Mentally Retarded Persons[70] and the Declaration on the Rights of Disabled Persons.[71] The declarations recognised disability as a human rights issue and thus incorporated most of the internationally recognised human rights. However, the disability movement viewed the declarations as being largely informed by the traditional medical and charity models and that they were 'tainted by paternalism'.[72] For example, the Declaration on the Rights of Retarded Persons uses words such as 'retarded' and 'handicap', which reinforce stigma and negative stereotypes and attitudes against PWMDs. The Declaration also provides that 'the mentally retarded person has, to the maximum degree of feasibility, the same rights as other human beings'[73] yet, as the UDHR proclaims, all human beings are born free and equal in dignity and rights.[74] The question here is: is there any enjoyment of equality since it is conditional to 'feasibility', which is a vague and subjective concept? The Declaration also provides for a 'qualified guardian to protect his [retarded person's] personal well-being and interests'.[75] However, guardianship has been sharply criticised. For example, Herr has noted that

> [g]uardianship intrudes on fundamental liberties and privacy rights, employs vague criteria, fails to tailor the scope of the guardian's authority, denies procedural safeguards, and lacks adequate monitoring and review.[76]

The Declaration on the Rights of Disabled Persons also incorporates international human rights and prohibits discrimination on disability grounds.[77] However, the Declaration adopts a negative attitude towards PWDs. For example, a disabled person is defined as

> any person unable to ensure by himself or herself, wholly or partly, the necessities of a normal individual and/or social life, as a result of a deficiency, either congenital or not, in his or her physical or mental capabilities.[78]

70 GA Res 2856 (XXVI), 26 UN GAOR Supp (no 29), 93, UN Doc A/8429 (1971).
71 GA Res 3447 (XXX), 30 UN GAOR Supp (no 34), 88, UN Doc A/1034 (1975).
72 Dimopoulous (n 33 above) 67.
73 Para 1 of the Declaration.
74 Art 1 of the Universal Declaration.
75 Para 5 of the Declaration.
76 S Herr 'Self-determination, autonomy, and alternatives to guardianship' in S Herr et al (eds) *The human rights of persons with intellectual disabilities* (2005) 430.
77 Para 2.
78 Para 1 of the Declaration.

The declaration aims at promotion of integration of disabled people 'as far as possible in normal life'.[79] This raises an important question: Are disabled persons not normal?

In the 1990s, the UN General Assembly adopted two instruments critical for the promotion of rights of PWMDs: the Principles for the Protection of Persons with Mental Illness and the Improvement of Mental Health Care (MI Principles)[80] and the Standard Rules on the Equalization of Opportunities for PWDs (Standard Rules).[81] According to the MI Principles, persons with mental illness (PWMI), 'have the right to the best available mental health care, which shall be part of the health and social care system'.[82] PWMI shall be treated with human dignity[83] and their autonomy protected.[84] PWMI have a right to be protected from exploitation, abuse or degrading treatment.[85] The MI Principles explicitly prohibit discrimination on grounds of mental illness[86] and proclaim the right of PWMI to exercise all civil, political, economic, social and cultural rights.[87] Aware of the limitations associated with institutionalised mental health care, the MI Principles stress that, '[e]very person with a mental illness shall have the right to live and work, to the extent possible in the community'.[88] On the importance of life in the community, Yamin and Rosenthal have observed as follows,

> [f]rom a human rights perspective, people are entitled to live in and receive care in the community not because it is more efficient, but because all human beings develop their identities within social contexts, and have rights to work and study, as well as being with family and friends.[89]

The MI Principles emphasise that determination of mental illness 'shall be made in accordance with internationally accepted medical standards'.[90] According to the principles,

> [n]o person shall be compelled to undergo medical examination with a view to determining whether or not he or she has a mental illness except in accordance with a procedure authorized by domestic law.[91]

79 Preamble to the Declaration.
80 A/RES/46/119, 17 Dec 1991 http://www.un.org/documents/ga/res/46/a46r119.htm (accessed 8 March 2015).
81 Res 48/96 annex, 20 Dec 1993 http://www.un.org/esa/socdev/enable/disre00.htm (accessed 8 March 2015).
82 Principle 1(1).
83 Principle 1(2).
84 Principle 1(6).
85 Principle 1(3).
86 Principle 1(4).
87 Principle 1(5).
88 Principle 3.
89 AE Yamin & E Rosenthal 'Out of the shadows: Using human rights to secure dignity and well-being for people with mental disabilities' (2005) 2 *PLOS Medicine* 296.
90 Principle 4(1).
91 Principle 5.

Key questions to be asked before a PWMI is compelled to undergo medical examination include: Has informed consent been obtained before medical examination? Has the patient been accorded an opportunity to seek a second opinion? Who performs such an examination?[92] The MI Principles require that all medical records and information should be kept confidential.[93]

As pointed out above, the MI Principles stress the importance of life in the community. Consequently, '[e]very patient shall have the right to be treated and cared for, as far as possible, in the community in which he or she lives'.[94] However, any treatment in a mental health facility should where possible be 'near his or her home or the home of his or her relatives or friends' and has 'the right to return to the community as soon as possible'.[95] A patient has a right to receive such care as appropriate to his or her health needs[96] and

> to be treated in the least restrictive environment and with the least restrictive or intrusive treatment appropriate to the patient's health needs and the need to protect the physical safety of others.[97]

Any medication should be only for therapeutic or diagnostic purposes but not as punishment or convenience of others.[98] The treatment must be based on an individually presented plan[99] and should be aimed at 'preserving and enhancing personal autonomy'.[100]

The MI Principles emphasise consent to treatment and thus treatment without a patient's consent is prohibited.[101] Informed consent is that consent, which is,

> obtained freely, without threats or improper inducements, after appropriate disclosure to the patient of adequate and understandable information in a form and language understood by the patient on (a) the diagnostic assessment; (b) purpose, method, likely duration and expected benefit of the proposed treatment; (c) alternative modes of treatment, including those less intrusive; (d) possible pain or discomfort, risks and side effects of the proposed treatment.[102]

92 WHO (n 20 above).
93 Principle 6.
94 Principle 7(1).
95 Principle 7(2).
96 Principle 8(1).
97 Principle 9(1).
98 Principle 10(1).
99 Principle 9(2).
100 Principle 9(4).
101 Principle 11(1).
102 Principle 11(2). Based on the principle of informed consent, the patient may refuse or stop treatment (principle 12(4)). For the exceptions to informed consent, see principle 11(6-8), (13) & (15). The exceptions may be summarised into three: (a) if he or she is held as an involuntary patient; (b) if an independent body is satisfied that the patient lacks capacity; and (c) if the independent body is satisfied that the proposed plan is in

The MI Principles stress the need for a judicial or other independent or impartial body established by domestic law and functioning in accordance with procedures laid down by domestic law.[103] The body shall periodically review cases of involuntary admission and must, as expected, observe the principles of natural justice, including a right to a fair hearing and observing the patient's right to legal representation.[104] The patient is entitled to access to information concerning his or her medical records.[105]

It is trite to state that like most human rights, the enjoyment of rights contained in the MI Principles may be limited in accordance with safeguards lain down by law.[106] Thus, according to the Principles,

> [t]he exercise of the rights set forth in the following Principles may be subject only to such limitations as are prescribed by law and are necessary to protect the health or safety of the persons concerned or of others, or otherwise to protect public safety, order, health or morals or the fundamental rights and freedoms of others.[107]

The MI Principles have been recognised as an important interpretative guide to international and regional human rights obligations in respect of persons with mental disability. For example, in *Victor Rosario Congo*,[108] it was noted that the MI Principles serve as a guide to states in the design of mental health systems. In *Purohit & Moore v The Gambia*,[109] in finding that the Gambian Lunatics Detention Act contravened various provisions of the ACHPR, the African Commission on Human and Peoples' Rights (the African Commission), pursuant to article 60 of the Charter, drew inspiration from MI Principle 2 on human dignity.[110]

It should be recalled that in the 1970s, the UN General Assembly declared 1981 the International Year of Disabled Persons.[111] Its major outcome was the World Programme of Action concerning Disabled Persons,[112] which recognised 'the right of disabled persons to participate fully in the social life and development of their societies and to enjoy living

the best interests of the patient's health needs. Any decision regarding involuntary admission must be made by a medical practitioner (principle 16).

103 Principle 17.

104 For procedural safeguards see, principle 18(1) - (8).

105 Principle 19.

106 On the scope of limitation of rights in the context of public health, see Chapter 5 above.

107 General limitation clause.

108 The Inter-American Commission on Human Rights Report 29/99, case 11, 427, adopted in sess 1424, OEA/ser/L.V/11) Doc 26, 9 March 1999, para 54. See also E Rosenthal & LS Rusbenstein 'International human rights advocacy under the "Principles for the protection of persons of mental illness"' (1993) 16 *International Journal of Law and Psychiatry* 257.

109 (2003) AHRLR 96 (ACHR 2003).

110 Para 60.

111 GA Res 31/123 of December 1976.

112 GA Res 37/52 of 3 December 1982.

conditions equal to those of their fellow citizens'.[113] The UN set aside a decade (1983-1992) to implement the World Programme of Action and in order to guide state action, the UN General Assembly adopted the Standard Rules.[114] For the first time, handicap was defined as a function of the relationship between PWDs and their environment.[115] According to the Standard Rules, people may be disabled by physical, intellectual or sensory impairment or mental illness.[116] The Standard Rules stress that PWDs are members of society and have the right to remain within their local communities'.[117] According to the Standard Rules, the Universal Declaration, ICCPR, CESCR, CRC, CEDAW and the World Programme of Action 'constitute political and moral foundation for the rules'.[118] Thus,

> [a]lthough the rules are not compulsory, they can become international customary rules when they are applied by a great number of states with the intention of respecting a rule of international law.[119]

The Standard Rules further enjoin states to take action to raise awareness in society about PWDs, their rights, needs, potential and contribution. This can be achieved through education, communication and information campaigns.[120] States should ensure the effective provision of medical care[121] and rehabilitation services to PWDs 'in order for them to reach and sustain their optimum level of independence and functioning'.[122] States are encouraged to recognise the principle that PWDs must be empowered to exercise their human rights, especially in the field of employment.[123] The Standard Rules require states to promote the full participation of PWDs in family life and respect for their right to personal integrity.[124] States should also ensure that laws do not discriminate against PWDs 'with respect to sexual relationships, marriages and parenthood'.[125] States are enjoined to create legal frameworks to achieve the objectives of full participation and equality for PWDs.[126] States should ensure that the legislation adequately addresses the rights and obligations of PWDs.[127] States are obliged to ensure that PWDs exercise their rights 'on an equal basis with other citizens'[128] and that organisations of PWDs participate in

113 Preamble.
114 Res 48/96 annex (n 81 above).
115 Para 18.
116 Para 17.
117 Para 26.
118 Introduction to the Standard Rules.
119 Para 14.
120 Rule 1.
121 Rule 2.
122 Rule 3.
123 Rule 7.
124 Rule 9.
125 As above.
126 Rule 15(1).
127 As above.
128 As above.

the development and evaluation of national legislation concerning the rights of PWDs.[129]

It can be seen that the Standard Rules adopt a broader approach to disability rights than the MI Principles since they focus on the equalisation of opportunities and participation in all aspects of society. However, both the rules and principles are complementary in the promotion and protection of the rights of PWMDs in general and PWMDs in particular.

4.3 The CPRD: A transformative paradigm shift

It should be noted that the disability movement criticised the soft law instruments above on grounds, inter alia that they are not legally binding and are largely formulated in programmatic language. The movement called for an international legally binding instrument, developed with their full participation, and specifically addressing the rights and obligations of PWDs. Indeed, in the 2000s, there were serious initiatives for a disabilities convention. For example, in April 2000, the UN Commission on Human Rights invited the UN High Commissioner for Human Rights to examine measures to strengthen the protection and monitoring of the human rights of PWDs.[130] In December 2001, the UN General Assembly established an Ad Hoc Committee to

> consider proposals for a comprehensive and integral international convention to promote and protect the rights and dignity of persons with disabilities, based on the holistic approach in the work done in the fields of social development, human rights and non-discrimination and taking into account the recommendations of the Commission of Human Rights and the Commission for Social Development.[131]

Following intensive meetings and negotiations, a draft convention was completed in 2004. On 13 December 2006, the UN General Assembly adopted the CRPD by consensus. The CPRD was opened for signature on 30 March 2007. The CRPD was drafted with active participation of disability organisations, including mental health service user representatives. The CRPD has been embraced widely by the disability movement as a universal standard for realisation of human rights of PWDs. It marks a transformative paradigm shift away from viewing PWDs as objects of charity and pity and as a problem whose solution lies only in medical intervention. It recognises PWDs as subjects with rights who are capable of claiming those rights. PWDs are viewed as active members of society who can make decisions for their lives based on their free and informed consent. The CPRD views PWDs as bearers of rights and responsibilities and with the capacity of self-determination. The

129 As above.
130 Res 2000/51.
131 Res 56/168.

CPRD adopts the position of the Universal Declaration, ACHPR and the Vienna Declaration and views human rights as indivisible, interdependent and interrelated.[132] According to the CRPD, disability 'results from the interactions between persons with impairments and attitudinal and environmental barriers that hinder their full and effective participation in society on an equal basis with others'.[133]

The CPRD has been hailed as a comprehensive human rights treaty that addresses the rights of PWDs in a holistic fashion. For example, the WHO has pointed out that the CPRD provides a comprehensive legal framework for ending the discrimination experienced on a daily basis by many people with mental health conditions.[134] Ngwena has also noted that '[t]he normative impetus behind the CRPD is inclusive equality. It is the imperative of securing equality and human dignity for disabled people in all socio-economic sectors'.[135] Burns has also observed that the CRPD has

> an explicit social development dimension and constitutes a significant global commitment to a human rights framework in which issues of achieving substantive equality and the full and unfettered rights of persons with disabilities are placed at centre stage.[136]

Albeit most of the substantive provisions of the CRPD are certainly relevant to issues of mental health, a detailed examination of the CRPD is beyond the scope of this chapter. What is important in this chapter is to examine the place accorded to mental disabilities within the CPRD. The purpose of the CRPD is to promote, protect and ensure the full and equal enjoyment of all human rights and fundamental freedoms of all PWDs, and to promote respect for their dignity.[137] The CRPD provides that PWDs 'include those who have long-term physical, mental, intellectual or sensory impairments which in interaction with various barriers may hinder their full and effective participation on equal basis with others'.[138] From this definition, it can be stated that mental health disabilities are recognised by the CRPD, which is guided by the principles of human dignity, autonomy, non-discrimination, equality, participation, and inclusion.[139]

132 Preamble.
133 As above.
134 See WHO *UN Convention on the rights of persons with disabilities: A major step forward in promoting and protecting rights* (2008) 49.
135 C Ngwena 'Western Cape Forum for Intellectual Disability v Government of the Republic of South Africa: A case study of contradictions in inclusive education' (2013) 1 *African Disability Rights Year Book* 139 141.
136 JK Burns 'The mental health gap in South Africa: A human rights issues' (2011) 6 *The Equal Rights Review* 99.
137 Art 1.
138 As above.
139 Art 3(a)-(f).On how words in the definition such as 'impairments', 'include', can be interpreted to include mental disabilities within the scope of the CPRD, see, G Szmukler et al 'Mental health law and the UN Convention on the rights of persons with disabilities' (2014) 37 *International Journal of Law and Psychiatry* 245.

The CRPD protects the right to life[140] and prohibits torture or cruel, inhuman or degrading treatment or punishment.[141] No scientific or medical experiment should be conducted on a PWD without his or her free consent.[142]

The CRPD views the individual as the primary decision maker, while recognising that the person with a disability may need some assistance in making and communicating a decision.[143] States parties are obliged to recognise that PWDs enjoy legal capacity on an equal basis with others in all aspects of life.[144] This provision means that PWDs are active subjects of rights, and not passive objects of social care. States should ensure that PWDs can effectively and fully participate in political and public life on an equal basis with others.[145] States are obliged to take appropriate measures to support PWDs in exercising their legal capacity.[146] However, in rendering the support, the rights and freedoms of PWDs should not be abused. In this vein, the CRPD provides as follows:

> States parties shall ensure that all measures that relate to the exercise of legal capacity provide for appropriate and effective safeguards to prevent abuse in accordance with international human rights law. Such safeguards shall ensure that measures relating to the exercise of legal capacity respect the rights, will and preferences of the person, are free of conflict of interest and undue influence, are proportional and tailored to the person's circumstances, apply for the shortest time possible and are subject to regular review by a competent, independent and impartial authority or judicial body. The safeguards shall be proportional to the degree to which such measures affect the person's rights and responsibilities.[147]

Other rights critical for the promotion of mental health include freedom from exploitation and abuse;[148] protection of integrity of the person;[149] privacy;[150] health;[151] an adequate standard of living and social protection;[152] and habitation and rehabilitation.[153] In order to ensure access to justice for PWDs, states parties are obliged to promote appropriate training for those in the field of justice, including police and prisons staff.[154]

140 Art 10.
141 Art 15(1).
142 As above.
143 Art 12.
144 Art 12(2).
145 Art 29.
146 Art 12(3).
147 Art 12(4).
148 Art 16.
149 Art 17.
150 Art 22.
151 Art 25.
152 Art 28.
153 Art 26.
154 Art 13(3).

5 The normative framework for realisation of mental health at the regional level

The ACHPR contains various civil, economic, political, social and cultural rights, which are vital for the promotion of mental health. The ACHPR guarantees everyone equal protection of the law.[155] Although the ACHPR does not explicitly include disability as one of the prohibited grounds of discrimination, it can be argued that disability is covered under the phrase, 'or other status'.[156] The ACHPR also provides that 'the disabled shall have the right to special measures of protection in keeping with their physical and moral needs'.[157] The ACHPR protects liberty and security of the person[158] and recognises the right to participate in government.[159] It also recognises 'the right to the best attainable state of physical and mental health'.[160] It also guarantees every person 'the right to the respect of the dignity inherent in a human being and to the recognition of his legal status'[161] and prohibits 'torture, cruel, inhuman or degrading punishment or treatment'.[162]

In *Purohit & Moore v The Gambia*,[163] the complainants, acting on behalf of patients detained in a psychiatric unit at a hospital, alleged that the legislation governing mental health – the Lunatics Detention Act – is outdated as it does not contain a requirement of consent to treatment or subsequent review of continued treatment. The complainants argued that the provisions of the Act that condemn persons described as 'lunatics'[164] to automatic and indefinite institutionalisation contravene articles 2 and 3 of the ACHPR, which provide for non-discrimination and equal protection of the law respectively. They further argued that since mental illness is a disability, the practice of detaining persons regarded as mentally ill indefinitely and without due process constitutes discrimination on the analogous ground of disability and thus contravenes article 2 and 3 of the Charter.

The African Commission observed that 'human dignity' is an inherent basic right to which all human beings, regardless of their mental disabilities, are entitled without discrimination.[165] The African Commission cited its earlier decision in *Media Rights Agenda v Nigeria*,[166]

155 Art 3 ACHPR.
156 Art 2.
157 Art 18(4).
158 Art 6.
159 Art 13.
160 Art 16(1).
161 Art 5.
162 As above.
163 (2003) AHRLR 96 (ACHPR 2003).
164 Sec 2 of the Act defines a 'lunatic' as including an idiot or person of unsound mind.
165 Para 57.
166 (2000) AHRLR 200 (ACHPR 1998).

where it held that the term 'cruel, inhuman or degrading treatment' in article 5 of the Charter is to be interpreted so as to extend the widest possible protection against abuses, whether physical or mental.[167] The African Commission held that the terms 'lunatics' and 'idiots' dehumanise and deny PWMDs any form of dignity in contravention of article 5 of the Charter. It stated as follows:

> [M]entally disabled persons would like to share the same hopes, dreams and goals and have the same rights to pursue those hopes, dreams and goals just like any other human being. Like any other human being, mentally disabled persons or persons suffering from mental illnesses have a right to enjoy a decent life, as normal and full as possible, a right which lies at the heart of the right to human dignity. This right should be jealously guarded and forcefully protected by all states party to the African Charter in accordance with the well established principle that all human beings are born free and equal in dignity and rights.[168]

The African Commission urged the government of the Gambia to ensure the enjoyment of the right to health of its people, paying special attention to PWMDs. The Commission observed that the right to health, 'which is vital to a person's life and well-being, and is crucial to the realization of all other fundamental human rights and freedoms',[169] includes the right to health facilities, access to food and services to be guaranteed to all without discrimination of any kind.[170] On implementation of the right to health under the ACHPR, the African Commission cautiously noted as follows:

> [In Africa], millions of people are not enjoying the right to health maximally because African countries are generally faced with the problem of poverty which renders them incapable to provide the necessary amenities, infrastructure and resources that facilitate the full enjoyment of this right. Therefore, having due regard to this depressing but real state of affairs, the African Commission would like to read into Article 16 the obligation on part of states party to the African Charter to take concrete and targeted steps, while taking full advantage of its available resources to ensure that the right to health is fully realised in all its aspects without discrimination of any kind.[171]

The Commission strongly urged the government of the Gambia to repeal the Lunatics Detention Act and replace it with a new legislation for mental health compatible with the African Charter and international standards and norms for the protections of PWMDs as soon as possible. In the meantime, the government should create an expert body to review cases of all persons detained under the Act and make appropriate recommendations for their treatment or release, and provide adequate medical and material care for PWMDs.

167 As above.
168 Para 61.
169 Para 80.
170 As above.
171 Para 84.

Another instrument critical for the promotion of mental health at the regional level is the Women's Protocol to the ACHPR. In addition to providing for other human rights recognised in international human rights instruments and the ACHPR, the Protocol enjoins states parties to ensure protection for women with disabilities and 'take special measures commensurate with their physical, economic and social needs to facilitate their access to employment, professional and vocational training as well as participation in decision making'.[172] States parties should also 'ensure the right of women with disabilities to freedom from violence, including sexual abuse, discrimination based on disability and the right to be treated with dignity'.[173] The African Charter on the Rights and Welfare of the Child (ACRWC) also obliges states parties to provide special protection to mentally and physically disabled children, who unfortunately are referred to as 'handicapped children'.[174] It should be noted that the regional provisions on disability are largely informed by the charity/medical models rather than the social and rights models of disability and are subject to progressive realisation and the availability of resources. Consequently, the Working Group on Older Persons and People with Disabilities in Africa[175] has drafted a Protocol to the African Charter on the Rights of Persons with Disabilities in Africa, which is informed by the social and rights based approaches to disability.[176]

6 The normative framework for realisation of mental health at the domestic level

6.1 General disability rights law

In addition to other human rights and freedoms, Uganda's Constitution recognises the rights of PWDs.[177] However, the Constitution restricts the liberty of the so-called persons of unsound mind 'for the purposes of the care or treatment of that person or protection of the community'.[178] Parliament has also enacted a fairly progressive legislation,[179] which obliges the state and other actors to create an environment conducive to PWDs realising their full potential. The Act aims at providing legal protection of PWDs pursuant to articles 32 and 35 of the Constitution.

172 Art 23(a).
173 Art 23(b).
174 Art 13.
175 Established by the African Commission in accordance with Resolution 143/45 of 2009.
176 The draft is available at http://www.achpr.org/news/2014/04/d121 (accessed 25 March 2015). For an elaborate analysis of the Draft Protocol, see, H Combrinck & LM Mute 'Developments regarding disability rights during 2013: The African Charter and African Commission on Human and Peoples' Rights' (2014) *African Disability Rights Yearbook* 309.
177 Art 32 & 35.
178 Art 23(1)(g).
179 The Persons with Disabilities Act.

'Disability' is defined as 'a substantial functional limitation of daily life activities caused by physical, mental or sensory impairment and environmental barriers resulting in limited participation'.[180] Given that the definition of disability includes mental or sensory impairments, it can be confidently stated that the Act applies to PWMDs.

The Act, which adopts the social and rights models of disability, has noble objectives, which include: the promotion of the dignity and equal opportunities of PWDs; participation of PWDs in all aspects of life as equal citizens of Uganda; elimination of all forms of discrimination of PWDs on ground of their disabilities; and promotion of positive attitude and image of PWDs as capable and contributing members of society, sharing the same rights and freedoms as other members of society.[181] The Act re-echoes such constitutionally guaranteed rights as health;[182] rehabilitation;[183] privacy;[184] freedom from cruel, inhuman or degrading treatment;[185] family rights;[186] and participation in political and public life, including decision-making.[187] The state, its agencies and all persons are obliged to uphold the rights and freedoms in the Constitution.[188] The Act prohibits discriminative medical examination[189] and thus an employer shall not conduct any test or examination to establish whether an applicant is a PWD.[190] However, an employer may make pre-employment inquiries into the ability of an applicant to perform job related functions.[191]

6.2 Mental health legislation

The main legislation in Uganda in the area of mental health is the Mental Treatment Act (the Act),[192] which came into force on 31 August 1938 during the colonial period and seeks to provide for 'the care of persons of unsound mind and the management of mental hospitals in Uganda'.[193] The Act stresses detention, treatment and care under custody in a facility for example a mental hospital. According to the Act,

> [a]ny magistrate, upon the information on oath in the prescribed form of any informant to the effect that the informant has good cause to suspect and believe some person to be of unsound mind and a proper subject to be placed

180 Sec 2.
181 Sec 3(a) - (e).
182 Secs 7 & 8.
183 Sec 10.
184 Sec 35.
185 Sec 34.
186 Sec 36.
187 Sec 37.
188 Sec 32.
189 Sec 14.
190 Sec 14(1).
191 Sec 14(2).
192 Cap 279.
193 Long title to the Act.

> under care and treatment, may, in any place which he or she deems convenient, see and question the person suspected to be of unsound mind, and in the same place, may hold an inquiry in private as to the state of mind of that person.[194]

In handling the complaint, the magistrate has powers to conduct an inquiry 'as if the suspected person were a person against whom a complaint for an offence punishable by a magistrate's court had been laid'.[195] Where the magistrate receives information on oath that a person suspected to be of unsound mind 'is at large or is dangerous to himself or herself or others, or is not under proper care or control or is cruelly treated or neglected',[196] the magistrate may order any police officer to apprehend and bring him or her to the magistrate for purposes of inquiring into his or her state of mind.[197] The suspected person may be detained in a mental hospital or other place deemed suitable by the magistrate for purpose of medical examination or for the welfare and safety of himself or herself or others.[198]

A magistrate conducting the inquiry shall appoint two medical practitioners who shall separately examine the suspected person, and if satisfied that he or she is of unsound mind, each practitioner shall sign a certificate to that effect.[199] Where the magistrate is satisfied that the person is indeed of unsound mind, he or she shall adjudge that person as being of unsound mind and issue a reception order for the care and treatment at a special mental hospital.[200] It should be noted that a police officer not below the rank of assistant inspector, a medical officer, or a chief may issue an 'urgency order' for the detention of a person alleged to be of unsound mind for the safety of the public or for the welfare of that person.[201] A person detained in a mental hospital may be discharged on the order of the chief medical officer.[202] He or she may be discharged at the request of relatives or friends who may be willing to undertake the care of that person.[203] The magistrate may require these relatives or friends to give an undertaking that the person shall be properly taken care of and he or she shall not injure himself or others.[204]

The Act encourages prejudice, stigma, discrimination and abuse of PWMDs, and violates almost all the rights recognised in the Constitution and international and regional human rights considered above. The Act

194 Sec 2(1) of the Mental Treatment Act.
195 Sec 2(2).
196 Sec 2(3).
197 Sec 2(3).
198 Sec 2(4).
199 Sec 3(1).
200 Sec 4(1).
201 Sec 6.
202 Sec 17.
203 Sec 18(1).
204 Sec 1(2).

uses derogatory language against a person with mental illness by referring to him or her as a 'person of unsound mind',[205] which means 'an idiot or person who is suffering from mental derangement'.[206] The Act views the challenge purely from a medical point of view whereby the person is treated as a mental patient. Yet, mental illness is simply one aspect of mental health. Mental health moves beyond mental illness and encompasses various mental conditions. The Act simply treats all PWMDs as persons of unsound mind, who should, following medical examination be detained or put under care in a mental hospital. It should also be noted that some PWMDs such as women and girls suffer double discrimination and thus require special attention to their health needs. They may be subjected to sexual violence and other forms of abuse. As the CRPD has correctly provided, 'women and girls with disabilities are subject to multiple discrimination'[207] and states should 'take measures to ensure the full and equal enjoyment by them of all human rights and fundamental freedoms'.[208]

The Act denies PWMDs the right to recognition before the law, prohibits them from providing evidence in court, denies them the right to administer their property, and abrogates the right to marry and the right to employment. This retrogressive legislation is fortified by the erroneous protective and paternalistic societal perception towards PWMDs that they do not have the capacity to distinguish between right or wrong and thus decisions and choices should be made on their behalf.

The Act relies on institutional care, yet contemporary approaches to mental health strongly recommend deinstitutionalisation and promotion of community based care.[209] The legal framework lacks mechanisms to enable PWMDs to contest or appeal their detention in mental health facilities or to stop the violence and abuse perpetrated against them. It is even not clear how a police officer or chief who may be untrained in mental health issues can make a decision of detention and subsequent admission of a PWMD. In any case, as Nyombi et al have correctly observed,

> the Act has not been well enforced. Mental health cases are rarely subject to review by the magistrates, leaving doctors to make decisive decisions without checks or balances. Legal recourse is a rare route no matter the case and

205 Sec 1(f).
206 As above.
207 Art 6(1) of the CRPD.
208 As above.
209 ML Perlin 'International human rights and comparative mental disability law: The role of institutional psychiatry in the suppression of political dissent' (2006) 39 *Israel Law Review* 69.

> admissions to hospital are mainly voluntary through self-referral or at the request of a relative.[210]

It is important to point out that if a person's liberty is deprived without a legal basis, then the deprivation of liberty is unlawful. For example, in *HL v UK*,[211] HL was a person who had difficulty speaking and with limited understanding. Following an incident where he had harmed himself at the day centre he was attending, he was admitted to hospital where he was retained for several months. However, HL's carers challenged the legality of his admission. The applicant alleged that his informal admission to hospital amounted to detention, which violated the provisions on liberty in the European Convention on Human Rights (ECHR).[212] The European Court of Human Rights held that the absence of safeguards and procedural rules regulating informal admissions failed to protect against arbitrary deprivation of liberty, thus violating art 5(1) of the ECHR. The court observed as follows:

> As a result of the lack of procedural regulation and limits, the Court observes that the hospital's health care professionals assumed full control of the liberty and treatment of a vulnerable incapacitated individual solely on the basis of their own clinical assessments completed as and when they considered fit ...[213]

It should be noted that there are efforts geared towards repeal or revision of the Act. The objects of the Mental Health Bill, which is a product of wide stakeholder consultation and follows a rights-based approach to mental health are to:

> (a) provide for community care and treatment for people with mental illness; (b) provide for the admission in, for the treatment and for the discharge from, health units and mental health units of persons with mental illness; (c) ensure that people with mental illness are enabled to seek treatment voluntarily; (d) ensure the safety and human rights of people with mental health problems and the people who come into contact with them; and (e) establish the Mental Health Advisory Board.[214]

210 C Nyombi et al'A critique of the Uganda Mental Health Treatment Act, 1964' (2014) 3 *Mental Health Law and Policy Journal* 50 51. For an analysis of the Act, see also M Mulumba 'Analysis of the Uganda Mental Treatment Act from a human rights and health perspective' http;//www.pages.ssm.com/so13/papers.cfm?abstract-id=10006 230 (accessed 18 May 2015).

211 (2005) EHRR 32.

212 Art 5.

213 Para 124. See also *Ashingdane v United Kingdom* 93 ECtHR (Ser A) at 19 (1985); L Gostin 'Human rights of persons with mental disabilities' (2000) 23 *International Journal of Law and Psychiatry* 125 152; LO Gostin & L Gable 'The human rights of persons with mental disabilities: A global perspective on application of human rights principles to mental health' 2004 (63) *Maryland Law Review* http://scholarship/ law.georgetown.edu/cgi/viewconte (accessed 18 December 2014).

214 Sec 3 of the Bill.

The Bill defines mental illness as

> a recognizable and persistent disturbance in the behaviour, thoughts, feelings, perceptions, mood, volition, orientation, awareness and memory of an individual that impairs the ability to cope with daily tasks and that impairs judgment or behaviour to a significant extent ...[215]

The Bill highlights key values such as human rights promotion and protection, deinstitutionalisation, integration of mental health care and community care, quality and safety, social inclusion, and inter-sectoral collaboration.[216]

7 Conclusion

The legal framework for realisation of the rights of PWDs in general and PWMDs in particular exists, especially at the international level. However, there is need to reform or repeal the Act to ensure that the new legislation is informed by contemporary psychiatry and human rights approaches. In any case, by ratifying the international and regional human instruments discussed in this chapter, the government of Uganda undertook to bring its domestic laws and practice in conformity with the standards and norms contained in these instruments.

The Proposed Mental Health Bill considered above is a move in the right direction. Any legislation that is eventually enacted should largely be guided by the social and rights models of mental disability. The legislation should also be guided by the standards laid down by the WHO[217] and could draw lessons from legislative developments in other jurisdictions such as South Africa[218] and Ghana.[219] The importance of legislation in the promotion of mental health need not be over-emphasised. Commenting on the utility of mental health legislation, the Mental Health and Poverty Project observed as follows:

> The fundamental aim of mental health legislation is to protect, promote and improve the lives and mental well-being of citizens ... Mental health legislation is not only concerned with care and treatment, but it guides the provision and setting up of institution-based health services. The mental health law is also essential for complementing and reinforcing the mental health policy by providing a legal framework for meeting its goals. Such legislation should ensure protection of human rights, enhancement of the

215 Sec 2 of the Bill.

216 For a discussion of the Bill, see, C Nyombi 'A critical review of the mental health treatment bill' (2011) 18 *East African Journal of Peace and Human Rights* 499.

217 WHO *Mental health care law: Ten basic principles* (1996); WHO *Mental health legislation and human rights* (2003); WHO *Resource book on mental health, human rights and legislation* (2005).

218 Mental Treatment Care Act, 2002.

219 Mental Health Act, 2012.

> quality of mental health services and promotion of the integration of people with mental disorder in their communities.[220]

The advantages of public interest litigation were considered in chapter four. Thus, there is a need for public spirited individuals or organisations to challenge the Act in Ugandan courts and the African Commission on grounds that it violates the human rights and freedoms guaranteed in the Constitution and international human rights instruments, which Uganda has ratified.

It should be pointed out above that given that the stigma and discrimination against PWMDs is deeply rooted in cultural and societal perceptions and attitudes, the above juridical strategies may be inadequate to promote mental health. The strategies should be augmented by public awareness and sensitisation of society, including key stakeholders such as the police and other law enforcement officers and health care professionals about the fact that like other human beings, PWMDs are entitled to a dignified life. PWMDs should be assisted or supported where necessary to realise their human rights. Their rights, needs, potential and contribution must be recognised.

220 Mental Health and Poverty Project 'Mental health reform in Uganda' Policy Brief 3 http://r4d.dfid.gov.uk/PDF/Outputs/MentalHealth_RPC/MHPB_Uganda3.pdf (accessed 3 July 2015).

7

HEALTH CARE PROFESSIONALS AND THEIR REGULATION

1 Introduction

It should be noted from the outset that like other professions, the health care professional patient relationship is based on trust. A patient trusts that the professional is competent, and possesses the requisite training, qualifications, skills and expertise to handle his or her health challenge. In Uganda, there are a number of health care professional councils that regulate the conduct of medical and dental practitioners, nurses and midwives, pharmacists, and allied health professionals. These councils are established by statute and their main functions include maintaining registers for the relevant practitioners, disciplining those unfit to practise, overseeing professional education, and guiding the practitioners on the question of professional ethics. The law encourages professional self-regulation by creating councils to ensure that health care professionals promote the interests of patients and the public. This chapter examines the law regulating health care professionals in Uganda with particular attention to the establishment, functions and composition of the various councils, registration of practitioners, and the questions of discipline and professional competence.

2 Medical and dental practice

2.1 The Medical and Dental Practitioners' Council

The practice of medicine and dentistry is governed by the Medical and Dental Practitioners' Act (the Act),[1] which establishes the Medical and Dental Practitioners' Council.[2] The council is

1 Cap 272 Laws of Uganda.
2 Sec 2(1) of the Act.

> a body corporate with perpetual succession and a common seal and may sue or be sued in its corporate name and, subject to this Act, may do or suffer all things and acts as bodies corporate may lawfully do or suffer.[3]

The functions of the council are generally: to monitor, supervise, maintain professional medical and dental education standards and ethics; to exercise disciplinary control over dental and medal practitioners; to protect society from abuse of medical and dental care and research on human beings; and to disseminate to the medical and dental practitioners and the public, ethics relating to doctor-patient rights and obligations.[4]

According to the Act, the council is composed of the chairperson, who shall be a senior practitioner appointed by the Minister; the director general of health services; two representatives of the faculties of medicine of all the universities established by law in Uganda; two representatives of the Uganda Medical Association; one representative of the Uganda Dental Association; and one practitioner representing the Uganda private medical and dental practitioners.[5] The term of office for a member of the council is three years from the date of appointment and is eligible for reappointment.[6] He or she may resign his or her office by writing to the chairperson of the council.[7] Where the council member's office becomes vacant other than by expiry of time, the Minister may appoint another person to fill the vacancy.[8]

The registrar shall be the chief executive officer and head of the secretariat[9] and secretary to the council.[10] Although the secretary may participate in the deliberations of the council, he or she has no right to vote.[11] The registrar shall be a public officer appointed by the Health Service Commission from amongst the registered practitioners.[12] The functions of the registrar shall be to keep and maintain registers of medical and dental practitioners; to make alterations in the register or remove names of practitioners as directed by council. The registrar may also remove from the register the name of a deceased practitioner, any entry which might have been incorrectly or fraudulently made in the register; and with the consent of the person concerned, the name of a person who has ceased to practise.[13] The registrar also has powers to inspect and have full access to all medical and dental health units. He or she is also obliged to record all minutes of meetings and to have custody of the seal of the

3 As above.
4 For the functions of the Council see, sec 3(a) - (i) of the Act.
5 Sec 1(a) - (c).
6 Sec 4(3).
7 Sec 4(4).
8 Sec 4(5).
9 Sec 7(1).
10 Sec 4(2).
11 As above.
12 Sec 7(1).
13 On the functions of the registrar see sec 8(1)(a) - (h).

council, and to perform any other function as may be conferred on him or her by council.[14] He or she is responsible for the funds and property of the council and day-to-day administration.[15]

The meetings of the council shall be as is provided for under the First Schedule to the Act.[16] The first meeting of the council shall be convened by the chairperson as soon as practicable after appointment of the first council.[17] After the first meeting, the council shall meet for transactions of business at such places and at such times as may be decided by the council.[18] In any case, the council must meet at least once every three months.[19] The chairperson may at any time call a special meeting of the council upon a written request by a majority of the members of the council.[20] The quorum for council meetings shall be a third of all the members.[21] The decisions of the council shall be by a majority of the members present and in case of equality of the votes, the person presiding shall have a casting vote in addition to his or her deliberative vote.[22] To avoid conflict of interest, a member who has a direct or pecuniary interest in a matter before council must disclose the nature of his or her interest as soon as possible to the council.[23] Subject to the requirements of the Act, the council may regulate its own procedure.[24]

2.2 Registration of medical and dental practitioners

The registrar shall maintain the following registers of medical and dental practitioners: a main register; a provisional register; and a temporary register.[25]The registrar shall also maintain a register for specialist medical and dental practitioners; and a register for health units.[26]The registrar shall publish all up-date registers and lists of practitioners and health units in the Gazette.[27]Any person who holds himself or herself out as a registered medical or dental practitioner commits an offence and is liable on conviction to a fine of not less than three hundred thousand shillings and not more than three million shillings or to imprisonment for not less than three months and not more than one year or to both.[28]

14 As above.
15 Sec 8(2).
16 Sec 5.
17 Rule 3(1) of the First Schedule.
18 As above.
19 As above.
20 Rule 2.
21 Rule 4.
22 Rule 5.
23 Rule 6(1).
24 Rule 8.
25 Section 19(1)(a) - (f).
26 As above.
27 Secs 19(2), (3) & 30.
28 For the general penalty section see sec 47.

Any person who qualifies to be registered may apply to council for registration.[29] The application shall be in the prescribed form and shall be accompanied by documentary proof of the qualifications and the prescribed fees.[30] Where the council is satisfied that the applicant is eligible for registration, it shall authorise the registrar to enter his or her name on the register. On registration, the applicant shall be issued with a certificate of registration[31] and may engage in medical or dental practice.[32] A person who does not qualify to be registered may apply to council for provisional registration, which shall cease to have effect upon attainment of full registration.[33] Persons holding the following minimum qualifications are eligible for registration as medical and dental practitioners: (a) a degree of Bachelor of Medicine, Bachelor of Surgery or Bachelor of Dental Surgery granted by a university established in Uganda by law; and (b) a medical or dental qualification recognised by the council for the purposes of registration.[34] In addition to these qualifications, every practitioner engaged in active public or private practice must undergo a minimum continuing medical or dental education prescribed and organised by the council.[35] The council may delegate its power to prescribe and organise the education to the Uganda Medical Association, the Uganda Dental Association or any other dental or medical association as it deems fit.[36]

The applicant for registration should satisfy council that he or she has acquired experience by serving a full-time internship in a hospital approved by the council.[37] The council may grant temporary registration to non-citizens of Uganda[38] and may also recognise the qualifications from a university not established in Uganda by law taking into account admission requirements and the curriculum followed.[39] It should be pointed out that the council may require a person whose qualifications are not recognised in Uganda by law to attend an interview or sit an oral or written examination or both for the purpose of having his or her qualifications recognised by the council.[40] The council may, after interviewing or examining that person, require him or her to undergo a period of training or undertake further examination.[41]

It is important to point out that for those persons who intend to engage in private practice, a certificate of registration is not enough. According to

29 Sec 21(1).
30 Sec 21(2).
31 Secs 21 & 22.
32 Sec 24.
33 Sec 23(1) & (2).
34 Sec 17(1)(a) - (b).
35 Sec 44(1).
36 Sec 44(3).
37 Sec 17(2).
38 Sec 17(4).
39 Sec 18(1).
40 Sec 20(1).
41 Sec 20(2).

the Act, no person is permitted to engage in private practice unless he or she has obtained a licence.[42] A registered medical or dental practitioner may apply to the council for a licence to engage in private practice either as a general practitioner or as a specialist in his or her area of specialisation.[43] The application shall be accompanied by a copy of the certificate of registration.[44] If the council is satisfied that the applicant possesses the requisite qualifications, it may grant him or her a licence for private practice subject to such conditions as it may determine.[45] In order for a person who is granted a private licence to practice as a full time private medical or dental practitioner, the council must be satisfied that he or she has acquired experience by rendering service in a full-time employment in an approved hospital or health unit for a period of three years.[46]

It should also be pointed out that the registered practitioner may demand reasonable charges for medical, surgical or dental advice given; for the attendance or treatment rendered; for the performance of any medical, surgical or dental appliance; or for any drugs prescribed or supplied.[47] The practitioner is entitled to institute legal proceedings for the recovery of the charges and any associated costs.[48] It is important to note that there are no regulations or guidelines to determine what amounts to 'reasonable charges'. The determination of the charges seems to be influenced by the discretion of the practitioner and the forces of supply and demand. However, in the absence of health insurance and a functioning social security system, this is likely to preclude the poor and marginalised from accessing health services. It may therefore be necessary to regulate or control charges payable in respect of health services rendered.

It should be noted that following an inquiry, the council may cause the removal of the name of a registered practitioner from the register under the following circumstances: where he or she is convicted by any court of law of a criminal offence involving moral turpitude; where he or she is found guilty of professional misconduct; where his or her name has been removed from the medical or dental practitioners register of any other country or has been suspended from practice.[49] The name of the person who has been removed from the register may be restored by the council at its own motion.[50] The name may also be reinstated upon an application by the aggrieved person and after carrying out due inquiry into the circumstances of the removal.[51] In conducting the inquiry, the council

42 Sec 27(1).
43 Sec 28(1).
44 As above.
45 Sec 28(3).
46 Sec 28(4).
47 Sec 42(1)(a) - (d).
48 As above.
49 Sec 25(1)(a) - (c).
50 Sec 26(1).
51 Sec 26(2).

must, like other tribunals, adhere to the principles of natural justice. In *Marko Matovu v Mohamed Sseviri*,[52] it was held that the cardinal rule of natural justice is so central to Uganda's justice system that it must be observed by both judicial and administrative tribunals. The council must avoid bias, because where this is proved, the proceedings will be declared a nullity.[53] The council should also ensure that the practitioner in question is given an opportunity to give his or her evidence and call witnesses and cross-examine witnesses testifying against him.[54]

2.3 Inquiry into professional misconduct

The council may hold an inquiry into an allegation of professional misconduct against a medical or dental practitioner.[55] It has quasi-judicial powers for purposes of adjudicating over complaints of professional misconduct against medical and dental practitioners. Patients may find it more convenient to lodge complaints with the council because unlike the courts, it is informal, cheaper and specialised. Although the council is informal in procedure, it must, as pointed out above, adhere to the principles of natural justice.

The Act does not define what amounts to professional misconduct. However, in the Guidelines developed by the council, the following are listed as examples of 'unprofessional or unethical conduct' by registered practitioners: failure to update one's continuing medical education and obtain annual practicing licence; advertising; professional incompetence; disclosure of information regarding a patient without his or her permission; lack of respect for colleagues; giving false certificates or evidence; and receiving or giving a bribe.[56] Other examples are: deliberate failure to obtain consent from a patient; rudeness to patients; failure to refer a patient where it is clearly indicated; abandonment of a patient under one's care; abuse of drugs and alcohol; offences involving forgery, dishonesty or violence; sexual relationships with patients and/or attendants; professional negligence that leads to maiming or death; conducting bio-medical research without following established guidelines; and intentionally administering a lethal chemical to a patient.[57]

The complaint alleging the professional misconduct must be in writing, signed by the complainant or his or her legal representative or any other person acting on his behalf, and must be forwarded to the registrar.[58]

52 (1979) HCB 174.
53 See eg *Obiga v Electoral Commission & Another* Election Petition 4/2011.
54 See for example, *Rosemary Nalwadda v Uganda AIDS Commission* Misc Cause 45/2010.
55 Sec 33.
56 Uganda Medical and Dental Practitioners Council (UMDPC) *Guidelines in Respect of Complaints against medical and dental practitioners* (2002) 6-7 (the Guidelines). See also UMDPC/USAID *Code of Professional Ethics* (2013).
57 As above.
58 The Guidelines (n 56 above) 2.

The complaint should be comprehensive, containing the names and practice of the relevant practitioner, all the relevant dates and facts and all documents to be produced at the inquiry.[59] Thus, the charges against the practitioner should clearly bring out the material facts to enable him or her adequately prepare a defence. In *Hutchinson v General Dental Medical Council*,[60] charges were brought by the respondent's committee against the appellant in respect of hygiene related matters. His fitness to practice was found to be impaired and the respondent's professional conduct committee made an order for erasure from the register. The appellant challenged the decision on grounds that the bringing of certain of the charges against him amounted to an abuse of process. Although the court accepted that there was a considerable degree of vagueness in the charges especially in terms of the timing, they were explicit in terms of the behaviour alleged and thus did not render fair hearing impossible. The court found that there was no documentary or other evidence to prove the allegations on a balance of probabilities and thus the decision of the committee was wrong. On that basis, rather than the ground of abuse of process, the court quashed the committee's decision.

The registrar shall in consultation with the chairperson of the council, convene a meeting for purposes of holding an inquiry.[61] A 21-days written notice signed by the registrar indicating the date, place and time of the inquiry shall be served personally on or sent by courier to the person whose conduct is the subject of inquiry.[62] The notice shall specify the particulars of the alleged misconduct and shall be accompanied by relevant documents to be produced at the inquiry.[63] In *De Souza v Tanga Township*,[64] it was held that the rules of natural justice require that the party should be given adequate notice, which should clearly specify the time and venue where the hearing of a particular matter is to take place. The registrar shall request the practitioner concerned to provide a written explanation with a caution that it may be used as evidence against him or her.[65] A person whose conduct is the subject of inquiry is entitled to appear and to be represented by an advocate of his or her own choice.[66] Where the person fails to appear and the council is satisfied the he or she was duly served with the notice, it may proceed with the inquiry in his or her absence.[67] In *Varma v General Medical Council*,[68] it was held that the Fitness

59 As above.
60 (2008) EWHC 2896 (Admin).
61 Sec 34(1) of the Act. It should be noted that the Act permits the council to appoint committees for the purpose of better carrying out its functions. Consequently, complaints against practitioners are heard by the Ethics or Disciplinary Committee of the Council. After receiving the complaint, the Committee may decide whether there are grounds – *prima facie* evidence – for an inquiry to be held or not.
62 Sec 34(2).
63 Sec 34(3).
64 (1961) EA 337.
65 The Guidelines (n 56 above) 3.
66 Sec 34(4).
67 Sec 34(5).
68 (2008) EWHC 753 (Admin).

to Practice Panel had properly borne in mind that it had to balance the appellant's private rights against the public interest of having serious allegations properly investigated and had justifiably treated the appellant's failure to attend the hearing as a voluntary decision to be absent.

The council may order and enforce the attendance of any witness.[69] The summons for the attendance shall be signed and issued by the registrar.[70] All persons appearing before the council must be truthful; any false statements will amount to perjury.[71] The council has the discretion to hold the inquiry in public or private.[72] The council may appoint an advocate to advise it on questions of law.[73] The council shall notify the person who is subject to an inquiry of its decision within 30 days after the conclusion of the inquiry.[74] The council may cause the report and decision of the inquiry to be published in a manner that it deems fit.[75] The following are the possible sanctions that may be imposed on a practitioner who has been found guilty: a verbal warning; a written warning; a serious written warning with a copy to the employer; placement on probation; suspension from practice for a prescribed period; erasure from the register; and any other penalty the council may deem necessary in the circumstances.[76]

2.3.1 Examples of complaints to the council

It should be noted that pursuant to its mandate under the Act, the council has inquired into a number of allegations of professional misconduct against medical practitioners. Although the rulings of the council are not binding in terms of precedent, they serve to illustrate that the council takes questions of alleged professional misconduct against practitioners seriously. For example, in *An inquiry by the council into alleged professional misconduct by Dr Asinja Kapuru*, Dr Kapuru was alleged to have substituted a medical record for another leading to the loss of a baby at Mulago national referral hospital. He was found guilty of gross professional misconduct and suspended from medical practice for a period of two years. It was alleged that the live baby boy was wilfully swapped with a dead baby girl at the hospital. Dr Kapuru admitted that he filed two reports: one

69 Sec 34(7).
70 Sec 34(8).
71 Sec 34(6) provides that the provisions of chapter X of the Penal Code Act and sec 131 of the Evidence Act shall apply in relation to any inquiry held by the council. The relevant provisions of Chapter X are: perjury and subornation of perjury; contradictory statements; false statements by interpreters; fabricating evidence; false swearing; deceiving witnesses; destroying evidence; conspiracy to defeat justice; and interference with witnesses. Sec 131 of the Evidence Act, cap 6 is to the effect that a witness shall not be excused from answering a question on ground that the answer will incriminate him or her.
72 The Guidelines (n 56 above) 5.
73 Sec 35(1).
74 Sec 36.
75 Sec 37.
76 The Guidelines (n 56 above) 5.

indicating that the baby was a male, and the other showing that the baby was female. He argued that he was convinced to change the record by a nursing sister. On the professional misconduct of the doctor, the Council observed as follows:

> The matter under consideration is a question of professional misconduct by a medical practitioner. Professional misconduct is the kind of conduct outside the bounds of what is considered acceptable or worthy of its membership of the governing body of [the] profession. Such behaviour usually manifests in negligence and/or failure to make reasonable provision for the safeguarding of life, health or property of a person who may be affected by the work for which the professional is responsible. The fact that substituting a medical record for another by a medical practitioner is wrong and unbecoming is beyond debate. The motive of such conduct is a matter of concern. It is simply a matter of lack of responsibility. A responsible doctor records information on the basis of his actual findings and not on the basis of 'rumours' from nurses or colleagues. When a practitioner handles a patient, he or she assumes full responsibility for that patient. It is disgraceful for Dr Kapuru to claim [or plead] that he made the second theatre report because of pressure. It is unbelievable that a fully trained medical practitioner could be cowed by a nurse to do something he knew as unethical and illegal.[77]

In *An inquiry by the council into the death of Mrs Mercy Ayiru at the Women's Hospital and Fertility Centre*, Ayiru was admitted for the purposes of an operation to remove fibroids. Dr Sali, the proprietor of the hospital advised the patient that the fibroids could be removed through laparoscopic surgery. She consented to the operation. However, she died. The pathologist was of the view that she died due to the negligence of the doctors who worked on her. In his defence, Dr Sali argued that the operation was carried out by Dr Rafique Parker and that Mrs Ayiru died due to cardiac arrest caused by 'lack of oxygenation into lungs' during induction of anaesthesia. According to Dr Parker, this was an anaesthetic accident. The Council found that the patient was under the care of Dr Sali; she was admitted to the hospital one hour before she was taken to the theatre; the intubation tube was wrongfully placed into the oesophagus; and Dr Parker was not a registered practitioner. The council ruled that as a doctor and proprietor of the facility, Dr Sali had the primary duty of care, and was thus fully responsible for the death of Mrs Ayiru. Dr Sali was issued with a strong reprimand while Dr Parker was suspended from practising medicine in Uganda for five years.

In *An inquiry into allegations of negligence against Uganda Martyrs Hospital Namugongo*, the complainant's wife, Tendo Grace went for a routine check-up at the hospital and was seen by Dr Opegu Titus who decided that she needed an urgent caesarean section. The patient was operated on and the baby was given to the parents but she looked exhausted. When they requested the doctor to check the baby, they were informed that he was

77 Ruling of the Council 2.

busy operating on another patient. They requested to be referred to another facility but there was inordinate delay. A specialist came to see the baby after six hours and referred them to Kadic hospital where the baby was put on oxygen. The hospital referred them to Mulago hospital where the baby died. The council found that Dr Opegu was responsible because he performed a caesarean section without adequate preparation and facilities to handle a distressed baby; there was a delay in referring the baby to a facility that would handle the problem; and the hospital, especially the theatre lacked adequate surgical facilities. The council ordered the suspension of Dr Opegu for three months and to do 50 hours of continuing professional development in one year. The council also ordered the closure of Uganda Martyrs hospital's inpatient facility, X-ray services and theatre until there is proof that those facilities are up to the acceptable standards.[78]

2.3.2 Appeal against decisions of the council

As I pointed out above, in handling complaints against a medical or dental practitioner, the council must follow the rules of natural justice, especially the right to a fair hearing,[79] which is guaranteed by the Constitution and is non-derogable.[80] The Constitution provides that

> [a]ny person appearing before an administrative official or body [such as the council] has a right to be treated justly and fairly and shall have a right to apply to a court of law in respect of any administrative decision taken against him or her.[81]

Consequently, the Act grants a person who is aggrieved by the decision of the council a right to appeal to the High Court within 90 days from the date of notification of the decision of the council.[82] However, medical practitioners seem more inclined to quietly serve their sentences or settle matters out of court. Indeed, in Uganda, there is an extremely dearth of cases where practitioners have challenged the decision of the council in the High Court.

In *Tumukurate Espildon v Uganda Medical and Dental Practitioners' Council*,[83] the appellant operated a medical practice in a township of Lyantonde, Rakai district. The disciplinary proceedings against him were based on a letter written to the council by persons who referred to themselves as concerned citizens. In the letter, they made grave allegations

78 For examples of other complaints, see, Inquiry into allegations of negligence against the administration and staff of Lubaga hospital, which led to the death of Nansubuga Judith; and an inquiry into allegations of negligence at Entebbe hospital that led to the death of Mrs Patricia Gitta.
79 Art 28.
80 Art 44(c).
81 Art 42.
82 Sec 38(1) of the Act.
83 High Court Civil Appeal 1999 (unreported).

against the appellant that he defiles young school girls but due to his wealth, he influences the police not to take any action; that he seduced a girl, made her pregnant and subsequently procured an abortion in his own clinic; and that he molests and attempts to rape women who attend his clinic. On appeal to the High Court, his counsel argued that the appellant was denied a fair hearing at the inquiry, that he was denied an opportunity to listen to evidence against him and cross examine witnesses and that the council relied on hearsay evidence to conclude that he was guilty of professional misconduct. Counsel also argued that the appellant was denied the right to legal representation. The issues before the court were whether the appellant received a fair trial; and whether or not there was sufficient evidence to justify the conclusion reached by the council. The court held that the inquiry was substantially flawed in procedure and the evidence adduced was not sufficient to justify the finding that the applicant was guilty of professional misconduct. The court observed that convincing evidence should have been sought by the council before reaching a finding that the applicant was guilty. That what was required during the inquiry was observance of the rules of natural justice and an objective scrutiny and evaluation of the evidence to determine whether the applicant was guilty of unethical or professional misconduct. That although the council cannot be expected to base its findings on proof beyond reasonable doubt, the evidence adduced against the medical practitioner must be subjected to serious scrutiny.

It should be noted that according to the Act, the Chief Justice is mandated to make rules regulating appeals to the High court.[84] Unfortunately these regulations have not been made. In *Tumukurate* above, counsel for the defendant argued that since the rules had not been made, the appellant could not challenge the decision of the respondent. In dismissing the objection, the court held that absence of the rules does not deprive an aggrieved party of a remedy. The court was of the view that the Constitution commands the court to 'administer justice without undue regard to technicalities'.[85] In any case, according to the Judicature Act, the High Court shall in exercise of its jurisdiction, grant 'all such remedies as any of the parties to a cause or matter is entitled to in respect of any legal or equitable claim properly brought before it'.[86]

In other jurisdictions, medical practitioners have also challenged decisions by their professional bodies. For example, in the Kenyan case of *Praxades Okutoyi v Medical Practitioners and Dentists Board*,[87] the applicant was suspended by the board on 29 November 2007 from practising medicine as a paediatrican aesthetist for a period of three years. He was also ordered to undergo remedial training before being re-admitted to

84 Sec 38(2).
85 Art 126(2)(e) of the Constitution.
86 Sec 33 of the Judicature Act, cap 13.
87 (2008) EKR http://www.kenyalaw.org (accessed 26 April 2015).

practise medicine. The decision followed an inquiry by the board pursuant to a complaint by Dr John N Ondeko, whose 17 year old son, suffered cardiac arrest and permanent brain damage while in the care of the applicant. The son had been admitted at Nairobi hospital on 15 February 2007 for a simple day surgery to correct his nose structure but left the hospital with permanent head damage. The board found the applicant guilty of infamous or disgraceful conduct.

The applicant appealed against the board's decision arguing that it was tainted with bias and thus unlawful and applied to court for a stay of the decision of the board. Counsel for the applicant argued that the applicant stood a grave risk of suffering not just substantial but also irreparable harm if the decision was not stayed pending the appeal and that the applicant's professional standing continued to be eroded by negative publicity accruing from the decision of the board. Counsel for the applicant also argued that the country was suffering a substantial loss from the illegal conviction and suspension of the applicant since there were only three paediatrican aesthetists, including the applicant. The court agreed with counsel for the board that the applicant had not demonstrated that the applicant would suffer substantial loss if the decision was not stayed. In dismissing the application, the court held that public interest expounded by the medical board in this case far outweighed the applicant's interest to earn a living. Lifting the suspension could seriously compromise the interests of the public. The court observed that had the applicant undergone remedial training as ordered by the board and was working under supervision, the court may have ruled differently.

In the Nigerian case of *Olaye v Chairman, Medical and Dental Practitioners Disciplinary Tribunal,*[88] the appellant and three other medical practitioners were charged before the respondent disciplinary tribunal for negligence due to their non-attendance to a patient contrary to the ethics of the medical profession. Although the appellant denied liability, the tribunal found him liable and directed that his name be struck off the register of medical and dental practitioners in Nigeria. However, the Nigerian Court of Appeal allowed the appeal on the ground that the tribunal had not observed the principles of natural justice. In another Nigerian case, *Denloye v Medical and Dental Practitioners Disciplinary Tribunal,*[89] the appellant was charged with neglecting a patient who was seriously ill in a prolonged manner between 29 June 1966 and 10 July 1966. The appellant was also charged with extortion of money from the patient's father as an inducement for him to treat the patient. The tribunal found him guilty of infamous conduct and ordered removal of his name from the register. However, the Court of Appeal set aside the decision of the tribunal on grounds of natural justice.

88 (1977) NMLB 506.
89 (1969) 1 All NLR 306.

In yet another Nigerian case, *Medical and Dental Practitioners Disciplinary Tribunal v Okonkwo*,[90] a patient, a 29 year old woman, and her husband belonged to a religious faith known as Jehovah's witnesses, who regard blood transfusions as going against the Bible. The patient was admitted to a hospital where a blood transfusion was recommended for her ailment. The patient and her husband explicitly refused to give their consent to the blood transfusion. The respondent treated the patient without transfusing blood and the patient died. The respondent was charged before the tribunal with negligence arising from the fact that he failed to administer a life saving measure to his patient. The tribunal referred to the code of ethics which stated that a doctor should not allow anything, including religion to intervene in his relationship with the patient and must take measures to preserve life. The tribunal found the respondent guilty on three counts and suspended him for six months on each of the charges to run concurrently.

The respondent appealed to the Court of Appeal where the questions to be determined were whether the allegations in the charge amounted to criminal offences so as to take them out of the jurisdiction of the tribunal; and whether the tribunal should have found him guilty when the patient and her husband had refused to give consent to the blood transfusion. The Court of Appeal allowed the appeal and set aside the decision of the tribunal and the latter appealed to the Nigerian Supreme Court, which dismissed the appeal. On the balance between public interest and a patient's right to refuse medical treatment, Agoola, JSC stated:

> The scope and limit of the duty of a practitioner faced with a patient's refusal to give informed consent to life saving medical treatment cannot be considered in isolation of the right of the patient ... It is expedient at the outset to recognize that a consideration of a religious objection to medical treatment involves a balancing of several interests, namely: the constitutionally protected right of the individual, state interest in public health, safety and welfare of society, and, the interest of the medical profession in preserving the integrity of medical ethics and, thereby, its own collective reputation. To give undue weight to these other interests over the rights of the competent adult may constitute a threat to liberty of the individual, unless legally recognised circumstances justify that weight should be ascribed to one over the others. Where for instance, the health and safety of society is under threat, for instance in an epidemic, public health and safety may be given a higher weight than an individual's human rights. Where, however, the direct consequence of a decision not to submit to medical treatment is limited to a competent adult patient alone, no injustice can be occasioned in giving individual right supremacy. In my judgment, any rule of ethics or professional conduct that ignores the need to balance these interests or that gives undue weight to individual circumstances will be out of touch with reality and may lead to unjust consequences.[91]

90 (2002) AHRLR 159 (NgSC 2001).
91 Para 72.

In the South African case of *Health Professionals Council of South Africa v Dewald de Bruin*,[92] Dr de Bruin, while a 32 year old clinical assistant specialising in urology, had a sexual relationship with the complainant, a 21 year old student, which resulted in her pregnancy. Over a period of about four months, Dr de Bruin attempted to abort the fetus in various ways, including physical intervention and the prescription of medication to the complainant without following the prescribed means acceptable to the medical profession. The complainant ultimately aborted in November 1993, under traumatic circumstances. Dr de Bruin was formally charged before the tribunal and an inquiry conducted by the disciplinary committee of the council followed. He was found guilty of disgraceful conduct in February 1998 and his name was struck off the register. He appealed to the Supreme Court of Appeal under section 20 of the Health Professions Act.

Dr de Bruin admitted that he made an error of judgment and was deeply ashamed with what he had done. The Supreme Court of Appeal held that his conduct was indeed reprehensible and deserved severe censure. However, the court took into account Dr de Bruin's professional integrity, his competence as an urologist, his dedication to his patients, his high ethical standards and the excellent service rendered to his community, all of which were collaborated by members of the medical profession. The court also found that the council had breached the principles of natural justice by not allowing the appellant's legal representative to make an oral presentation. Consequently, the court quashed the council's decision and substituted the penalty of striking the practitioner's name from the register with a suspension of two years.

In order for the High Court to clearly understand how the inquiry was conducted by the council, it is necessary for the appellant to avail a record of proceedings to the court. In the Tanzanian case of *Shiva v Minister of Health & another*,[93] the appellant averred that the first respondent's medical council, which found him guilty of negligence, was constituted by three members who had previously conducted a probe against him and that this was contrary to the principles of natural justice. The appellant further averred that the decision of the council was tainted with an error of law since it did not address itself to the patient's record. The court refused to quash the decision of the council since the appellant did not make available to court the proceedings of the council, including the pleadings, documents relied upon and the ruling. In dismissing the appeal with costs, the court observed that in the absence of the record of proceedings, there was no evidence to prove that the members took part in the proceedings and influenced the decision of the council.

92 2004 (4) All SA 392 (SCA).
93 (2008) TZHC 10.

3 Nursing and midwifery

3.1 The Nurses and Midwives Council

The Nurses and Midwives Act (the Act)[94] defines a midwife as 'a person who is trained and qualified in the care of women in relation to childbirth and in the care of infants and who is registered or enrolled'.[95] A nurse is defined as 'a person who is trained and qualified in the promotion of health, the prevention of disease and the care of the sick and who is registered or enrolled'.[96] Although the Act defines a traditional birth attendant (TBA) as 'a person recognized by her community as being able to assist women in child birth',[97] it does not provide for their regulation, yet they play a critical role in assisting pregnant women, especially in rural areas.

The Act provides for the training, registration, enrolment and discipline of nurses and midwives of all categories and establishes the Nurses and Midwives Council. The council

> shall be a body corporate with perpetual succession and a common seal and may sue or be sued in its corporate name and, subject to this Act, may do or suffer all other things and acts as bodies corporate do suffer.[98]

The functions of the council shall be: to regulate the standards of nursing and midwifery in the country; to regulate the conduct of nurses and midwives and to exercise disciplinary control over them; to approve courses of study for nurses and midwives; to supervise and regulate the training of nurses and midwives; to grant diplomas or certificates to persons who have completed the respective courses of study in nursing or midwifery; to supervise the registration and enrolment of nurses and midwives; and to exercise general supervision and control over the two professions.[99] Given the increased adoption of a human-rights-based approach (HRBA) to health programming, it may be necessary for the Act to expressly provide for the promotion and protection of human rights as one of the functions of the council.

The council shall consist of the following: a chairperson who shall be a senior registered nurse or midwife (or both) appointed by the Minister; two members elected by the Uganda Nurses and Midwives Association; two tutors representing all nursing and midwifery schools in Uganda; one representative elected by public health nurses; one representative elected

94 Cap 274.
95 Sec 1(i).
96 Sec 1(k).
97 Sec 1(q).
98 Sec 2(1).
99 Sec 3(a) - (h).

by psychiatric nurses; two representatives of nurses and midwives working in non-government organisation hospitals; one representative of the Uganda Private Midwives Association; one representative of the Uganda Community-based Health Care Association; one representative of the Uganda Medical and Dental Practitioners Council; and one representative of the Uganda Allied Health Professionals Council.[100] The council also has the following ex-officio members: the commissioner for nursing services; the chief training officer (nursing); the registrar; the senior principal nursing officer Mulago Hospital; the senior principal nursing officer, Butabika hospital; and the head of the department of nursing, Makerere University.[101]

No person shall be appointed a member of the council if he or she has been declared bankrupt or has entered into any composition with his or her creditors; has been convicted of an offence involving moral turpitude; is unable in the opinion of the medical board, by reason of infirmity of mind or body, to perform the duties of a member; or has been disqualified from practice under this Act or under the Medical and Dental Practitioners Act.[102] The registrar shall be the secretary to council.[103] The term of office for the members of the council shall be three years from the date of appointment and shall be eligible for reappointment for not more than two terms.[104]

The meetings of the council are conducted in accordance with the Schedule to the Act. The council shall meet for the transaction of business at places and times as may be decided by the council, but it must meet once every three months.[105] The chairperson shall, upon a written request by a majority of the members, call a special meeting of the council.[106] All questions proposed at a meeting of the council shall be decided by simple majority and in case of an equality of votes, the presiding person shall have a casting vote in addition to his or her deliberative vote.[107] A decision may be made without a meeting by circulation of the relevant papers among members of the council and by the expression of the views of the majority of members.[108] However, any member may require that the decision should be deferred and considered at a meeting of the council.[109] A member who has a direct or indirect pecuniary interest in a matter to be considered at a meeting of the council should disclose the nature of his or

100 Sec 4(1)(a) & (c)(i) - (ix).
101 Sec 4(b)(i) - (vi).
102 Sec 4(4)(a) - (d).
103 Sec 4(5).
104 Sec 5.
105 Rule 3(1) of the Schedule.
106 Rule 2(3).
107 Rule 5(1).
108 Rule 5(2).
109 As above.

her interest to the council.[110] The council may, subject to the Act, regulate its own procedure.[111]

3.2 Registration and enrolment of nurses and midwives

The registrar shall be the chief executive officer of the council and the head of the secretariat and shall keep and maintain a register and roll of nurses and midwives, indicating the address of contact; the date of entry; qualifications and additional qualifications; and such other particulars as council may determine.[112] A person holding any of the following minimum qualifications shall be eligible for registration or enrolment in the appropriate category to which the qualifications relate: a degree of Bachelor of Science in nursing recognised by the council; and a certificate or diploma in nursing issued by the council.[113] A person who produces evidence, which is satisfactory to the council that he or she has been registered or enrolled as a nurse or midwife in any other country, may also be eligible for registration or enrolment by the council.[114] The council may also recognise other qualifications for purposes of nursing and midwifery registration or enrolment.[115] A person not holding the requisite qualifications may apply to the council, which may make arrangements for him or her to attend an interview and sit for an oral or written examination.[116] After the examination, the council may direct that person to undergo a period of training or to undertake further examination as it may specify.[117] Where council is satisfied with the results of an interview or examination, it shall authorise the person's registration or enrolment.[118]

A person who qualifies to be registered or enrolled as a nurse or midwife may apply to council for registration or enrolment, and if council is satisfied that he or she has met the necessary requirements, it shall authorise the registrar to enter the person's name on the register or the roll.[119] An application for registration or enrolment shall be in the prescribed form and shall be accompanied by the applicant's qualifications and the prescribed fee.[120] The registrar shall, if satisfied that all the requirements for registration or enrolment have been met, issue the applicant with a certificate of registration or enrolment with the seal of the council affixed on it.[121] A registered nurse or midwife practicing in a

110 Rule 6(1).
111 Rule 8.
112 Sec 22(1)(a) - (d). For an outline of the functions of the registrar, see sec 11(1) & (2).
113 Sec 19(a) & (b).
114 Sec 19(c).
115 Secs 19(d), 20(1) & (2).
116 Sec 21(1).
117 Sec 21(2).
118 Sec 21(3).
119 Sec 23(1).
120 Sec 23(3).
121 Sec 24.

health unit, whether public or private shall apply to council for a practising licence.[122] The application for the licence shall be accompanied by a certificate of registration.[123] If the council is satisfied that the applicant possesses the relevant qualifications, it shall grant him or her the licence.[124] The registration or enrolment of a nurse or midwife shall not entitle him or her to practise medicine, surgery or dentistry; to grant any medical certificate or certificate of death; or to undertake the charge of cases of abnormality or disease in connection with parturition.[125] Every registered or enrolled nurse or midwife engaged in active public or private practice shall undergo a minimum continuing education course as prescribed by the council in order to be maintained on the register.[126] Any person who procures registration by fraud commits an offence.[127] Any person who holds him or herself out directly or indirectly as being a registered or enrolled nurse or midwife commits an offence.[128]

A registered or enrolled midwife who has served in a hospital or health unit for not less than five years may apply to the council for a licence to engage in private practice. The licence permits him or her to 'undertake the care of women in relation to childbirth and of infants and to manage common health conditions in the community'.[129] In order for a registered nurse to apply for a licence to engage in private practice, he or she should have served in a hospital or health unit for not less than ten years. The licence permits the nurse to manage common health conditions in the community.[130] If the council is satisfied that the nurse or midwife possesses the relevant qualification, it shall authorise the grant of the licence.[131] The nurse or midwife shall not stockpile, retail or wholesale drugs at his or her health unit or maternity home unless he or she first obtains a special licence.[132] He or she shall not, in the interest of good practice and the welfare of patients, carry out procedures 'beyond common conditions and health problems and shall refer all cases beyond his or her ability to a medical practitioner'.[133] The nurse or midwife engaged in private practice is entitled to demand reasonable charges for the attendance on, treatment of or service rendered and may sue for or recover the same with all associated costs in a court of competent jurisdiction.[134]

122 Sec 25(1).
123 Sec 25(2).
124 Sec 25(3).
125 Sec 27(a) - (c).
126 Sec 52(1).
127 Sec 51.
128 Sec 53.
129 Sec 30(1).
130 Sec 30(2).
131 Sec 30(4).
132 Sec 34(1).
133 Sec 34(2).
134 Sec 49.

It is important to point out that advances in nursing and midwifery education and training, locally and internationally, have resulted in a new cadre of nurses and midwives with higher levels of specialisation and qualifications at Bachelors, Masters and more advanced degrees. Given the shortage of medical practitioners in the country, nurses and midwives who have acquired more training and qualifications should be able to render more services to the public than is envisaged in the current legislation. Midwives who have undergone further relevant training for example should handle some of the complications related to child birth provided the relevant facilities are available. There is thus a need to review the Act to ensure that it takes into account advances in nursing and midwifery education and practice. Some of the midwives who have acquired additional training and qualifications should not be restricted to the so-called common health conditions in society. They may be able to perform some of the roles traditionally reserved for medical practitioners provided they are provided with relevant additional training.

3.3 Inquiry into professional misconduct

It should be noted that the council may cause the removal of a nurse or midwife from the register or roll when he or she is convicted by a court of law of a criminal offence involving moral turpitude; is found guilty of professional misconduct by the council; or is suspended from practice.[135] The disciplinary committee of the council[136] may inquire into the conduct of a registered nurse or midwife if: he or she is convicted of an offence under the Act or under the Medical and Dental Practitioners Act; he or she is convicted of any offence involving dishonesty or fraud; he or she is alleged to have committed any scandalous conduct in respect of his or her professional calling; or his or her name has been struck off the register or roll of any board, hospital, university or other body recognised by the council.[137]

For purposes of holding an inquiry into the conduct of a nurse or midwife, the registrar shall convene a meeting of the committee.[138] The nurse or midwife shall be personally served with a 28 days' written notice signed by the registrar. The notice may also be sent by registered post at his or her last known address informing him or her of the place and time fixed for the inquiry. The notice shall be accompanied by all documents relevant for the inquiry.[139] The nurse or midwife shall be entitled to be present at the inquiry and shall, if he or she wishes, be represented by an advocate of his or her choice.[140] Should the nurse or midwife fail to appear at the

135 Sec 28(1)(a) - (c).
136 For the composition of the committee, see sec 36(1)(a) - (g).
137 Sec 37(1)(a) - (d).
138 Sec 37(2).
139 Sec 37(3).
140 Sec 37(4).

inquiry without a reasonable excuse, and the committee is satisfied that he or she was duly served, it may proceed with the inquiry in his or her absence.[141] In *R (Raheem) v Nursing and Midwifery Council*,[142] the Administrative court held that there had been no proper exercise of discretion by the conduct and competence committee of the respondent as to whether it had been appropriate to continue in the absence of the applicant in respect of a hearing conducted to decide whether she had been guilty of misconduct. It was held that the decision to proceed in absence of the nurse or midwife must be exercised with care and caution. The appeal was allowed and the Committee was directed to rehear the whole matter. In *Jatta v Nursing and Midwifery Council*,[143] it was held that where the Panel is satisfied that the notice of hearing has been served, hearing of the complaint may proceed notwithstanding that the notice was not received by the respondent or appellant. The court held that there was no procedural irregularity when the Panel proceeded in Mr Jatta's absence.

In *Faulkner v Nursing and Midwifery Council*,[144] it was alleged that the appellant had caused stress to a patient and engaged in inappropriate sexually related activity. The court dismissed the appeal on grounds that the respondents conduct and competence committee had not made an error in exercising its discretion to hear allegations against the nurse in his absence, and then to find the allegations proved and ordering that she be struck off the register. In *Ward v Nursing and Midwifery Council*,[145] the appellant, a registered nurse at a private residential care home, faced four allegations before a panel of the respondent's conduct and competence committee. She was charged with failure to maintain accurate contemporary records, failing to undertake assessments prior to administering treatment to a resident, and dishonestly documenting that a percutaneous endoscopic gastronomy feed had been commenced when it had not. The appellant argued that the panel erred in proceeding in her absence and that it inappropriately admitted hearsay evidence against her. The court found that the appellant had voluntarily absented herself from the hearing and upheld the decision of the conduct and competence committee that her fitness to practice is impaired and the she be struck off.

An inquiry by the committee shall be deemed to be a judicial proceeding and any false statements shall amount to the offences of perjury and subornation of perjury and fabricating evidence under the Penal Code Act.[146] The committee shall have the powers of the High Court to summon witnesses and call for the production of any documents and to examine witnesses and parties on oath.[147] Any person who without

141 Sec 37(5).
142 (2010) EWHC 2549 (Admin).
143 (2009) EWCA Civ 924.
144 (2009) EWHC 3349 (Admin).
145 (2014) EWCA 1158 (Admin).
146 Secs 94 & 99 of the Penal Code Act.
147 Sec 38(1).

reasonable excuse fails to obey the summons; refuses without reasonable cause to answer all questions put to him or her by the committee; or wilfully interrupts the proceedings of the committee or insults any member of the committee, commits an offence.[148]

After the inquiry, the committee may recommend to the council the removal of the registered or enrolled nurse or midwife from the register or the roll; order the suspension of the nurse or midwife for a period that it may deem fit; or reprimand the nurse or midwife.[149] All the proceedings before the committee at any inquiry shall be recorded and signed by the presiding person.[150] Any aggrieved person may within one month of the notification of the decision of the council, appeal to the High Court.[151] The appeal shall be by petition, stating the facts and grounds, and a copy shall be served on the registrar.[152] At the close of the proceedings of the inquiry, the party shall be informed of his or her right to appeal.[153] The appeal may, as I illustrated above, allege non-compliance with the principles of natural justice. For example, in *R (Johnson) v Professional Conduct Committee of the Nursing and Midwifery Council*,[154] the appellant argued that the charges against him were insufficiently particularised, which was unfair and contrary to article 6(3)(b) of the European Convention on Human Rights, which provides that a person charged with an offence has the right to adequate time and facilities for the preparation of his defence. It was held that the charges must be sufficiently particularised to enable a person charged to know, with reasonable clarity, the case he or she has to meet and to prepare a defence.

4 Allied health profession

4.1 The Allied Health Professionals Council

Although the Act does not define AHPs, they belong to clinical health care professions, distinct from medicine, dentistry, nursing and midwifery. AHPs play a critical role in the provision of health services in the country. They include, dental technologists; medical clinical officers, anaesthetic clinical officers, ophthalmic clinical officers, and psychiatric officers; laboratory technologists and laboratory technicians; dispensers; orthopaedic clinical officers and technicians; physiotherapists and occupational therapists; health inspectors, health assistants and assistant field officers for entomology; and radiographers.

148 Sec 39.
149 Sec 40.
150 Sec 41.
151 Sec 42(1).
152 Sec 42(2).
153 Sec 42(3).
154 (2008) EWHC 885 (Admin).

The AHPs are governed by the Allied Health Professionals Act,[155] which provides for their regulation, supervision and control. The Act establishes the Allied Health Professionals Council, which shall be a body corporate and has the following functions: to regulate the standards of AHPs in the country; to regulate the conduct of AHPs and to exercise disciplinary control over them; to regulate the education, training of AHPs and approve their qualifications; and generally to exercise general supervision and control over the allied health profession.[156] The council shall consist of a chairperson who shall be a senior AHP; a representative of the director general of health services; the assistant commissioner of health services responsible for AHPs; one person representing each of the professions of dentistry; pharmacy; clinical medicine; medical laboratory technology; orthopaedic technology; physiotherapy; public health; and radiography.[157] The council also consists of one representative for each of the following: the Medical and Dental Practitioners Council, the Nurses and Midwives Council; all faculties of medicine of all universities in Uganda established by law; and the National Drug Authority.[158] No person shall become a member of the council if he or she has been declared a bankrupt or has entered into a composition with his or her creditors; has been convicted of an offence involving moral turpitude; is unable by reason of infirmity of mind or body, to perform the duties of a member; or has been disqualified from practising or carrying out his or her profession or calling.[159]

4.2 Registration of AHPs

The council may recognise training institutions for AHPs and approve their courses of study and qualifications.[160] Holders of the following qualifications awarded by institutions recognised by the council shall be eligible for registration: a degree of Bachelor of Science in any of the disciplines of allied health professions awarded by a university established in Uganda by law; and a certificate or diploma in any of the disciplines of allied health professions.[161] The council may also recognise qualifications obtained from a foreign country provided it is satisfied that the standard of training and examinations is not inferior to the standard set by the council.[162] A person who does not possess the requisite qualifications may apply to the council, which may make arrangements for him or her to attend an interview or sit an oral or written examination. The council may direct the applicant to undergo a period of training or undergo further

155 Cap 268 Laws of Uganda.
156 Sec 4 of the Act.
157 Sec 5(1)(a) - (d).
158 Sec 5(1)(e) - (f).
159 Sec 5(4).
160 Sec 19 & 20.
161 Sec 21(a) - (b).
162 Sec 21(1)(c) & (2).

examination. If the council is satisfied with the results of the interview or examination, it shall authorise his or her registration. It should be noted that the council may appoint a committee to assess the suitability of the applicant's registration, and the committee shall submit its findings to the council for its decision.[163]

A person who qualifies for registration as an AHP shall apply to the council for registration and if it is satisfied that he or she possesses the requisite qualifications, it shall authorise the registrar to enter his or her name on the register. The application shall be in the prescribed form and shall be accompanied by evidence of the qualifications and the prescribed fee.[164] The registrar shall keep and maintain a register of AHPs and shall enter therein the address of contact; the date of entry; qualifications; and such other particulars as the council may determine.[165] The registrar shall cause the publication of the names of registered AHPs in the Gazette.[166] On registration, the registrar shall issue the registered person with a certificate of registration.[167] It should be noted that registration of an AHP does not permit him or her to practice medicine or dentistry. He or she is also not permitted to grant any medical certificate or certificate of death except for the disciplines that fall under his or her profession. He or she is also not permitted to undertake the charge of cases of abnormality or disease in connection with parturition.[168] It should also be noted that registered AHPs shall undergo minimum continuing education as prescribed by the council. Any person who procures registration by fraud or passes off as registered whereas not, commits an offence.[169]

A registered AHP may apply to the council for a licence to engage in private practice in the discipline of his or her area of specialisation. The application for the licence shall be accompanied by a certificate of registration. The applicant should have worked full-time in a hospital or health unit approved by the council for a period of not less than four years.[170] The AHP engaged in private practice may demand reasonable charges for the services rendered and may recover the same with full costs in a court of competent jurisdiction.[171]

4.3 Inquiry into professional misconduct

Where the council receives an allegation against an AHP, which if proved would constitute professional misconduct, it may refer it to the disciplinary

163 Sec 22(1) - (4).
164 Sec 23(1) - (2).
165 Sec 24(1)(a) - (c).
166 Sec 24(2).
167 Sec 25.
168 Sec 26.
169 Sec 53 & 55.
170 Secs 29 - 31.
171 Sec 51.

committee to hold an inquiry into the conduct of the professional. The registrar shall on the receipt of the complaint summon a meeting of the disciplinary committee. A 28 days written notice signed by the registrar shall be served personally on the professional or sent to him or her by registered post at his or her last known address. The notice shall contain the substance of the allegation made against him, the date, time and venue of the inquiry and copies of relevant documents.[172] The professional shall be entitled to be present at the inquiry or be represented by an advocate of his or her choice. If the professional fails to appear without any reasonable excuse, the committee may conduct the inquiry in his or her absence.[173]

In *Abdalla v Health Professions Council,*[174] the appellant, a radiographer claimed that the committee's decision to proceed in her absence was in breach of her rights under article 6(1) of the European Convention on Human Rights, and alternatively it was in breach of the rules of natural justice since the committee proceeded in her absence. The court rejected the appellant's argument and held that lack of funds to pay for legal representation would not justify an adjournment where there was no realistic prospect that the position would change in the reasonably near future. That if the appellant chose not to avail herself with the opportunity to attend the hearing, then the committee was entitled to proceed in her absence. In deciding whether to proceed in the appellant's absence, the disciplinary body must have regard to all the circumstances of the case. In *R v Jones (Anthony),*[175] the House of Lords held that the discretion to commence and conduct proceedings in the absence of the appellant should be exercised with the utmost care and caution and that the panel must carefully balance fairness of the appellant and the wider public interest.

The committee shall have the powers of the High Court to summon witnesses and order the production of all relevant documents.[176] After the inquiry, the committee may recommend to the council the removal of the professional or order his or her suspension for a period it may deem fit.[177] The registrar shall notify the professional in writing of the decision of the council within three months after the conclusion of the inquiry.[178] A person who is aggrieved by the decision of the council may appeal to the High Court within one month from the notification of the decision. The committee shall inform the professional of his or her right of appeal. The appeal shall be by petition in writing stating the facts and grounds of appeal and a copy shall be served on the registrar.[179]

172 Sec 28(1) - (3).
173 Sec 38(5).
174 (2009) EWHC 3948.
175 (2003) 1 AC 1; (2002) UKHL 5.
176 Sec 39(1).
177 Sec 41.
178 Sec 43(1).
179 Sec 44(1) - (4).

The committee must permit the professional to summon witnesses where necessary. In *R (Thompson) v General Chiropractic Council,*[180] the appellant challenged the decision of the committee of the respondent to hold a substantive hearing when a particular witness, whom the appellant promised to call, would not be available. The court analysed the issue as being one of procedural fairness of the proceedings before the committee. The court noted that the expert witness in question was crucial to the appellant's defence and held that although courts would be slow to interfere with case management decisions taken by a professional body, this was subject to the supervisory jurisdiction of the court to ensure that the parties were given a fair hearing.

5 Pharmacy

5.1 The Pharmaceutical Society of Uganda

The Pharmacy and Drugs Act,[181] which provides for the regulation of the profession of pharmacy establishes the Pharmaceutical Society of Uganda, which 'shall be a body corporate having perpetual succession and a common seal and may sue and be sued in its corporate name'[182] and 'may hold, acquire and dispose of any property, movable or immovable'.[183] For a person to be a member of the society, he or she should have passed the qualifying examinations for membership of the society and completed the relevant practical training as approved by the council.[184] He or she should hold a degree, diploma or other qualification as approved by the council.[185] No person shall be enrolled as a member of the society unless he or she is 21 years old and has paid the prescribed fees. A person shall not be enrolled if he or she has been adjudged by a court to be of unsound mind; or has been convicted by a court whether in Uganda or elsewhere of any offence involving fraud or dishonesty; or has been adjudged a bankrupt or insolvent.[186] The registrar shall keep the register of all pharmacists in the prescribed form.[187] The registrar shall issue a certificate of registration to an applicant provided he or she is of good character and a member of the society.[188] In case the pharmacist for any reason ceases to be a member of the society, his or her name shall be deleted from the

180 (2008) EWHC 2499 (Admin).
181 Cap 280 Laws of Uganda.
182 Sec 6(1).
183 Sec 6(2). For the procedure for the meetings of the society, see the First Schedule to the Act.
184 Sec 7(1)(a).
185 Sec 7(1)(b).
186 Sec 8(a) - (c).
187 Sec 13(1).
188 Sec 13(2).

register.[189] The registrar shall cause the names of all registered pharmacists to be published in the Gazette.[190]

According to the Act, the governing body of the society shall be a council, which shall consist of twelve members. The core functions of the council are to enforce standards of pharmacy; regulate the conduct and discipline of all pharmacists; maintain a register of registered pharmacists; ensure that pharmacy training institutions conform to set standards; approve all pharmacy practice outlets whether public or private; and conduct continuing pharmacy education.[191]

5.2 Inquiry into professional misconduct

Where a complaint is made against a pharmacist and the registrar is of the opinion that there is a cause for an inquiry, he or she may, after consulting the chairperson of the disciplinary committee, which is a committee of the Pharmacy Board,[192] serve a notice on the pharmacist requiring him or her to give an explanation in writing within six weeks.[193] The registrar shall lay a copy of the notice, plus the pharmacist's explanation and all relevant documents before the disciplinary committee.[194] Where the committee is satisfied that there is a cause for an inquiry, it shall order that the inquiry be held. The complainant, pharmacist and any other person who may assist the committee shall be summoned to appear before the committee.[195] The concerned pharmacist or his legal representative should appear on the day fixed for hearing. However, where the pharmacist or his representative fails to appear, the complaint may be heard in his absence. In *Yusuf v Pharmaceutical Society of Great Britain*,[196] where the pharmacist voluntarily chose not to attend or be represented and the tribunal exercised its discretion with utmost caution, it was held that the tribunal's decision was fair, measured and unassailable.

Should the committee find the pharmacist guilty, it may impose any one or more of the following sanctions: reprimand the pharmacist; order him or her to pay a fine of two-hundred shillings; order the cancellation or suspension for a specified period of his or her certificate of registration.[197] Any pharmacist aggrieved by the decision of the committee may appeal within one month after the date of the order to the High Court.[198] The

189 Sec 13(4).
190 Sec 14.
191 Sec 21(1) & 2. See also Ministry of Health 'The Pharmacy Council' http://www.health.go.ug (accessed 23 September 2013).
192 Established under section 1 of the Act.
193 Sec 16(1). For acts or omissions that amount to professional misconduct, see the second schedule to the Act.
194 Sec 16(2).
195 Sec 16(3).
196 [2009] EWHC 867 (Admin).
197 Sec 16(4).
198 Sec 18(1).

appeal shall be made by petition in writing bearing a stamp of twenty-one shillings.[199]

In spite of the above statutory right appeal, I have not come across any Ugandan case where a pharmacist has challenged the decision of the committee. However, in other jurisdictions, some pharmacists have appealed against the decisions of their professional bodies. For example, in the South African case of *Simon v South African Pharmacy Council & Others*,[200] the appellant, a pharmacist registered under the Pharmacy Act 53 of 1974 appealed against the decision of an appeal committee of the first respondent, the South African Pharmacy Council. He was a party to a number of transactions in which at the request of a customer an invoice was made out containing a false description of the goods and products supplied to the customer. The purpose of this was to enable the customer lodge a claim with his or her medical aid scheme. The appellant was convicted of fraud and sentenced to 18 months' imprisonment and suspended for a period of 5 years. Pursuant to the conviction, the Council instituted disciplinary proceedings under section 39 of the Pharmacy Act, against the appellant. He was found guilty of misconduct and struck off the register of pharmacists and ordered to pay costs of the disciplinary inquiry.

He appealed against the sanction by the disciplinary committee. Counsel for the appellant argued that the sanction unreasonably limits the applicant's participation in his chosen trade, profession or occupation, and the decision being in the nature of an administrative action, was arbitrary, capricious or irrational. Counsel for the first respondent submitted that as far as sanctions or penalties imposed by a professional tribunal are concerned, the power of the court to interfere in the exercise of the tribunal's discretion is limited. The court agreed with counsel for the respondent that the power of the court to interfere in the exercise of the discretion by a tribunal is very limited. A court of appeal will only interfere if it is shown, that the tribunal, in imposing a sanction, misdirected itself in such a nature, degree or seriousness that it shows, directly or by inference that the tribunal did not exercise its discretion at all or exercised it improperly or unreasonably. In dismissing the appeal with costs, the court observed that by his conduct, the appellant brought the honour of his chosen profession into disrepute.

5.3 The scope of a pharmacist's responsibility

Before concluding this section, it is necessary to inquire into the pharmacist's scope of responsibility. I have pointed out above that a complaint may be lodged against a pharmacist before a disciplinary body.

199 Sec 18(2)(a).
200 (2006) ZAWHC 14. See also, *Simman v South African Pharmacy Board* 1980 (1) SA 764 (T); *Rosenberg v South African Pharmacy Board* 1981 (1) SA 22 (A).

The question is: do pharmacists have a duty to warn or even explain to patients about the potential risks of the medications prescribed by a doctor? Simply walk into a pharmacy in Kampala or a town near you in order to appreciate the situation. Perhaps because most pharmacies are not designed to be conducive for private inquiries or discussion about highly personal or intimate matters, very few people discuss with the pharmacist the prescription from the doctor. Some pharmacists may not insist that the patient buys the full dose as prescribed by the doctor. More often than not, a patient presents the prescription from his/her doctor and the pharmacist simply dispenses the drugs without any question. As health professionals, both the doctor and pharmacist should be concerned about the health, care and safety of the patient. So, does the responsibility to warn lie with the pharmacist or it remains with the patient's doctor?

Generally, the role of pharmacists is to follow instructions of doctors accurately, and dispense the medication in accordance with the prescription from a particular doctor. Albeit there are no local cases on the subject, comparative case law may be persuasive. For example, in *Hooper v Capoblanco,*[201] the California Supreme court held that except for special circumstances, pharmacists are not required to warn patients of potential side effects of drugs. In *Kampe v Howard Stark Professional Pharmacy,*[202] a patient alleged that a pharmacy failed to 'warn, counsel, evaluate, or verify the appropriateness of prescriptions, including controlled substances'.[203] In fact, evidence showed that the pharmacist had warned, counselled and evaluated the prescription. The court held that the pharmacy had only 'a limited duty to fulfil lawful prescriptions'.[204] That a pharmacist fulfils professional duties by accurately filling a prescription and that there is no duty for a pharmacist either to monitor therapy or to warn patients.

However, over the years, courts have held that a pharmacist's responsibility or duty extends far beyond accurate order processing. Given that pharmacists are possessed with a unique body of knowledge, when a pharmacist knows of a potential problem with a particular drug therapy, he or she has a duty to act to protect the patient from harm. However, in absence of knowledge of the problem, the pharmacist's duty is limited. In *Horner v Spalitto,*[205] a patient was prescribed ethchloryunol 750mg and diazepam 10mg, each to be taken every eight hours. The pharmacist dispensed the medications accurately. However, six days later, the patient died. An autopsy attributed his death to the drugs' adverse effects. The claim by the Horner family was based on the pharmacist's alleged failure to question the therapy and to warn the patient of the potential side effects or adverse reactions when these medications are taken together. The

201 No 99 A S01792 (Cal Sup Ct Nov, 15, 2000).
202 841 SW.2d 223 (1992).
203 As above.
204 *Hooper* (n 201 above) 226.
205 1 S.W.3d 5 19 (Mo Ct App 1999).

pharmacist was found not guilty. On appeal, it was held that the pharmacist's duty extends beyond mere prescription of drugs and that pharmacists have the training and skills to recognise when a prescription dose is outside a normal range. Thus, they are in the best position to discuss the appropriateness of a patient's drug regimen. Consequently, the court reinstated the case against the pharmacist.

The question whether a pharmacy has a duty to warn its customers of the potential side effects of the prescription drugs it dispenses was also considered in *Cottam v CVS Pharmacy*,[206] where it was held that the pharmacy has no duty to warn. However, when the pharmacist assumes the duty to warn the patient of some side effects, he or she must warn of all potential side effects. In *Happel v Wal-Mart Stores*,[207] it was also held that pharmacists are professionals and thus under certain narrow circumstances, they have a duty to do more than just an accurate order filler. They have a limited duty to warn. Albeit this duty would not require a pharmacist to learn about the patient's condition and render medical judgment, in giving information to the patient, he or she should warn of potential danger. The court observed that when a pharmacist has special knowledge that a particular patient has an increased risk of harm if she takes a particular medication, he or she has a duty to counsel the patient about the risk.

In *Morgan v Wal-Mart Stores*,[208] a child died due to hypereosinophilic syndrome resulting from the use of desipramine prescribed for attention-deficit hyperactivity disorder. The defendant pharmacy was alleged to have been negligent for dispensing the medication without warning the child's parents of this rare disorder. The question before the court was whether pharmacists have a duty under Texas law to warn of potentially adverse reactions to prescription drugs. The court stated:

> To impose a duty to warn on the pharmacists would be to place the pharmacist in the middle of the doctor-patient relationship, without the physician's knowledge of the patient ... [T]he duty of the manufacturer runs to the physician and not the patient. Therefore it is illogical and unreasonable to impose a greater duty on the pharmacist who properly fills a prescription than is imposed on the drug's manufacturer.[209]

The court dismissed the case and held that the dispensing pharmacist simply had no knowledge of the particular risks of desipramine in this particular patient. However, the court acknowledged that pharmacists owe patients a duty beyond accurately filling a prescription 'based on the

206 764 NE 2D 814 (Mass 2002).
207 766 NE 2d 1118 (Ill 2002).
208 No 03-99-00700.CV (Tex App Dist 3 08/10/2000) http://www.versuslaw.com (accessed 21 April 2015).
209 Para 43.

presence of additional factors, such as known contraindications, that would alert a reasonably prudent pharmacist to a potential problem'.[210]

6 Traditional medical practice

6.1 Understanding traditional medicine

The World Health Organisation (WHO) defines traditional medicine (TM) as,

> Diverse health practices, approaches, knowledge and beliefs incorporating plant, animal, and/or mineral based medicines, spiritual therapies, manual techniques and exercises applied singularly or in combination to maintain well-being, as well as treat, diagnose or prevent illness.[211]

According to the National Council of Traditional Healers and Herbalists Associations of Uganda (NACOTHA), TM refers to 'ways of protecting and restoring health that existed before the arrival of modern medicine with medicinal plants being the world's oldest known health-care products'.[212]

TM plays a critical role in the promotion of health of the people especially in rural areas. People, especially in the rural areas, may find TM more physically and economically accessible and culturally acceptable than modern or conventional medicine.[213] They may identify with the traditional medical practitioners who may more easily appreciate their situation than the modern health practitioners whose attitude may be patronising and condescending. TM is perceived to be more 'natural and safer' than conventional therapies[214] and is an important and often underestimated part of prevention and treatment health services.[215] For example, in a study concerning rural poor women's access to maternal health care rights in south western Uganda, I found that some women utilise the services of traditional birth attendants (TBAs) for labour and delivery care although they receive antenatal care (ANC) at health centres.[216] In eastern Uganda, TM has been used for the treatment of

210 Para 52.
211 WHO *Traditional Medicine Strategy 2002-2005* (2002) 7.
212 National Council of traditional Healers and Herbalists Associations of Uganda (NACOTHA), http://www.blackherbals.com.nacotha1.htm (accessed 12 April 2014).
213 As above.
214 WHO *Guidelines on developing consumer information on proper use of traditional, complementary and alternative medicine* (2004).
215 WHO *Traditional medicine strategy 2014-2023* (2013)11.
216 BK Twinomugisha 'Protection of rural poor women's right of access to maternal health care in Uganda: The case of Kashambya sub-county, Kabale district' unpublished LLD thesis, Makerere University, 2004.

diabetes because of difficulties in accessing hospitals.[217] There is also evidence that herbal medicines are used by infertile women in order to achieve parenthood.[218] TM is also used to treat sexual and erectile challenges in men.[219] In fact, in Uganda, between 70-80 per cent of the population use TM to meet their health care needs.[220] The importance and contribution of TM to the improvement of health has been underlined by the WHO Director General as follows:

> [T]raditional medicines, of proven quality, safety, and efficacy, contribute to the goals of ensuring that all people have access to care. For many millions of people, herbal medicines, traditional treatments, and traditional practitioners are the main source of care. This is care that is close to their homes, accessible and affordable. It is also culturally acceptable and trusted by large numbers of people. The affordability of most traditional medicines makes them all the more attractive at a time of soaring health-care costs and nearly universal austerity. Traditional medicine also stands out as a way of coping with relentless rise of chronic non-communicable diseases.[221]

It should however be noted that in spite of the importance of TM to the health of the people, it raises questions of safety and quality.[222] There are reports that quack traditional healers have taken advantage of desperate and hapless patients.[223] Consequently, the government has been urged to develop legal and policy frameworks to regulate the activities of traditional medical practitioners.[224]

6.2 Regulation of traditional medical practice

There is no law in Uganda that specifically addresses the registration, practice and discipline of traditional medical practitioners. The NDA has established guidelines for the manufacture, registration and sale of herbal medicines. However, the guidelines do not cover the practice of herbal medicine, which 'will be handled under the auspices of the various

217 E Rutebemberwa et al 'Use of traditional medicine for the treatment of diabetes in eastern Uganda: A qualitative exploration of reasons for choice' (2013) 13 *BMC International Health and Human Rights* 1.

218 HF Kaadaga et al 'Prevalence and factors associated with use of herbal medicines among women attending infertility clinic in Uganda' (2014) *BMC Complementary & Alternative Medicine* 14.

219 M Kamatenesi-Mugisha & H Oryem-Origa 'Traditional herbal remedies used in the management of sexual impotence and erectile dysfunction in western Uganda' (2005) 14 *Africa Health Sciences* 40.

220 As above.

221 Speech by WHO Director General, Dr Margaret Chan, at the International Conference on Traditional Medicine for South-East Asian Countries, New Delhi, India 12-14 February 2013, cited in WHO *Traditional medicine strategy* (2013) 16.

222 See eg, LS Otieno et al 'Acute renal failure following the use of herbal remedies' (1991) 14*East African Medical Journal* 2 993-998.

223 R Ninsiima 'Fake traditional healers threatening African medicine' *The Observer* 19 February 2013.

224 As above.

professional organizations that unite herbalists in the country'.[225] Consequently, traditional medical practitioners are self-regulated through NACOTHA, which is a loose association of traditional healers and herbalists in the country. Some of the functions of NACOTHA include: the promotion, research and the development of TM in the country and to 'increase public awareness and understanding about the value of traditional medicine and other healing practices through improving health, prevention and management of diseases'.[226] The WHO has advocated for the regulation of TM in order to ensure the safety and efficacy of its products and practices.[227] The goals of the WHO strategy are: (a) harnessing the potential contribution of TM to health, wellness and people-centred health care; and (b) promoting the safe and effective use of TM by regulating, researching and integrating TM products into health systems where appropriate.[228]

TM may be integrated into the mainstream health care system as in China or operate parallel with modern or conventional medicine as in India.[229] However, as Sonya has cautioned, integrating TM in the health care system as advocated by the WHO may withhold power from traditional practitioners.[230] Thus, although there is an urgent need to regulate the practice of TM in the country, the process should be formal, inclusive and participatory. NACOTHA should be actively involved in the design and implementation of any proposed legislative framework on TM.

7 Conclusion

The legal framework for regulation, supervision, control and discipline of various categories of health professionals in the country exists. However, it suffers from a number of weaknesses. In the first place, all the statutes treat health care as a commodity to be determined by the market without state regulation. As expected, health care professionals engaged in private practice are entitled to demand and recover reasonable charges and other costs from the patients. However, there is no mechanism to determine the reasonableness of the charges. There is a need to provide for the regulation of private health providers and the control of fees and charges in respect of medical treatment and other services rendered by these providers.

The legal framework does not adequately recognise advances in health training and education, which have produced a new cadre of health

225 NDA *Guidelines for regulation of traditional or herbal medicines in Uganda* (2004) 2.
226 http://www.blackherbals.com/nacothal.htm (accessed 20 May 2014).
227 WHO *Traditional Medicine Strategy 2014-2023* (2012).
228 WHO (n 227 above) 11.
229 GS Cheng *Regulation of the practice of traditional medicine in China, India, and Malaysia* (2012).
230 D Sonya 'Unintended consequences of regulating traditional medicine' (2013) 2 *World Health Organisation South East Asia Journal of Public Health* 131.

professionals in the country. For example, it may be necessary to review the Nurses and Midwives Act to take into account the fact that many midwives have acquired further training and qualifications entitling them to perform some of the roles traditionally reserved for medical practitioners. Midwives give care and supervision to women during pregnancy, labour and the postpartum period and care for the new born babies and infants. With further training and the availability of necessary facilities and equipment, midwives should be able to assist women who have developed complications and require emergency obstetric services such as a caesarean section, which has hitherto been performed by gynaecologists and obstetricians. There is also a need to regulate the work of traditional medical practitioners who assist many people especially in rural areas.[231] These practitioners should actively participate in the design and implementation of the relevant legal and policy frameworks intended for their benefit.

Although there is an increased recognition of the role played by human rights in health programming, the legal framework regulating health care professionals does not explicitly provide for the promotion and protection of human rights especially the right to health. It may not be enough to merely provide for human rights issues in various codes of ethics. These should be explicitly provided for in the statutes or in regulations or as schedules to the statutes so that their legally binding nature may not be challenged.

Unlike the statutes regulating medical and dental practitioners, nurses and midwives, and AHPs, the Pharmacy and Drugs Act, which regulates pharmacists, is poorly drafted, disorganised and outdated. It has many bodies: the Pharmacy Board, Pharmaceutical Society of Uganda and the Pharmacy Council. The functions and roles of these bodies appear duplicated, conflicting and confusing. For example, albeit the council, which is the governing body of the society, is 'charged with the general responsibility for securing the highest practicable standards in the practice of pharmacy',[232] disciplinary matters are handled by either the board or the disciplinary committee.[233] The functions of the board and society are not clearly defined. Some of the sanctions are also outdated. For example, one of the penalties that may be imposed on the pharmacist is a maximum

231 Lessons can be drawn from Tanzania's Traditional and Alternative Medicines Act 2002, which provides for the promotion, control and regulation of traditional and alternative medicines practice. The Act establishes a Traditional and Health Practitioners' Council (sec 4) whose functions are laid out in sec 6(a) - (n). The functions include supervision, control, registration and discipline of traditional and alternative health practitioners.

232 Sec 21(1).

233 Sec 4(1) provides that '[T]he chairperson of the board may, by summons under his or her hand, require any person to appear before the board or the disciplinary committee at an inquiry held in connection with any of the functions of the board or the disciplinary committee'. The boundary between the board and the disciplinary committee in so far as disciplinary matters are concerned is not clearly demarcated.

of two hundred shillings. Although pharmacists deal in drugs, their relationship with the National Drug Authority is also not provided for by the Act. The Act also does not provide formatters critical for the pharmacy profession such as continuing pharmacy education and the regulation of private practice. Thus, there is a need for a review of the Act to ensure that it clearly demarcates the functions of the various organs and caters for new and emerging issues in the pharmacy profession.

8

MALPRACTICES IN HEALTHCARE

1 Introduction

The preceding chapter looked at the regulation of health care professionals through various professional bodies or councils established by law and ethics governing the professions. A person aggrieved by the conduct of a health care professional may decide either to lodge a complaint with the relevant disciplinary body or go to court. In the first instance, malpractice litigation[1] serves a number of purposes. It is an avenue through which health care professionals may be held accountable for their actions in court. Second, litigation may act as an incentive to the professionals to ensure that they maintain a high standard of care since they may fear paying out money once successfully sued for poor practice. Thirdly, the patient may want the professional punished for the injury caused. In this case, litigation may act as retribution against the professional who may have caused injury to the complainant. Above all, if the patient wins the case, he or she receives damages as compensation, which is supposed, in so far as money can do, to restore him or her to the position he or she would have been if the injury had not occurred. Thus, because a patient needs compensation, he or she may choose to go to court rather than a professional body.

Malpractice litigation is largely based on the law of negligence. The plaintiff has to prove three things: first, that the defendant health care professional owed him or her a duty of care; second, that the defendant was in breach of that duty by failing to provide care in accordance with a standard required by the law; and third, that the plaintiff suffered injury or harm as a result of the breach, which was not so unforeseeable to be

1 A malpractice may be defined as professional misconduct or demonstration of an unreasonable skill with the result of injury, loss or damage to the patient. Thus, malpractice litigation is where the patient challenges a health care professional's conduct in court.

regarded in law as too remote. Against the above backdrop, this chapter examines these elements in detail in order to determine the extent to which health care professionals may be held accountable through litigation. The chapter also considers the defences that may be available to a health care professional who has been sued for negligence.

2 What the plaintiff must prove in a malpractice action

2.1 The duty of care

According to the law of negligence,[2] the plaintiff must prove that the defendant owed him or her a duty of care in the circumstances of the particular case. The law will recognise a duty of care only where the relationship between the parties is seen as giving rise to that duty. Each case must be judged on its own facts. The duty of care may not be difficult to establish where patients are in a hospital or clinic because it may be presumed that the health care professionals in these units are responsible for their care. However, except where there is an established duty of care, the law does not impose any obligation upon doctors to provide treatment to those who require it. A doctor generally owes a duty of care only to patients who are on his or her list.

Assuming John, a medical doctor, comes across a road accident where a number of people whom he has never attended to have been injured and simply drives away, can he be held accountable in law for failing to assist? He may have a professional ethical or social obligation to do so but no legal obligation arises. In other words, he does not owe a duty of care to the injured persons. He can only be bound when he is already under such a duty because of his job. There must be a clearly established doctor-patient relationship. The relationship begins when the patient presents himself or herself and the doctor initiates diagnostic or treatment measures. The situation would be different if the injured persons were brought to the hospital casualty department where John was working at the time. He would be obliged to provide care to them.[3]

2 Negligence is usually an unintentional action, which occurs when a person either performs or fails to perform an action that a reasonable person would or would not have committed in a similar situation. Charges of negligence against a doctor or other health care professional arise because the patient or family is not happy with the result of the diagnosis, treatment or care. On the detailed explanation of the tort of negligence see, WVH Rogers *Winfield & Jolowicz on Tort* (2006) 250. In the Nigerian case of *Diamond Bank Ltd v Partnership Investment Co Ltd* (2010) WRN 42 52, Ogbuagu JSC stated as follows: 'Negligence is generally defined as the failure to exercise a standard of care that a reasonable prudent person would have exercised in a similar situation; any conduct that falls below the legal standard established to protect others against unreasonable risk of harm'.

3 See for example, *Barnett v Chelsea & Kensington Hospital Management Committee* (1968) 1All ER 1068.

2.2 Breach of the duty of care

In addition to showing that the defendant owed him or her a duty of care, the plaintiff must prove the breach of that duty by the defendant. It should be noted that 'breach' is the essence of negligence. It describes the defendant's behaviour that actually injures the plaintiff. Thus, the question in negligence cases is: has the defendant measured up to the standard of behaviour or care in the particular circumstances of a given case? A defendant is required to exercise reasonable care in the performance of his or her duties. He or she must have acted properly and exhibited a standard of care required of him or her by the law of negligence. In other words, he or she should not have breached the duty of care owed to the plaintiff. The relevant questions here are: what is the standard of care required of the professional? What amounts to reasonable care? Who must prove failure to observe the standard of care? Under the general law of negligence, in order to render the defendant liable, the plaintiff must satisfy what is known as the 'neighbour principle', which was laid down in *Donoghue v Stevenson,*[4] where Lord Atkin stated as follows:

> You must take reasonable care to avoid acts or omissions which you can reasonably foresee would be likely to injure your neighbour ... [neighbour's being]: persons who are so closely and directly affected by my act that I ought reasonably to have them in contemplation as being so affected when I am directing my mind to the acts or omissions which are called in question.[5]

However, Lord Atkin's foreseeability test may not be appropriate in situations involving defendants who actually possess or hold themselves out as possessing special skills or expertise.[6] Defendants in such cases are judged by the appropriate professional standard of care, which in the health care context was established in *Bolam v Friern Hospital Management Committee.*[7] In this case, the plaintiff was a psychiatric patient suffering from depressive illness. He was advised by a consultant attached to the defendant hospital, to undergo electro-convulsive therapy. He signed a consent form but was not alerted to the risk of fracture that can occur because of fit-like convulsions that such treatment induces. In due course, he received this treatment, but he was not given any relaxant drugs. Consequently, he suffered several injuries, which included dislocation of

4 (1932) AC 562.

5 *Donoghue* (n 4 above) 579.

6 Courts have added the condition of 'proximity' to the foreseeability test under negligence cases. In *Alcock v Chief Constable of the South Yorkshire Police* (1992) 1 AC 310 411, Lord Oliver stated: '[T]he concept of proximity is an artificial one which depends more on the court's perception of what is the reasonable area for the imposition of liability than upon any logical process of analytical deduction'. In *Peabody Donation Fund v Parkinson* (1985) AC 210, Lord Keith observed that in addition to foreseeability and proximity, it must also be just and reasonable to impose a duty of care.

7 (1957) 2 All ER 118; (1957) 1 WLR 582. The case was approved by the House of Lords in later cases such as *Whitehouse v Jordan* (1981) 1 All ER 267; *Maynard v West Midlands Regional Health Authority* (1985) 1 All ER 635; (1984) 1 WLR 634.

the hip joints and fracture of the pelvis. The plaintiff claimed damages from the defendant hospital alleging that the provision of electro-convulsive therapy without the prior administration of relaxant drugs, or without restraining his convulsions manually, amounted to negligence. The court held that: 'A doctor is not guilty of negligence if he has acted in accordance with a practice accepted as proper by a responsible body of medical men skilled in that particular art'.[8] McNair J observed as follows:

> In the ordinary case which does not involve any special skill, negligence in law means this: some failure to do some act which a reasonable man in the circumstances would do, or doing some act which a reasonable man in the circumstances would not do; and if that failure or doing of that act results in injury, then there is a cause of action. How do you test whether this act or failure is negligent? In an ordinary case, it is generally said, that you judge that by action of the man in the street. He is the ordinary man. In one case it has been said that you judge it by the conduct of the man on top of a Clapham omnibus. He is the ordinary man. But where you get a situation which involves the use of some form of special skill or competence, the test as to whether there has been negligence or not is not the test of a man on the top of a Clapham omnibus because he has not got this special skill. The test is the standard of the ordinary skilled man exercising and professing to have that skill.[9]

Other cases have also emphasised the need for professionals to perform their duties with the necessary skill and care. For example, in *Lanphier v Phipos*[10] the court stated as follows:

> Every person who enters a learned profession undertakes to bring to the exercise of it a reasonable degree of care and skill. A surgeon does not undertake that he will perform a cure; nor does he undertake to use the highest possible degree of skill, as there may be persons of higher education and greater advantage than himself; but he undertakes to bring a fair, reasonable, and competent degree of skill; and in an action against him by a patient, the question is whether the injury complained of must be referred to the want of a proper degree of skill and care in the defendant or not.[11]

In *Achutrao Haribhau Khodawa v State of Maharshtra*,[12] the Supreme Court India also stated as follows:

> The skill of medical practitioners differs from doctor to doctor. The very nature of the profession is such that there may be more than one course of treatment which may be advisable for treating a patient. Courts would indeed be slow in attributing negligence on the part of a doctor if he has performed his duties to the best of his ability and with due care and caution. Medical opinion may differ with regard to the course of action to be taken by a doctor

8 (1957) 2 All ER 118 121.
9 As above.
10 (1838) 8 C & P 475. See also *Dryden v Survey* (1936) 2 All ER 535.
11 As above.
12 AIR 1996 SC 2377.

> treating a patient, but as long as a doctor acts in a manner which is acceptable to the medical profession and the court finds that he has attended on the patient with due care, skill and diligence and if the patient still does not survive or suffers a permanent ailment, it would be difficult to hold the doctor to be guilty of negligence.[13]

It should be noted that both parties to the case may adduce expert medical opinion as to what constitutes a responsible body of professional practice. The difference in opinion may lead to difficulties in determining whether the defendant has been negligent as illustrated by the case of *Maynard v West Midlands Regional Health Authority*,[14] where two consultants, employed by the defendant health authority, were treating the plaintiff for a chest complaint. Albeit they believed her to be suffering from tuberculosis (TB), they thought that there was a possibility that it might be Hodgkin's disease, which is fatal unless treated in its early stages. Given this situation, the consultants decided that, rather than wait for the results of a sputum test, to ascertain whether she had TB, it was sensible to conduct an exploratory operation to determine whether she had Hodgkin's disease. The operation was conducted properly but showed that she had TB and not Hodgkin's disease. The plaintiff claimed damages from the defendant health authority arguing that there was negligence. The trial judge agreed with the expert witness who gave evidence on behalf of the plaintiff that this was a case of TB and that it was wrong to carry out the operation. The trial judge gave judgment to the plaintiff. The Court of Appeal reversed the decision but the plaintiff appealed to the House of Lords, which dismissed the appeal. Lord Scarman observed as follows:

> A case which is based on an allegation that a fully considered decision of two consultants in the field of their special skill was negligent clearly presents certain difficulties of proof. It is not enough to show that there is a body of competent professional opinion which considers that there was a wrong decision, if there also exists a body, equally competent, which supports the decision as reasonable in the circumstances. It is not enough to show that subsequent events show that the operation need never have been performed, if at the time the decision to operate was taken it was reasonable in the sense that a responsible body of medical opinion would have accepted it as proper ... [A] doctor who professes to exercise a special skill must exercise the ordinary skill of his specialty. Differences of opinion and practice exist, and will always exist, in the medical as in other professions.[15]

Thus, it can be seen from the above discussion that health care professionals are to be judged against the standards of their peers. A defendant may win a negligence suit if an expert in his or her field can give a professional opinion in court that his or her actions were proper. However, as the court held in *Bolitho v City & Hackney Health Authority*,[16]

13 As above.
14 (1985) 1 All ER 635.
15 *Maynard* (n 14 above) 638.
16 (1997) 4 ALL ER 771 (HL); (1997) 3 WLR 115.

the professional opinion relied upon by the defendant in cases of diagnosis and treatment must be reasonable or responsible. Montgomery has also pointed out that,

> the standard of care to be expected of professionals is that required of those skilled in the particular specialty in question ... [A] general medical practitioner is not to be judged against the standards of consultant specialists but against what is reasonable to expect of a general practitioner.[17]

The 'peer standard' may also be applied to situations where the professional is alleged not to have warned his or her patient of the risks inherent in the operation. In *Sidaway v Bethlem Royal Hospital Governors,*[18] the plaintiff who suffered persistent pain in her back and shoulders was advised to have an operation on her spinal column. She was warned by the surgeon of the possibility of disturbing a nerve root and its possible consequences but the surgeon did not mention the possibility of damage to the spinal cord, the risk of which was very small-only one percent. Unfortunately, though the operation was performed with due care, the plaintiff suffered injury to her spinal cord which made her severely disabled. In a suit for damages, the plaintiff contended that the surgeon had been in breach of a duty owed to her to warn her of all possible risks inherent in the operation and so her consent for the operation was not an informed one. The House of Lords held that the test of liability in respect of a doctor's duty to warn his patients of risks inherent in treatment recommended by him was the same as the test applicable to diagnosis and treatment, namely that the doctor was required to act in accordance with a practice accepted at the time as proper by a responsible body of medical opinion. The court decided that since the surgeon's non-disclosure of the risk of damage to the plaintiff's spinal cord accorded with a practice accepted as proper by a responsible body of neuro-surgical opinion, the defendants were not liable to the plaintiff.

2.3 Damage suffered

In addition to proving that there was a duty of care, which was breached, the plaintiff must show that he or she suffered damage caused by the defendant. In other words, the plaintiff must prove what is known as causation: that the harm or injury suffered was caused by the defendant's breach of duty.[19] The traditional approach to causation in negligence is the 'but for' test, which is decided on a balance of probabilities. The plaintiff must show that *but for* the defendant's negligence, he or she would not have suffered the harm in respect of which he or she is seeking damages. In other

17 J Montgomery *Health Care Law* (2003) 177.
18 (1985) 1 All ER 643
19 On causation and remoteness in negligence, see generally the cases of *Re Polemis*: *The Wagon Mound (No1)* (1961) UKPC 1; *Nevil & Another v Cooper & Another* (1958) EA 594.

words, the plaintiff would not have suffered the harm had the defendant not been negligent.

The question to be addressed by the court is: in the absence of the defendant's negligence, would the patient have avoided the harm? In *Barnett v Chelsea & Kensington Hospital*,[20] the plaintiff's husband had experienced persistent vomiting after drinking tea and had gone to the casualty department of a hospital. The doctor on duty refused to see him and he subsequently died from arsenical poisoning. The court found that the doctor's refusal to see him, though negligent, was not a cause in fact of his death. The doctor's conduct was considered causally irrelevant, for there was little or no chance that effective treatment could have been given in time. The court noted that the drinking of poisoned tea would have brought about his death whether or not he was treated in hospital.

The 'but for' test is generally a good guide in determining whether a given factor was a cause in fact. The test may be easily applied in typical cases of negligence for example in a car accident where proof of causation may be a simple matter requiring witness accounts and physical examination of the accident scene by the police to establish what happened. However, in certain cases involving scientific or medical uncertainty, it may be difficult to pin point the actual cause of the injury. The 'but for' test assumes that there was, at the moment in question, a single set of conditions sufficient to cause the harm or injury. It becomes difficult to prove that the injury was caused by the defendant where there are multiple causal agents at work. The plaintiff may also find difficulty in proving that any exacerbation of his or her illness was attributable to the negligence of the doctor or other health care professional rather than a simple progression of his or her illness. In any case, like other fields involving scientific inquiry, medical knowledge has its own limits: some issues may even not be easily understood by those engaged in medical practice. The chain of causation may also be broken by the plaintiff where for example he or she refuses to follow the doctor's advice by not taking the prescribed drugs.

Because of the difficulties associated with the traditional approach to causation, courts have substituted it with the rather weaker causal requirement that the defendant's negligence must be shown to have increased the risk to which the plaintiff was exposed. In *Mc Ghee v National Coal Board*,[21] the plaintiff, a worker in a brick kiln contracted industrial dermatitis through exposure to brick dust. Since the risk of dermatitis was part of the job of a kiln worker, exposure to brick dust in the kilns was inevitable. However, the defendant employers had negligently increased the period of exposure by failing to provide showering facilities at the

20 (1969) 1 QB 428.
21 (1973) 1 WLR 1. See also *Wilsher v Essex Area Health Authority* (1988) AC 1074.

workplace with the result that the brick dust was left caked on the bodies of the kiln workers until they got home. It was not clear whether the plaintiff contracted dermatitis as a result of his cumulative exposure to the brick dust or as a result of a single abrasion caused by the dust. The House of Lords held in favour of the plaintiff on the basis that the increase in the risk of dermatitis could be treated as having made a substantial contribution to the injury. In *Fairland v Glenhaven Funeral Services,*[22] the House of Lords confirmed the *McGhee* case but strictly limited its application to cases in which scientific or medical uncertainty makes it virtually impossible to determine the true cause of the plaintiff's injury.

Another case in which the 'but for' test was not followed because of special circumstances, is *Chester v Afsher,*[23] where the claimant suffered from severe back pain. A neurosurgeon that she consulted advised for surgery but negligently failed to inform her of the minimal risk of paralysis inherent in such operation. The operation was conducted without any negligence but unfortunately the very risk which the surgeon had failed to inform her of materialised and the patient suffered partial paralysis. In her claim for damages, the claimant did not prove that she would never have had the operation had she been told about the risk. She simply proved that she would not have consented to the operation which was performed resulting in the injury. Although the risk, of which the patient was not warned, was not created or increased by the failure to warn, it was held that the patient had to succeed. Because of the special circumstances of the case, the 'but for' test of causation was not applied. It can be seen that had the 'but for' test been applied, the plaintiff would have been deprived of a remedy although there was a breach of duty on the part of the defendant.

3 Vicarious liability

The plaintiff may decide to bring a negligence action directly against the health care professional. However, since the principal reason for bringing a malpractice action is to obtain compensation, patients may be reluctant to only sue individuals who may lack the financial resources to pay damages. Thus, patients may decide to sue the hospital or other employer of the health care professional under the doctrine of vicarious liability. This doctrine refers to liability that falls on one person as a result of an action of another person. The liability is thus not personal. The hospital or other employer of the health care professional is made to account for the damage caused by the professional.

In *Cassidy v Ministry of Health,*[24] the plaintiff underwent an operation on his hand at the defendant's hospital, which was performed by a full-time

22 (2002) UKHL 22.
23 (2004) 4 All ER 587 (HL).
24 (1951) 1 All ER 574; (1951) 2 KB 343.

assistant medical officer. After the operation, his hand and forearm were bandaged for two weeks. During this period, the plaintiff complained of pain but nothing was done by either the doctor who had operated or the house surgeon, who were both hospital employees. The plaintiff was simply given sedatives. When the bandages were removed, the hand had become stiff and useless for purposes of his work, which involved using a pick and shovel. The plaintiff alleged negligence against the defendant hospital and claimed damages. Denning LJ held as follows:

> [W]hen hospital authorities undertake to treat a patient and themselves select and appoint and employ the professional men and women who are to give the treatment, they are responsible for the negligence of those persons in failing to give proper treatment, no matter whether they are doctors, surgeons, nurses and radiographers ... I can see no possible reason why they should not also be responsible for the house surgeons and resident medical officers on their permanent staff ... Hospital authorities accepted the plaintiff as a patient for treatment and it was their duty to treat him with reasonable care. They selected, employed, and paid all the surgeons and nurses who looked after him. He had no say in that selection at all. If those surgeons and nurses did not treat him with proper care and skill, then the hospital authorities must answer for it, for it means that they themselves did not perform their duty for him.[25]

It should also be noted that the patient may decide to sue both the doctor and the hospital. Assuming a patient is injured by a doctor working in hospital B, the patient may sue not only the doctor personally, but also the doctor's employer, hospital B. The hospital will have been sued under vicarious liability.

In order for the doctrine of vicarious liability to apply, there must be a relationship between the employer or master and the employee or servant. The employee must have committed a tort, that is, the injury or harm complained of; and that tort must have been committed in the course of employment of the employee.[26] The burden of proving that the employee – the health care professional – was acting in the course of his employment lies on the plaintiff.[27] In *Muwonge v Attorney General*,[28] Newbold, P succinctly summarised the doctrine of vicarious liability as follows:

> The law is that an act may be done in the course of a servant's employment so as to make his master liable even though it is done contrary to the orders of the master; and even if the servant is acting deliberately, wantonly, negligently or even criminally, or for his own behalf, nevertheless, if what he did is merely

25 As above. Lord Denning cited the case of *Cassidy* in the subsequent cases of *Roe v Ministry of Health* (1954) 2 QB 66 and *Jones v Manchester Corporation* (1957) 2 All ER 125.

26 On the application of the doctrine of vicarious liability, see also *Mukalazi v Davis Kisule* (1995) III KALR 42; *Regina Nalukwago v Dr Phillip Byaruhanga & 2 Others* (1995) III KALR 106.

27 See *Sheik Kateregga & Another v UEB* (1995) III KALR 143.

28 (1967) EA 17.

> a manner of carrying out what he was employed to carry out then his master is liable.[29]

4 The burden of proof

The plaintiff has the burden to prove that the defendant has failed to meet the standard of care demanded by law. In some cases, the plaintiff may not point exactly to the person(s) to blame for his or her injury. For example, the plaintiff may wake up after an operation in a hospital to find a swab or other object inside his or her body. In such a case, the court may be persuaded to infer negligence by the defendant, unless the latter can offer an acceptable explanation of the circumstances under which the swab or object was left in the body. In such a situation, the plaintiff would have pleaded what is known as *res ipsa loquitur* – the thing speaks for itself.

In order to successfully rely on the doctrine of *res ipsa loquitur*, the plaintiff must show three things. First, that he or she has been injured and that there is no explanation of how the injury arose. Second, that his or her injury arose in circumstances in which such an injury would not normally occur. Third, that the defendant was in control of the situation in which context the injury occurred.[30] Once the plaintiff pleads *res ipsa loquitur*, the defendant explains what took place and brings some evidence to rebut the allegation. In effect, the burden shifts to the defendant to prove that he or she was not negligent. In *Embu Public Road Services Ltd v Riimi*,[31] the court stated as follows:

> The doctrine of *res ipsa loquitur* is one which a plaintiff, by proving that an accident occurred in circumstances in which an accident should not have occurred, thereby discharges, in the absence of an explanation by the defendant, the original burden of showing negligence on the part of the person who caused the accident. The plaintiff in those circumstances does not have to show any specific negligence, he merely shows that an accident of that nature should not have occurred in the circumstances, which leads to the inference, the only reasonable inference, that the only reason for the accident must therefore be the negligence of the defendant.[32]

Under certain circumstances, therefore, where a defendant does not satisfactorily explain to the court how the accident happened, the doctrine of *res ipsa loquitur* may be invoked to hold him or her vicariously liable for negligence. In *Alex Wanigina v Attorney General*,[33] the plaintiff, a field

29 *Muwonge* (n 28 above) 45.
30 See *Jack Busingye & 2 Others v TMK* (1992-1993) HCB 171; *Bikwatirizo v Railways Corporation* (1971) EA 82. On the effect of the doctrine of *res ipsa loquitur* on the burden of proof, see M Jones*Medical Negligence* (2008).
31 (1968) EA 22.
32 *Riimi* (n 31 above) 24. On the nature and scope of the doctrine of *res ipsa loquitur*, see the South African cases of *Naude v Transvaal Boot & Shoe Manufacturing Co* 1983 AD 379; *Monteoli v Woolworths (Pty) Ltd* 2000 (4) SA 735 (W).
33 (1985) HCB 102.

assistant aged 49 went to a public hospital with a fractured left wrist which was put in plaster of Paris. After this he was given a pothidine injection on his right arm. On receiving this injection, his right arm began swelling. He was given a largactil injection. He developed gangrene as a result of which his right thumb and right middle finger were amputated. The right little and ring fingers could not be fully bent or straightened. His right hand though functional, was severely impaired because he could neither button his shirt nor shake hands or write with it. The plaintiff lost his job since he was no longer active. He sued the defendant for general and special damages for the injuries sustained. The court held that since the defendant did not call evidence to explain how the gangrene had developed after the injection, he would be held vicariously liable on the doctrine of *res ipsa loquitur.*

It should be noted that given the difficult conditions under which doctors sometimes work, courts may be reluctant to apply the doctrine of *res ipsa loquitur*. In *Pope John's Hospital & Another v Baby Kasozi*,[34] the appellants were sued in the High Court by the respondent – through his father as a next friend – for negligence arising out of the delivery of the respondent by forceps and of the alleged failure of the hospital to properly treat the baby's eye injury. The action was brought against the doctor who affected the delivery and the defendant hospital where the birth took place. The birth was difficult and prolonged and delivery was eventually carried out by forceps and it was in the course of this delivery that the baby's left eye was so badly injured as to cause complete blindness in the eye. The High Court found the doctor negligent for not checking the position of the forceps or applying them properly and that the doctrine of *res ipsa loquitur* applied. The hospital was found negligent because it had not referred the child to an eye specialist in time. On appeal, it was found that the facts did not show that the doctor was negligent and that the injury to the eye was caused by the operation and not by any failure to refer the child to an eye specialist. The court held that where evidence has established what happened, the doctrine of *res ipsa loquitur* cannot apply. That the doctrine cannot apply to a mistake or error of judgment of a surgeon during a very difficult situation. Sir William Duffus, P observed as follows:

> I have not however, come across a case where it [*res ipsa loquitur*] has been applied to a mistake or error of judgment by a surgeon in a difficult and tricky operation and the forceps delivery of a baby according to the evidence in this case clearly comes within that description. It would be placing an impossible burden on a surgeon if the doctrine applied and the surgeon, in any operation not entirely successful, had the onus of justifying every moment in his operation: It would hamper the exercise of initiative and skill in a surgeon.[35]

34 (1974) EA 220.

35 *Baby Kasozi* (n 34 above) 225. The judge cited the case of *Roe v Ministry of Health* (1954) 2 All ER 132 139, where the court observed that in medical cases, the fact that something has gone wrong is not in itself any evidence of negligence. Lord Denning noted that: 'But it would be doing a disservice to the community at large if we were to

The question as to whether a mistake or error of judgment imputes negligence was also considered in *Bitumaka Appolinali v The Trustees of Uganda*,[36] where the plaintiff aged 22 years, injured his knee during a football match and was sent to the defendant's hospital. The doctor in charge performed an operation to remove the torn part of the cartridge of the knee joint. She used a thin scalpel which broke in the cartilage but failed to trace the broken part. She closed the knee joint, demobilised it to prevent further injury and sent the plaintiff to Mbarara hospital for X-ray and further operation. The operation was performed but the foreign body could not be traced. The plaintiff was sent to Mulago hospital but she refused a further operation. An expert witness testified that he would have expected a solid knife to have been used for such an operation. The court held that the occurrence was a mere accident and not negligence on the part of the defendant. Katinti J cited the case of *Mahon v Osborne*,[37] where Lord Denning laid out the legal measure of a professional's duty as follows:

> If he possesses an art, he must be reasonably skilled in it. There is no doubt that the surgeon was that. He must also be careful, but the standard of care which the law requires is not insurance against accidental slips. It is such a degree of care as a normally skilful member of the profession may reasonably be expected to exercise in the actual circumstances of the case in question. It is not every slip or mistake which imports negligence, and in applying the duty of care to the case of a surgeon, it is peculiarly necessary to have regard to the different kinds of circumstances that may present themselves for urgent attention.[38]

5 Defences to a malpractice action

Since malpractice is a form of negligence, many of the defences allowed against general negligence claims may also be viable against claims of malpractice. A health care professional who has been sued for malpractice may, unless he or she admits the facts as alleged by the plaintiff, rely on a number of defences, which are considered below.

5.1 Denial

Except where *res ipsa loquitur* is successfully pleaded as discussed above, the burden of proving negligence lies on the plaintiff. In his or her defence, the

impose liability on hospitals and doctors for everything that happens to go wrong. Doctors would be led to think more of their own safety than of the good of their patients. Initiative would be shifted and confidence shaken. A proper sense of proportion requires us to have regard to the conditions in which hospitals and doctors have to work. We must insist on due care for the patient at every point, but we must not condemn as negligence that which is only a misadventure'.

36 (1974) HCB 96.

37 (1939) 1 All ER 535.

38 *Mahon* (n 37 above) 548.

defendant may totally deny the plaintiff's version of facts and leave the plaintiff to strictly prove his or her claim. In law, this defence is called a *traverse*. The defendant will aver that he or she was not in any relationship with the plaintiff and thus did not owe him or her a duty of care. In other words, he or she never diagnosed or treated the patient.

5.2 Peer acceptance: Invoking the *Bolam* test

Although the defendant may admit that he or she owed a duty of care to the plaintiff, he or she may introduce expert evidence to show that he or she exercised reasonable care as accepted by his or her profession. The defendant may bring an expert witness to show that he or she met the standard of care and can thus not be held liable for negligence. An expert witness such as a doctor is that person, who because of his or her training, education and experience in the medical field, has knowledge beyond that of the ordinary person. Because of his or her expertise in that field, the expert is permitted by the court to give an opinion, which may exonerate the defendant.

5.3 Contributory negligence

Often times, health care professionals may not be entirely blamed for the injury. If the defendant can show that the injury would not have occurred had it not been for the negligent act by the patient, he or she may have a valid defence against a malpractice action. This defence is known as contributory negligence, which refers to conduct on the part of the plaintiff that is a contributing cause of harm or injury. For example, where a patient mixes prescriptions against the doctor's orders or advice or fails to disclose to the doctor past and present medical conditions and treatments and any familial or genetic conditions he or she may be aware of, he or she may be found to have contributed to the negligence. In *Jenkins v Bogalusa Community Medical Centre*,[39] a patient being treated for arthritis was told not to get out of bed without ringing for assistance. He however attempted to get out of bed and fell, fracturing his hip. He subsequently died from embolism following hip surgery. It was held that he contributed to his own death by failing to follow instructions.

5.4 Voluntary assumption of risk

This defence, which is expressed in the Latin maxim, *volenti non fit injuria*, literary means that no injury is done to one who voluntarily consents. The defence has three elements: knowledge of the risk in question, the *sciens* element; a voluntary exposure to the risk, the *volens* element; and an

39 340 So 2d 1065 (1976).

assumption of risk. It is a 'free will or consent' defence where the plaintiff is said to have voluntarily assumed the risk. If a plaintiff, with full knowledge accepts the risk of injury, he or she will not recover damages. Thus, *volenti non fit injuria* is a complete defence to an action in negligence.

The defendant may aver that he or she explained to the patient the potential side effects or inherent risks of the operation or procedure. To support his or her case, the defendant may produce an informed consent form signed by the patient or the person authorised so to sign. The form should indicate that the health professional explained the procedures, that the patient understood the risks involved, accepted that risk, and consented to the treatment. The point is that the patient should have clearly understood the risk involved and the choice to accept that risk must be voluntary. For example, a doctor shows Denis, his patient who has a lung related problem the following health warning on a cigarette packet: 'Do not smoke: Tobacco is harmful to your health and kills!' The doctor explains to him the side effects of tobacco smoking and how his situation will deteriorate if he does not stop the habit. The patient refuses and continues smoking leading to extensive damage to his lungs. In such a situation, the patient is said to have voluntarily accepted the risk inherent in tobacco smoking.

5.5 Where the action is time barred

The law provides the time in which actions in negligence should be brought to court. According to the Limitation Act,[40] no action founded in tort can be brought after the expiry of six years from the date on which the cause of action arose.[41] However actions for damages for negligence or breach of duty must be instituted within three years.[42] The Civil Procedure and Limitation (Miscellaneous Provisions) Act[43] also limits the period in which actions founded in tort may be brought against the government, local authority and scheduled corporations to two years.[44] Thus, the defendant may aver that the plaintiff is barred from bringing a claim because the period in which such claim should have been instituted has expired. The rationale behind the limitation period is to avoid situations where evidence may fade or be confused due to a lapse of time. Expiry of the limitation period provides a defendant a complete defence to a claim unless the plaintiff can prove to court that he or she was under a disability.[45] Once a claim is statute barred, subsequent developments

40 Cap 80.
41 Sec 3(1).
42 As above.
43 Cap 72.
44 Sec 3.
45 Sec 21(1) of the Limitation Act, Cap 80; sec 5 of the Civil Procedure and Limitation (Miscellaneous Provisions) Act, Cap 72.

cannot revive it. Time begins to run from the date when the cause of action occurred.[46]

6 Remedies

6.1 Damages

In most malpractice actions, the plaintiff claims damages, which refer to any injuries or harm or loss caused by the defendant. The plaintiff may claim damages for permanent physical or mental disability; personal injuries; pain and suffering; and medical and hospital expenses. He or she may receive compensatory damages, in form of general or special damages. General damages are for payment for the emotional pain and suffering or injury suffered. Special damages are the actual loss of income, loss of wages, profits and medical expenses.

As pointed out above, the burden to prove that the defendant's breach of duty resulted in damage lies on the plaintiff. Similarly, the plaintiff has the onus to prove the damages claimed from the defendant. The general principles for the award of damages apply in malpractice cases. Courts try as much as possible to assess what the patient has lost. Special damages may be easily proved through production of documents such as receipts. However, determining the quantum of damages for disability, or pain and suffering is a daunting task. This challenge was expressed by Ouma J in *Mukalazi v Davis Kisule*[47] as follows:

> Damages, which are to be awarded, are those so far as money can compensate or will give the injured party reparation for the wrongful act and for natural and direct results of the wrongful act. Money is awardable so that something tangible may be procured to replace something of a like nature which has been destroyed or lost. Money however, cannot renew a physical frame that has been shattered. All that a judge can do is to award money, which can be considered as giving reasonable compensation. There appears to be no meter stick a judge can apply to measure the amount to be awarded for pain and suffering or ensuing disability. And yet it is essential that judges must try to maintain some uniformity in the general method of awards. Further, it is essential that as far as possible, comparable injuries ought to be compensated by comparable awards.[48]

The plaintiff may also claim punitive damages, which are also known as exemplary damages. The purpose of punitive damages is to serve as a punishment to the defendant who may harm the plaintiff in a malicious or wilful way and a warning to others not to engage in similar behaviour. In

46 See *Miramago v Attorney General* (1979) HCB 24.
47 (1995) III V KALR 42.
48 *Mukalazi* (n 47 above) 45.

George Ongom and Another v Attorney General & 2 Others,[49] the court noted that

> exemplary damages are awarded over and above the compensatory damages where aggravating circumstances have been created such that due to the conduct or intervention of the defendant, the plaintiff is a victim of an arbitrary, oppressive and unconstitutional behaviour of a government official.[50]

The court further observed that exemplary damages 'are not intended to enrich the plaintiff but to punish the defendant and deter him from repeating his wrongful conduct'.[51] The court may also grant nominal damages to a patient as token payment to demonstrate that while there may not have been any material harm done, the patient's rights were violated.[52]

6.2 Alternative dispute resolution (ADR)

It should be noted that claiming damages through the court process is usually lengthy and expensive. Given the poverty levels in the country, cases may only be brought by those who can afford the litigation expenses involved. There is also limited specialisation by legal practitioners in medical negligence litigation. Obtaining the services of doctors willing to act as expert witnesses for patients may also be difficult. There is also the onerous task of proving fault in medical negligence cases. In any case, the majority of the patients and their families may not be aware of their rights and the procedure for claiming them. Thus, it may be necessary to pursue ADR mechanisms. ADR is a structured negotiation process through which parties to a dispute may negotiate their own settlement with the assistance of an intermediary who is a neutral person and possesses the necessary training in ADR techniques. Parties – the patient or family and the health care professional or authority – may, instead of going to court to resolve their dispute, agree to refer it for ADR, which takes the form of arbitration, conciliation and mediation. The advantage of ADR is that it saves the parties time and expenses and promotes reconciliation as opposed to litigation, which is adversarial, formal and may involve a substantial amount of legal costs. It should also be pointed out that the court may also encourage or order the parties to explore ADR strategies. ADR may help in clearing the backlog, which is faced by courts of judicature in the country.

49 (1979) HCB 267.
50 *George Ongom* (n 49 above) 269.
51 As above.
52 As above.

7 Criminal liability for negligence

Before concluding this chapter, it is important to interrogate circumstances under which a health care professional may be held responsible for his or her errant actions under criminal law. Although medical malpractice may lead to a negligence action, which may result in the award of damages, certain acts may give rise to criminal liability. For example the Penal Code Act penalises negligent acts likely to spread infection of disease. It provides as follows:

> Any person who unlawfully or negligently does any act which is and which he or she knows or has reason to believe to be likely to spread the infection of any disease dangerous to life commits an offence and is liable to imprisonment for seven years.[53]

In *Uganda v Namubiru Rosemary*,[54] the accused who is a senior nurse and HIV positive is alleged to have pricked herself with a needle and then negligently injected a child with the same needle. Post exposure prophylaxis (PEP) was administered on the child and she tested HIV negative. However, the accused was charged under section 117 of the Penal Code before the Buganda Road Chief Magistrates' Court. She was convicted and sentenced to three years' imprisonment and appealed to the High Court. The High Court agreed with the trial magistrate that she was negligent. The court stated:

> The appellant was a healthcare provider. She acted so recklessly that she exposed a baby to the risk of infection of a disease [HIV], which is dangerous to life. There is need to protect society from such reckless behaviour. This country continues to grapple with various life threatening diseases. Court cannot shut its eyes from the reality of the situation in which we live. The confidence and trust put in health care professionals by the people should not be abused, or misplaced.[55]

It should be noted that grave instances of malpractice or gross negligence resulting in the death of a patient may also result in criminal prosecution of the health care professional.[56] According to the Penal Code Act,

> any person who, by any rash or negligent act not amounting to manslaughter, causes the death of another person is liable to imprisonment not exceeding seven years or to a fine not exceeding seventy thousand shillings or both.[57]

53 Sec 171.
54 HCT-00-CR-CN-0050-2014 (Unreported).
55 *Namubiru Rosemary* (n 54 above) 10.
56 See, A McCall-Smith 'Criminal negligence and the incompetent doctor' (1993) 1 *Medical Law Review* 33.
57 Sec 227 of the Penal Code Act.

Examples of rash or negligent acts include where a person 'gives medical or surgical treatment to any person whom he or she has undertaken to treat'[58] or 'dispenses, supplies, sells, administers or gives away any medicine or poisonous or dangerous matter'[59] thereby causing harm or injury to that person.

The question is: what amounts to gross negligence? In *R v Bateman*,[60] the court held that for a person to be liable for gross negligence it must be shown that he or she owed the deceased a duty of care, he was in breach of that duty and the breach caused the death. It must be shown that the negligence was gross in the sense that there was such a disregard for the life and safety of other persons so as to constitute a crime and be worthy of punishment. In *R v Adamako*,[61] an anaesthetist in the course of an eye operation failed to notice that the tube used to assist the patient's breathing had become disconnected. After nine minutes, the patient suffered a cardiac arrest and died. Expert evidence described the defendant's failure to identify the problem and remedy it as 'abysmal' and as a 'gross dereliction of care'. He was convicted of manslaughter and appealed to the House of Lords on the basis that the gross negligence test was not the proper test for involuntary manslaughter. Lord Mackay observed as follows:

> [I]n my opinion the principles of the law of negligence apply to ascertain whether or not the defendant has been in breach of a duty of care towards the defendant who has died. If such breach is established the next question is whether that breach of duty caused the death of the victim. If so, the jury must go on to consider whether that breach of duty should be characterized as gross negligence and therefore a crime. This will depend on the seriousness of the breach of duty committed by the defendant in all the circumstances in which the defendant was placed when it occurred. The jury will have to consider whether the extent to which the defendant's conduct departed from the proper standard of care incumbent upon him, involving as it must have done a risk of death to the patient, was such that it should be judged criminal.[62]

The jury found that the defendant's standard of care fell so far below the standard of a competent anaesthetist. It was held that his conduct went beyond a civil breach of his duty of care and amounted to gross negligence, which should attract criminal sanctions. The House of Lords dismissed his appeal and convicted him of gross negligence manslaughter.

58 Sec 228.
59 As above.
60 (1925) 19 CR App R 8.
61 (1994) 3 All ER 79; (1995) 1 AC 624.
62 As above.

8 Conclusion

A patient who is aggrieved by the conduct of a health care professional may lodge a complaint with the relevant professional body, which may discipline the professional. However, because of the desire to obtain compensation for the harm or injury suffered, the patient may pursue litigation against the professional or hospital or employer or both. Malpractice litigation is based on the law of negligence. Except for circumstances where the doctrine of *res ipsa loquitur* may apply, the burden of proof that the defendant was negligent lies on the plaintiff. Thus, the plaintiff must prove three essential elements of negligence: that the defendant owed him or her a duty of care; that he or she was in breach of that duty; and that the he or she suffered harm in consequence of that breach.

Because of the technicalities involved in proving negligence, it is important for the patient to hire a practicing advocate to handle the case. The advocate should carefully select expert witnesses who will assist in explaining the facts giving rise to the cause of action to the court. Malpractice actions move beyond the law: they are multi-disciplinary and encompass questions of law and medicine. Thus, the advocate must read widely in order to get acquainted with medical terminology and procedure. Civil Society Organisations (CSOs) engaged in matters of health rights should assist patients who may lack legal costs and expenses to institute malpractice actions.

In malpractice actions, defendants are judged by the standard of their peers. Thus, the defendant may raise a defence that what he did was in accordance with a practice accepted by his or her peers – that his or her conduct is deemed proper by his or her profession. He or she may produce expert evidence to support his or her position. Other defences available to the professional are denial, contributory negligence, voluntary assumption of risk and the limitation period. The defendant professional also needs an advocate to handle the intricate legal principles surrounding these defences. However, not all matters must end in court. The health care professional should reach out to the plaintiff to explore possibilities of settling the dispute out of court through ADR mechanisms such as mediation, arbitration and conciliation. These mechanisms do not only promote reconciliation, they save time and costs, unlike the adversarial court system, which is usually protracted. During mediation or arbitration, the defendant should try to explain to the patient and family what happened especially the difficult circumstances under which an operation or procedure was performed or conducted. He or she may even offer an apology to the patient and his or her family. Lastly, health care professionals need to take their duties to their patients seriously. Not only may they be subjected to a malpractice action through civil proceedings, they may be criminally prosecuted for negligence. This certainly affects the image, standing and career of the concerned professional.

9

FUNDAMENTAL RIGHTS OF PATIENTS

1 Introduction

In the preceding chapter, we saw that a health care professional may be held accountable for medical negligence through court action. In addition to liability for negligence, the professional may be held liable for violation of patients' rights, which revolve around the notion of consent to treatment. The professional may be held liable for trespass to the person where treatment is carried out without the patient's consent. Consequently, this chapter examines the question of consent to treatment, which is at the heart of patients' rights. The chapter analyses the circumstances under which a patient may consent to or refuse treatment in law. It also examines circumstances where treatment may be given without the consent of the patient. Before providing concluding remarks, the chapter considers factors that may vitiate consent to treatment.

2 Patients' Charter: Patient's rights and responsibilities

In a bid to promote awareness of patients' rights in the health care context, the Ministry of Health developed a Patients' Charter, hereinafter the 'Charter',[1] which outlines patients' rights and responsibilities. The rights in the Charter include: the right to medical care; prohibition of discrimination; participation in decision making; confidentiality and privacy; informed consent; and refusal of medical treatment.[2] The responsibilities of the patient include provision of information; compliance with instructions; and respect and consideration of other patients and health workers.[3] Whereas the Charter is not a legal document as such and

1 Ministry of Health *Patients' Charter* (2009).
2 See arts 1-19 of the Charter.
3 See arts 20-24 of the Charter.

may thus not have the force of law, it declares a number of principles, which have been recognised in human rights instruments and the common law.[4] At the heart of these principles is informed consent to treatment, which as this chapter illustrates is largely governed by tort law. On informed consent, the Charter provides as follows:

> Every patient has the right to be given adequate and accurate information about the nature of one's illness, diagnostic procedures, [and] the proposed treatment for one to make a decision that affects one of these elements. The information shall be communicated to the patient at the earliest possible stage in a manner that he/she is expected to understand in order to make a free, informed, and independent choice. However, the clinician may withhold the medical information if he/she strongly feels that by giving this information, it is likely to cause harm to the patient's mental or physical health.[5]

The Charter also provides for the manner in which consent may be given. According to the Charter, informed consent 'may be given verbally or in writing or demonstrated by [the] patient's behaviour. Consent should be witnessed'.[6] In a medical emergency, such consent 'shall be given as soon as possible afterwards'.[7]

The Charter also outlines the circumstances under which medical care may be provided without the consent of the patient. These include situations where '[t]he patient's physical or mental state does not permit obtaining his/her informed consent'[8] and or it is impossible to obtain the consent of the patient's representative or guardian or the patient is a minor or incapacitated.[9] According to the Charter, a patient may verbally or in writing refuse treatment 'provided such refusal does not endanger the health of others'.[10] Treatment against a patient's will, may be provided under the following circumstances:

- If the patient has received information as required to make an informed choice.
- If the treatment is anticipated to significantly improve the patient's medical condition.
- If there are reasonable grounds to suppose that after receiving treatment, the patient will give his/her retrospective consent.[11]

4 Currently, there is a Patients' Rights Bill before Parliament, which codifies all the principles in the Charter.
5 Art 10 of the Charter.
6 Art 10(a) of the Charter.
7 Art 10(b) of the Charter.
8 Art 11(a) - (b) of the Charter.
9 As above.
10 Art 12(a) of the Charter.
11 Art 12(b) - (c).

3 Why consent to treatment?

As the Charter has illustrated above, patients must give valid consent to medical treatment. Consent plays a number of roles in the doctor-patient relationship. Given that a health care professional is usually in a dominant position in his or her relationship with the patient, consent plays a critical role in ensuring that the interests of the patient are protected. The training and experience acquired by health care professionals equips them with knowledge and information concerning the patient's condition and places them in a powerful position over the patient. As McHale and Fox have pointed out:

> The requirement that the patient's consent be obtained thus operates as a constraint on the power of the health care professional. It is particularly important that the law protects this right given that the health professional, particularly the doctor, is in a powerful position vis-à-vis the patient, and that her role frequently involves touching, examining and operating upon patients. Given this power dynamic, control of information becomes a key feature in defining the balance of power between the health professional and the patient.[12]

Consent provides legal justification of care to avoid allegations of committing the tort of trespass to the person, which may take the form of assault or battery.[13] Treatment without consent may in some cases be treated as a crime, although in a health care context, it is much more likely that a civil action will be brought for trespass to the person, rather than a criminal action. Consent also provides a clinical function: it secures the patient's trust and cooperation.[14]

Consent represents the legal and ethical expression to one's autonomy and self-determination. In absence of evidence to the contrary, adult patients are presumed to have capacity of giving or withholding consent. An adult patient of sound mind can refuse treatment even if such treatment will save his or her life. Thus, where a health care professional attempts to treat a person without his or her valid consent, then the professional may be liable under both tort and criminal law.

12 J McHale & M Fox *Health care law: Texts and materials* (1997) 317.

13 According to Mullis & Oliphant, '[B]attery is where one person intentionally and without consent applies force directly to another. Where that person intentionally makes a threat that causes another reasonably to apprehend the immediate infliction of a battery on him, that is an assault'. Battery is a non-consensual touching and is a tort. See A Mullis & K Oliphant *Torts* (2003) 60. In *Collins v Wilcock* (1984) 1 WLR 1172, it was held that to be a battery, there must be 'something in the nature of overt hostility'. The judge observed that touching will only amount to a battery where it does not fall within the category of physical contacts generally acceptable in the conduct of general life. Battery is thus an intentional and offensive touching of another without lawful justification. See BA Garner (ed) *Black's law dictionary* (2003) 130. Consent is an affirmative defense to assault and battery.

14 See the case of *Re W* (1992) 4 All ER 627.

It should however be noted that though the court may technically find that there was trespass, it may award nominal damages especially if the treatment or operation was for the defendant's benefit. In *Njareketa v The Director of Medical Services and Another*,[15] the appellant, a 24 year old patient, had a malignant growth on his leg. The surgeon found it necessary to amputate the leg in order to save his life. The patient first consented to the operation but subsequently retracted the consent and expressly refused. The plaintiff asked for 30 000 shillings as damages. Although the court found that the surgeon committed trespass to the person, it only awarded the plaintiff nominal damages. On appeal, the court found that the operation was for the plaintiff's benefit: he was alive and apart from his disability, he was in excellent health. The court awarded him only one cent and observed as follows:

> It is not due to our lack of compassion for the appellant but to the realization that it is necessary to protect the Government Medical Department and all surgeons from unscrupulous claims of this nature that we reduce nominal damages awarded to the appellant to one cent and set aside the learned judge's order as to costs. The appellant may certainly be a fit subject for charitable assistance, but he is entitled to nothing in law, and should never have brought this action.[16]

4 Capacity to consent to treatment

The general rule is that a health care professional should presume that a patient has capacity to consent to or refuse treatment.[17] In the health care context, capacity refers to competence to make decisions with respect to medical treatment. The key question here is: does the patient have the competence to consent to or refuse treatment? In *F v West Berkshire Health Authority*,[18] the court held that a patient is competent if he or she is able to understand the nature and purpose of the treatment. That he or she must be able to understand the risks and side effects as explained by the health care professional. In this case, the plaintiff aged 36 had learning difficulties. She had been a voluntary in-patient at a mental hospital for over 20 years and had developed a sexual relationship with a male patient. Both the professionals and her mother thought that she should not have been pregnant and should be sterilised. Since she was unable to consent, a declaration was sought from court that the sterilisation would be lawful. The House of Lords held that it had no power to consent on her behalf. However, it examined whether it would be lawful for the operation to be performed without her consent. Lord Brandon held that a doctor who operates on a patient without consent commits the actionable tort of trespass.

15 (1950) 17 EACA 60.
16 *Njareketa* (n 15 above) 61-62.
17 See *Re T* (1992) 4 All ER 649, 661.
18 (1989) 2 All ER 545; (1990) 2 AC 1; (1989) 2 WLR 938.

Another case concerning capacity to consent to treatment is *Re T (Adult: Refusal of Treatment)*,[19] where T who was pregnant was involved in a car accident and went into premature labour which necessitated a caesarean section operation. T's mother was a Jehovah witness, albeit T was not. After a conversation with her mother, T told the hospital staff that she did not want a blood transfusion and signed a refusal to consent form. Prior to the conversation with her mother, T had not expressed any concern about the blood transfusion. The caesarean section operation was carried out without a blood transfusion but the baby was still-born. T's condition subsequently deteriorated. She was admitted to an intensive care unit where it was decided that without a blood transfusion she would die. The question before the court was whether T's refusal to consent was legally valid and whether it was invalidated by her mother's influence. Lord Donaldson, MR stated as follows:

> The law requires that an adult patient who is mentally and physically capable of exercising a choice must consent if medical treatment of himis to be lawful, although consent need not be in writing and may be inferred from the patient's conduct in the context of the circumstances. Treating a patient without his consent or despite a refusal of consent will constitute a crime. If however, the patient has made no choice and, when the need of treatment arises, is in no position to make one, the classic emergency situation with an unconscious patient [applies], eg the practitioner can lawfully treat the patient in accordance with his clinical judgment of what is in the patient's best interest.[20]

For consent to be valid, it must be real, genuine, free and voluntary. In *Chatterton v Gerson*,[21] Ms Chatterton suffered chronic intractable pain following a hernia operation. She was given an injection to block the pain. The injection was initially successful but the pain returned later. She had the procedure repeated. However, the pain was not relieved and she was left seriously disabled, unable to feel anything in her right leg and foot. She sued Dr Gerston arguing that she had not given any valid consent to the procedure since it had not been explained to her and in any case she doubted the doctor's explanation. Noting that the consent of the patient must be real, Bristow J held as follows:

> It is clear law that in any context in which consent of the injured party is a defence to what would otherwise be a crime or civil wrong, the consent must be real ... In my judgment what the court has to do in each case is to look at all the circumstances and say 'was there a real consent?' I think justice requires that in order to vitiate the reality of consent there must be a greater failure of communication between doctor and patient than that involved in a breach of duty if the claim is based on negligence. When the claim is based on negligence the plaintiff must prove not only the breach of duty to inform but

19 (1992) 4 All ER 649.
20 *Re T* (n 19 above) 652.
21 (1981) 1 All ER 257; (1981) QB 432; (1980) WLR 1003. See also S Mc Lean *A patient's right to know: Information disclosure, the doctor and the law* (1989).

> that had the duty not been broken she would not have chosen to have the operation. Where the claim is based on trespass to the person, once it is shown that the consent is unreal, then what the plaintiff would have decided if she had been given the information which would have prevented the vitiation of the reality of her consent is irrelevant ... [O]nce the patient is informed in broad terms of the nature of the procedure, which is intended, and gives her consent, that consent is real ...[22]

Thus, the patient must clearly know in broad terms what he or she is consenting to. In *Re MB*,[23] the court held that the patient must be able to comprehend and retain the information that is material to the decision – especially the likelihood of the consequences of having or not having the treatment in question – and that the patient must be able to use the information and weigh it in order to arrive at the decision as to whether to consent to or refuse the treatment. In *Re C*,[24] the court also held that in order to determine competence, it is necessary to ascertain whether the patient understood the nature, purpose and effects of the proposed treatment. That the patient should be able to comprehend and retain the information about the treatment, believe that information, and weigh it in the balance so as to arrive at a choice. In this case, the doctor recommended amputation of a patient's leg. The patient refused to consent to the procedure and sought a declaration from court that the amputation could not proceed without his consent. The court held that the patient was competent to withhold his consent. The court noted that the patient's general incapacity due to schizophrenia was irrelevant since it had not been proved that he had not understood the choice he was being asked to make. The court granted an injunction to prevent the hospital from amputating his leg.

In order to give a fully informed consent, the patient should be provided with information about the benefits and risks of the particular course of conduct or treatment. In *Sidaway v Bethlem RHG*,[25] the plaintiff had an operation on her spine to relieve pain. There were two possible risks: that a nerve root might be damaged in the area of operation and that the spinal cord might be damaged. Neither of these risks was statistically significant. However, the consequences were very serious if either risk was to happen. She was left severely disabled with partial paralysis and sued the doctor who had treated her. The Court of Appeal inferred that probably the doctor warned her about the first risk, damage to the nerve root, but not the second risk, damage to the spinal cord. On appeal, the House of Lords had to decide whether the failure to inform her of the risk of injury to the spinal cord was negligent. Lord Scarman held as follows:

22 *Chatterton* (n 21 above) 435.
23 (1997) 2 FCR 541.
24 (1994) 1 All ER 819.
25 (1985) 1 All ER 643.

> The right of self-determination; the description applied by some to what is no more and no less than the right of a patient to determine for himself whether he will or will not accept the doctor's advice, is vividly illustrated where the treatment recommended is surgery. A doctor who operates without the consent of his patient is, save in cases of emergency or mental disability, guilty of the civil wrong of trespass to the person; he is also guilty of the criminal offence of assault. The existence of the patient's right to make his decision, which may be seen as a human right protected by the common law ... known as the 'doctrine of informed consent', it amounts to this: where there is a 'real' or 'material' risk inherent in the proposed operation (however competently and skilfully performed) ... a patient has a right to be informed of the risks inherent in the treatment which is proposed. The [medical] profession, it is said should not be a judge in its own cause; or less emotively but more correctly, the courts should not allow medical opinion as to what is best for the patient to override the patient's right to decide for himself whether he will submit to the treatment offered to him.[26]

Lord Scarman cited the American case of *Canterbury v Spence*,[27] where the court enunciated four principles regarding informed consent. First, every adult person of sound mind has a right to determine what shall be done with his own body. Second, consent is the informed exercise of a choice, which entails an opportunity to evaluate knowledgeably the options available and the risks on each. Third, the doctor must disclose all 'material risks' and what is material is determined by the 'prudent patient' test. Fourth, the doctor has a 'therapeutic privilege', which enables him or her to withhold from his or her patient information as to risk if it can be shown that disclosure may pose a serious threat of psychological detriment to the patient. Although all the judges agreed with Lord Scarman that an inquiring patient has a right to be given the information which he or she requests, Lord Diplock and other judges rejected the *Canterbury* test in favour of the *Bolam* test, which was considered in chapter eight.

In the South African case of *Christian Lawyers Association v Minister of Health and Others*,[28] the High Court considered informed consent in the context of termination of pregnancy. The court stated that the concept forms the basis of the doctrine of *volenti non fit injuria* that justifies conduct that would otherwise have constituted a delict if it took place without a victim's informed consent. That the informed consent rests on three essential elements: knowledge, appreciation, and consent. In *Castell v De*

26 *Sidaway* (n 25 above) 648. On informed consent, see J Montgomery 'Power/knowledge/consent: Medical decision taking' (1988) 51 *Modern Law Review* 245; G Robertson 'Informed consent to medical treatment' (1981) 97 *Law Quarterly Review* 102. Garner (n 13 above) 346 defines informed consent as: 'A person's agreement to allow something to happen, made with full knowledge of the risks and alternatives ... A patient's knowing choice about a medical treatment or procedure, made after a physician or other health care provider discloses whatever information a reasonable prudent provider in the medical community would give to a patient regarding the risks involved in the proposed treatment or procedure'.

27 464 F 2d 772 (1972).

28 2005 (9) SA 509.

Greef[29] the court held that in exercise of his or her fundamental right to self-determination, it is the patient to determine whether or not to undergo an operation. It is irrelevant that the patient's attitude is unreasonable in the view of the medical doctor. The patient's right to bodily integrity and autonomy entitles him or her to refuse treatment. The ultimate decision to undergo or refuse any proposed treatment or intervention lies with the patient and not the doctor. In *Chester v Afshar*,[30] the court held that '... as a result of the surgeon's failure to warn the patient, she cannot be said to have given informed consent to the surgery in the full legal sense'.[31]

In the *Government of the Republic of Namibia v LM and Others*,[32] the Supreme Court of Namibia handled the question of informed consent in the context of sterilisation. In this case, three HIV positive women were sterilised while in labour. The Supreme Court held that the women had been forcefully sterilised, without proper consent during emergency caesarean deliveries. The court found that none of the women could have given informed consent as they were in varying degrees of labour and may not have fully and rationally comprehended the consequences of giving consent for the sterilisation procedures. The court further found that none of the respondents made any appointment or booking to confirm the intention to be sterilised before going into labour. The Supreme Court referred the matter to the High Court for determination of the quantum of damages due to the women. In emphasising the importance of consent as a component of the right to self-determination, the court stated:

> The right to found a family includes the right of a woman of full age to bear children and of men and women to choose and plan the size of their families. In the case of an unmarried woman, it is primarily her choice, in the exercise of the right to self determination, whether or not to bear children. Against this background, the decision of whether or not to be sterilised is of great personal importance to women. It is a decision that must be made with informed consent, as opposed merely to written consent. Informed consent implies an understanding and appreciation of one's rights and the risks, consequences and available alternatives to the patient. An individual must also be able to make a decision regarding sterilisation freely and voluntarily.[33]

The Supreme Court further stated as follows:

> The consent obtained was invalidated by the respondents' lack of capacity to give informed consent in light of the history of how the decision to sterilise them was arrived at and the circumstances under which the respondent's consent was obtained. It was merely written rather that informed consent, which in my opinion is not sufficient for the performance of a procedure as invasive and potentially irreversible as sterilisation. The important factor

29 1994 (4) SA 408 (C).
30 (2004) 4 All ER 587.
31 Para 24.
32 (2014) NASC 19.
33 Para 1.

> which must be kept in mind at all times is whether the woman has the capacity to give her consent for sterilisation at the time she is requested to sign consent forms. Therefore, it is not decisive what information was given to her during antenatal care classes or at the moment she signed the consent form if she is not fully comprehending the information or making a decision without any undue influence caused by the pain she is experiencing.[34]

Another case involving sterilisation without a woman's informed consent is *NB v Slovakia*,[35] where NB of Roma ethnic origin, went to a public hospital to give birth to her second child. During labour, she was given various medications including a drug that is used for its sedative, anxiety-relieving and muscle relaxing effects. After this medication was administered, NB was approached by a member of the medical staff who took her hand and helped her sign some papers. At that time, NB was intoxicated from the medication and lacked the strength to inquire about what the papers were about. NB later found that the paper she signed stated that she had requested a sterilisation procedure during delivery and that she had been informed about the irreversible nature of the procedure. She also alleged that she experienced inferior treatment at the hospital where the patients were segregated based on their ethnic origins and women of Roma origin were put in a 'Gypsy room'. She also maintained that this discrimination was one factor in the doctor's decision to sterilise her without her consent. The court held that the sterilisation affected her reproductive health status as well as her private and family life. The court also found that the state failed to carry out its positive obligation by not putting in place effective legal safeguards to protect the reproductive health of women such as the need to inquire informed consent for sterilisation. The court held that there is a violation of women's reproductive health rights if sterilisation is carried out without free and informed consent.

In the Nigerian case of *Medical & Dental Practitioners Disciplinary Tribunal v Okonkwo*,[36] the court stressed an adult competent patient's right to consent or refuse a medical procedure. The court held that treatment without consent can give rise to an action in trespass. That the patient has a right to determine his or her own treatment and that right is superior to the physician's duty to provide necessary care. The court stated:

> [A]n individual should be left alone to choose a course for his life, unless a clear and compelling overriding state interest justifies the contrary. The law's role is to ensure the fullness of liberty when there is no danger to public interest. Ensuring liberty of conscience and freedom of religion is an important component of that fullness. The courts are the institutions society has agreed to invest with the responsibility of balancing conflicting interests in a way as to ensure the fullness of liberty without destroying the existence and stability of society itself. It will be asking too much of a medical practitioner

34 Para 108.
35 Application 29518/10 (12 September 2012).
36 (2002) AHRLR 159.

> to expect him to assume this awesome responsibility in the privacy of his clinic or surgery, unaided by materials that are available to the courts or even by his training. This is why if a decision is to override the decision of an adult competent patient not to submit to blood transfusion or medical treatment on religious grounds is to be taken on grounds of public interest or recognized interest of others, such as dependent children, it is to be taken by the courts.[37]

In the South African case of *Nicola McDonald v Graham Wroe*,[38] the plaintiff had developed repeated bouts of an infection in the area of her wisdom teeth and the defendant correctly advised her that it was necessary for her wisdom teeth to be extracted. The plaintiff experienced numbness on the left side of her face after the operation. The numbness was a result of damage to her inferior nerve, which damage appeared to be permanent in nature. The risk of permanent nerve damage was an inherent risk arising from the surgery in that area, of which the defendant had failed to warn her prior to the surgery and when obtaining her consent to the procedure. The court held that a patient who relies on informed consent bears the burden to prove, on a balance of probabilities, that the medical practitioner was negligent in so far as he failed to warn his patient of the particular risk or complication, and the practitioner's negligent omission as such caused the damages suffered. The court stated:

> The defendant's wrongful and negligent failure to warn the plaintiff of the risk involved resulted in the plaintiff consenting to the defendant performing the surgery. He performed the surgery correctly without negligence. The experts were unable to fault the manner in which he performed the surgery in any way. The harm which the plaintiff suffered is due to a risk which is inherent in the surgical procedure. The harm which the plaintiff suffered, is harm she might equally probably have suffered in any event if the surgery had been performed by a specialist surgeon. There is therefore no direct causal link between the defendant's negligence (in failing to warn the plaintiff of the risk) and occurrence of the harm, unless it is shown that the plaintiff, upon being warned of risk, would not have undergone the procedure at all. That is not the plaintiff's case.[39]

5 Form of consent

Where there is no specific provision requiring a certain form, consent may be oral or written.[40] However, it is advisable for a health care professional to procure a written consent of the patient for evidential purposes before performing any procedure. A signed consent form provides good evidence in court. A patient who has signed the consent form may find it difficult to

37 Para 72.
38 2006 (3) All SA 565 (C).
39 Para 34.
40 According to sec 61 of the Evidence Act, Cap 6 Laws of Uganda, all facts except the contents of documents may be proved by oral evidence. Oral evidence must be direct; it should be by witnesses who saw, heard or perceived the facts (sec 62). On documentary evidence, see secs 63 - 64 of the Act.

deny his or her signature. In any case, if he or she denies it, the signature may be subjected to a hand writing expert who may confirm that it is the real signature in dispute.[41] It should be noted that evidence of consent may be gathered from clinical notes indicating that on the material date, an explanation was offered and the patient freely gave his or her consent. This is especially true in respect of those patients who are illiterate or unable to physically sign. It should also be noted that issues concerning whether the patient consented to or refused the treatment may be subjected to cross-examination in court in order to discover the truth.

6 Treatment without consent

Montgomery[42] has outlined four major circumstances under which a health care professional may provide care or treatment without consent:

- First, there are certain activities which may not require consent because they are insignificantly intrusive;
- Second, where the treatment is authorised by public policy, it may outweigh the refusal to consent. For example, care or treatment may be provided to a person against his or her will in order to stop the spread of a contagious or infectious disease.[43] Treatment may also be provided to a pregnant woman in order to benefit the fetus she is carrying;[44]
- Third, where consent cannot be obtained because there is no one who is legally capable of giving it on the patient's behalf, health care professionals may also proceed without consent; and
- Fourth, where treatment is required for a mental illness or disorder, professionals may also be absolved of the need to obtain consent.

In *F v West Berkshire Health Authority*,[45] the House of Lords upheld the decision by the lower court permitting the sterilisation of a mentally incompetent woman on grounds of necessity. After stating the general rule that adult patients of sound mind must consent to treatment, Lord Brandon alluded to examples where treatment may be given without consent under the 'best interests rule' as follows:

> There are however, cases where adult patients cannot give or refuse their consent to an operation. One case is where, as a result of an accident or otherwise an adult patient is unconscious and an operation or other treatment cannot be safely delayed until he or she recovers consciousness. Another case is where a patient, though an adult cannot by reason of mental disability

41 See sec 75 of the Evidence Act.
42 J Montgomery *Health care law* (2003) 190.
43 See for example art 23(1)(d) of the Constitution of the Republic of Uganda.
44 For example, in Uganda, Nevirapine, which is aimed at preventing transmission of HIV from the mother to the child is administered on every pregnant woman who seeks to deliver in a recognised health facility.
45 (1989) 2 All ER 545. See also, *Re T (Adult: Refusal of Treatment)*; M Braiser & M Loibojoit (eds) *Protecting the vulnerable: Autonomy and consent in health care* (1991).

> understand the nature or purpose of an operation or other treatment … In my opinion, the solution to the problem which the common law provides is that a doctor can lawfully operate on, or give other treatment to, adult patients who are incapable for one reason or another, of consenting to his doing so, provided that the operation or other treatment concerned is in the best interest of certain patients. The operation or other treatment will be in their best interests if, but only if, it is carried out in order to save their [patients who are incapable of giving consent] lives or to ensure improvement or prevent deterioration in their physical or mental health.[46]

The defence of necessity thus may play an important role in the treatment of persons without capacity to consent. Medical treatment of incompetent patients such as the mentally ill and the unconscious may be justified on grounds of necessity.[47] However, Lord Golf observed that for the defence of necessity to succeed, there must have been: (a) a necessity to act in circumstances where it was not practicable to communicate with the assisted person; and (b) the action taken must have been such as a reasonable person would in all the circumstances take, acting in the best interests of the assisted person. Lord Golf was of the view that albeit in non-medical cases the test is that of 'a reasonable man', in medical cases, the *Bolam* test should be applied. Thus, a doctor who acts in accordance with a responsible and competent body of professional opinion will not be held liable.

7 The position of children

The Convention on the Rights of the Child (CRC) defines a child as 'every human being below the age of eighteen years unless under the law applicable to the child majority is attained earlier'.[48] In Uganda, the Children's Act,[49] also defines a child as that person who has not attained the age of eighteen years.[50] Under the Contracts Act,[51] capacity to contract is eighteen years.[52]

In respect of a child's right to be cared for, the Constitution provides that, '[s]ubject to laws enacted in their best interests, children shall have the right to know and be cared for by their parents or those entitled to bring them up'.[53] According to the Children's Act, every parent shall have the responsibility for his or her child[54] and it is the duty of every parent or guardian to maintain a child.[55] The child has the right to medical

46 *F* (n 45 above) 548.
47 As above.
48 Art 1.
49 Cap 59 Laws of Uganda.
50 Sec 2.
51 Act 7 of 2010, Laws of Uganda.
52 Sec 11(1).
53 Art 34(1).
54 Sec 6(1).
55 Sec 5(1).

attention.[56] Children are entitled to protection from social or customary practices that are harmful to their health.[57] The Children's Act further provides that '[a]ny person having custody of a child shall protect the child from discrimination, violence, abuse and neglect'.[58] According to the Penal Code Act, a parent or guardian who neglects to provide necessities – such as medical care – to a child commits an offence.[59]

According to the CRC, children have such rights as health, self-determination, non-interference, and the right to make informed decisions. A child who is capable of forming his or her own views has the right to express such views freely in all matters affecting him or her.[60] The view of the child should be weighed in accordance with his or her age or maturity.[61] In all actions concerning children, the welfare and best interests of the child are paramount.[62] Any act, which is prejudicial to the child, is against his or her interest. What constitutes the best interests of the child depends on the circumstances of each case.

The legal position outlined above raises a number of questions: does a child have capacity to consent to treatment? In other words, is it legally permissible for a health care professional to treat a child without the consent of the parent or guardian? When is a child presumed to be mature enough to make his or her own decisions? In *Gillick v West Norfolk and Wisbech Area Health Authority & Another*,[63] Mrs Gillick objected to the provision of contraceptives to her daughters without her prior knowledge and consent so long as they were below16 years. The court recognised the right of a 'mature minor' to consent to her own medical treatment. Lord Fraser stated:

> It seems to me verging on the absurd to suggest that a girl or boy aged fifteen could not effectively consent, for example to have a medical examination of some trivial injury to his [or her] body or even to have a broken arm set. Of course the consent of the parents should normally be asked, but they may not be immediately available. Provided the patient, whether a boy or girl, is capable of understanding what is proposed, and of expressing his or her own wishes, I see no good reason for holding that he or she lacks the capacity to express them validly and effectively and to authorize the medical man to make the examination or give the treatment which he wishes.[64]

It should thus be noted that what is important is whether the care or treatment is in the 'best interests of the child'. Further, whether a child is

56 Sec 5(1)(f).
57 Sec 7.
58 Sec 5(2).
59 Sec 157 of the Penal Code Act.
60 Art 12(1).
61 As above.
62 Art (1).
63 (1985) 3 All ER 402.
64 *Gillick* (n 63 above) 405.

able to exercise a right of autonomy and seek medical treatment without a parent or guardian's consent largely depends on the maturity of an individual child. 'Mature children' should be supported in their decision making. Where a child clearly lacks the competence to make a choice about his or her health care, the parent or guardian should give the consent. In the absence of a parent or guardian that should consent to the treatment, the doctor may treat the child out of necessity.

Another question that arises in respect of children's health care is where a parent or guardian refuses to consent to a child's treatment on moral or religious grounds. Some people believe in the healing power of prayer and refuse to take their children for treatment. Others such as Jehovah's witnesses do not believe in blood transfusion. In *Re R (A Minor) (Blood Transfusion)*,[65] a ten month girl was suffering from B-cell lymphoblastic leukaemia and needed a blood transfusion. The parents who were devout Jehovah's witnesses refused to consent to the treatment. Guided by the welfare and best interests of the child, the court overrode the parents' wishes and directed that the child should receive blood transfusion as medical advice dictated.[66] On this question, the Ugandan Constitution is clear: it provides that, '[n]o child shall be deprived of medical treatment, education or any other social or economic benefit by reason of religious or other beliefs'.[67]

8 Factors that vitiate consent

8.1 Coercion and undue influence

Consent to treatment must be voluntary. It must be freely given and not forcefully extracted. Thus, any apparently valid consent may be invalidated by coercion or undue influence since it is not the voluntary consent of the patient. Although cases of coercion may be rare, there are instances where a person in a stronger position may unduly influence a patient to consent to or refuse treatment. In *Re T (Adult: Refusal of Medical Treatment)*,[68] where the refusal was allegedly in response to the influence of the mother, who was a practicing Jehovah's witness but T was not practicing that faith, it was held that blood could be provided in T's best interests since the refusal was unduly influenced by the mother. Lord Justice Staughton said that in determining whether the consent was obtained through undue influence, the key question to consider is: did the external influences cause the patient 'to depart from her own wishes to

65 (1993) 2 FLR 757; (1993) FCR 544. See also *Re O (A Minor) (Medical Treatment)* (1993) 2 FLR 149; *Re S (A Minor) (Medical Treatment)* (1993) 1 FLR 396.

66 For a discussion of the parameters of the 'best interests rule', see C Bridge 'Parental beliefs and medical treatment of children' (1994) *Butterworth's Family Law Journal* 131.

67 Art 34(3).

68 (1992) 4 All ER 649.

such an extent that the law regards it as undue'?[69] Lord Donaldson was of the view that in determining whether a patient has been unduly influenced in order to affect independence of judgment, it is necessary to consider the relationship that exists with the person influencing him or her.[70]

The patient's consent or refusal of treatment may be vitiated by the influence of another person in a stronger position for example a relative, close friend, teacher, parent or health care professional. The closer the relationship, the more difficult it becomes to resist the undue pressure. Once established that a relationship exists, the burden is on the stronger party to rebut the presumption that the influence was undue. It is necessary to look at the strength of the patient. In a situation where a patient is in pain, tired or depressed, he or she may be less able to resist the undue influence.[71] Court looks at whether the decision was made freely and voluntarily reflecting the patient's autonomy. Lord Donaldson observed as follows:

> A special problem arises if at the time the decision is made the patient had been subjected to the influence of some third party. This is by no means to say that the patient is not entitled to receive and indeed invite advice and assistance from others in reaching a decision particularly from members of the family. But the doctors have to consider whether the decision is really that of the patient ... The real question in each such case is, does the patient really mean what he says or he is merely saying it for a quiet life, to satisfy someone else or because the advice and persuasion to which he has been subjected is such that he can no longer think and decide for himself? In other words, is it a position expressed in form only, not in reality?[72]

It should be noted that Lord Donaldson correctly cautioned that cases involving undue influence in the law of property and contract may not be applicable to the different context of consent to medical or surgical treatment. He argued that unlike property and contract cases, the interest of the stronger party in medical consent cases is not necessarily to gain commercially.[73]

8.2 Fraud

Where information is deliberately withheld from a patient in bad faith in order to deceive them into agreeing to a certain type of treatment, then the apparent consent will be invalid. Thus, an apparent valid consent may be

69 *Re T* (n 68 above) 669.
70 *Re T* (n 68 above) 662.
71 As above. See also S Cameron & A Lynch 'Undue influence, consent and medical treatment' (2003) 96*Journal of the Royal Society of Medicine* 598; Montgomery (n 26 above); G Robertson (1981) 'Informed consent to medical treatment' 97 *Law Quarterly Review* 102.
72 As above.
73 *Re T* (n 68 above) 669.

vitiated if it is obtained by fraud, which includes the deliberate withholding of information from the patient in bad faith.[74]

9 Conclusion

Consent to treatment is at the heart of patients' rights, which are recognised by the common law and declared in the Charter. This chapter examined the circumstances under which a patient may consent to or refuse medical treatment. It also examined instances where treatment may be given without consent and factors that may invalidate an apparently valid consent. It was noted that given that a health care professional is usually in a dominant position in his or her relationship with the patient, consent plays a critical role in ensuring that the interests of the patient are protected. Consent provides the legal justification of care to avoid allegations of committing trespass to the person. The consent must be real, genuine, free and voluntary. Treatment may be provided without consent to persons who may be incapable of doing so for example, some mentally disabled persons and children, provided that such treatment is in their best interests. An apparently valid consent may be vitiated by factors such as coercion, undue influence and fraud.

It may be necessary to sensitise the people about patient's rights so that they may be able to claim them. The Ministry of Health should translate the Charter – or the Bill, once passed into an Act of Parliament – into local languages and disseminate the information therein on radio so that it may reach a wider audience especially in the rural areas. As pointed out in Chapter 7, the Uganda Medical and Dental Practitioners' Council should perform its statutory function: the dissemination of 'ethics in relation to doctor-patient rights and obligations' to the medical and dental practitioners and the public.[75]

74 See *Chatterson v Gerson* (1981) 1 All ER 257; *Appleton v Garrett* (1995) 34 BMLR 23; *Freeman v Home Office* (1984) 1 All ER 1036 1044.

75 Sec 3(h) of the Medical and Dental Practitioners Act, cap 272.

10

RESEARCH ON HUMAN PARTICIPANTS

1 Introduction

Research is invaluable in advancing knowledge in various fields, including the bio-medical, behavioural, and the social sciences. Over the years, physicians and researchers have investigated the causes of and potential treatments for various diseases. The research results have contributed to the understanding of prevention, diagnosis and treatment of new and emerging diseases. Benefits of research include vaccines for measles, antibiotics, medication for diabetes, blood pressure, and improved treatment of malaria, TB, HIV/AIDS and other diseases.[1]

It should however be noted from the outset that although research involving human participants is conducted for the benefit of society, it may also present burdens and risks to the volunteers or patients who may participate in the research.[2] Where the volunteers or patients are harmed or injured, the research project may have legal implications. Researchers or investigators must thus take due care not to injure the research participants. In order to minimise harm and maximise benefits for patients and volunteers, clinical research in Uganda is regulated and monitored by national regulatory authorities, including the Uganda National Council for Science and Technology (UNCST), the National Drug Authority (NDA) and various ethical and scientific committees. Against this backdrop, this chapter examines the legal, ethical and administrative frameworks available for scrutinising and regulating research involving

1 See for example, JN Sharyl et al *Beyond the HIPPA privacy rule: Enhancing privacy, improving health through research* (2009).

2 On the disastrous impact of certain medical experimentation, see for example HA Washington 'Medical apartheid: The dark history of medical experimentation on black Americans from colonial times to the present' (2007) 20 *Social History of Medicine* 620; MB Mason 'International protection of persons undergoing medical experimentation: Protecting the right to informed consent' (2002) 20 *Berkley Journal of International Law* 513.

humans as participants. Before providing concluding remarks, the chapter looks at the extent of liability in research involving human subjects.

2 Understanding research involving humans as participants

The Uganda National Council for Science and Technology (UNCST) defines research as 'any type of systematic investigation, testing and evaluation, designed to develop or contribute to generalisable knowledge'.[3] The UNSCT defines research involving humans as participants as,

> any study involving persons, and directed to the advancement of biomedical or other knowledge, that cannot be regarded as an element in established clinical management, public health or social practices and that involves either physical or psychological intervention or assessment or generation, storage, and analysis of records containing biomedical or other information referable to identifiable individuals and communities. Research involving humans as research participants also includes research on any material obtained from a research participant whether the participant is still living or has died.[4]

Research involving human participants includes clinical investigations; social-behavioural studies which involve interaction with or observation of people; basic scientific research to study the biology of persons or organs and specimens; and systemic collection, storage and analysis of data on humans'.[5] The next sections examine the legal and administrative frameworks for conducting research involving humans as participants.

3 The international framework

The Nazi regime atrocities[6] created an urgent need to regulate the conduct of clinical research in order to hold scientists and researchers accountable. Consequently, international human rights instruments such as the ICCPR and ethical documents such as the Nuremberg Code,[7] the Declaration of

3 Uganda National Council for Science and Technology (UNCST) *National guidelines for research involving humans as research participants* (2007).
4 UNCST (n 3 above) 47.
5 UNCST (n 3 above) 1.
6 German physicians conducted medical experiments on thousands of concentration camp prisoners during World War II without their consent. Most participants either died or were permanently disabled. An American military tribunal opened criminal proceedings against these physicians for their participation in war crimes and crimes against humanity. For details of these trials see, JM Mann et al (eds) *Health and Human rights* (1999) 284 - 300.
7 The Nuremberg Code followed the trial of the physicians who had committed the Nazi atrocities. The Code aimed at protecting the integrity of the research subject and is the first international document to emphasise voluntary participation and informed consent to research. The Code provided that participants must give consent and the benefits of research must outweigh the risks.

Helsinki,[8] the UNESCO Declaration,[9] the CIOMS International Ethical Guidelines,[10] and the UNAIDS/WHO Guidance Document[11] have been drawn up.

3.1 International human rights instruments

Various human rights instruments protect the rights of human subjects of scientific or medical experimentation. Both the Universal Declaration on Human Rights (Universal Declaration) and the International Covenant on Civil and Political Rights (ICCPR) provide that '[n]o person shall be subject to torture or to cruel, inhuman and degrading treatment or punishment'.[12] Following the Nazi atrocities, the ICCPR specifically provided that 'no one shall be subjected without his free consent to medical or scientific experimentation'.[13] According to the Human Rights Committee (HRC),[14] the aim of article 7 is to protect the dignity and the physical and mental integrity of the individual.[15] The provision does not allow any limitation and thus is non-derogable.[16] No justification or extenuating circumstance whatsoever may be invoked to excuse its violation.[17] The prohibition extends to both physical pain and mental suffering.[18] The HRC has emphasised that article 7 expressly prohibits medical or scientific experimentation without the free consent of the person concerned.

According to the HRC, special protection in regard to such experiments is necessary in the case of persons not capable of giving valid consent, and in particular those under any form of detention or imprisonment.[19] Such persons should not be subjected to any medical or

8 The 1964 Declaration by the World Medical Association has been revised a number of times: 1975, 1983, 1989, 1996, and 2000. See RV Kalsonet et al 'The revision of the declaration of Helsinki: Past, present and future' (2004) 57 *British Journal of Clinical Pharmacology* 695; D Human & S Fluss 'The World Medical Association's declaration of Helsinki: Historical and contemporary perspectives' http://www.wma.net/e/ethicsunit/pdf/draft_contemporary_perspectives.pdf (accessed on 3 February 2014).

9 UNESCO 'Universal declaration on bio-ethics and human rights' (2005) http://www.portal.unesco.org/en/ev.php.URL_ID=31058 (accessed 28 January 2014).

10 CIOMS 'International guidelines for bio-medical research involving human subjects' (2002) http://www.cioms.ch/publications/layout_guide2002.pdf (accessed 17 February 2014).

11 UNAIDS/WHO 'Guidance document: Ethical considerations in bio-medical HIV prevention trials' (2012) http://www.unaids.org/en/media/unaids/contentassets/documents (accessed 32 January 2014).

12 Art 5 of the Universal Declaration; art 7 of the ICCPR.

13 Art 7.

14 Human Rights Committee, General Comment 20: 'Article 7 (Prohibition of torture, or other cruel, inhuman or degrading treatment or punishment' Forty-fourth session, 1992, UN Doc/HRI/GEN/1/Rev 1 30.

15 Para 1.

16 Para 3.

17 As above.

18 Para 5.

19 Para 7.

scientific experimentation that may be detrimental to their health.[20] The Women's Protocol to the ACHPR also enjoins states parties to take appropriate and effective measures to 'prohibit all medical or scientific experiments on women without their informed consent'.[21]

3.2 The Declaration of Helsinki

The Declaration is a 'statement of ethical principles to provide guidance to physicians and other participants involving human subjects'.[22] It stresses the importance of informed consent and the requirement that research should be carried out by medically or scientifically qualified persons. It also emphasises the requirement that the risks of research should not exceed the benefits. The Declaration enjoins medical researchers to ensure that 'considerations related to the well-being of the human subject should take precedence over the interests of science and society'.[23] The Declaration stresses promotion and respect of health and human rights of all human beings and calls for special attention to the vulnerable and disadvantaged and those who are unable to give or refuse consent.[24]

According to the Declaration, it is the 'duty of every physician in medical research to protect the life, health, privacy and dignity of the human subject'.[25] The Declaration also stresses the respect of integrity and confidentiality of the research subject and declares that 'subjects must be volunteers and informed participants in the research subject'.[26] The research design and execution should conform to acceptable scientific principles[27] and the importance of the research objective should outweigh 'the inherent risks and burdens to the subject'.[28] The Declaration emphasises that 'medical research is only justified if there is a reasonable likelihood that the population in which the research is carried out stand to benefit from the results of the research'.[29]

It should be noted that the Declaration of Helsinki is a standard setting instrument for medical research in many countries, including Uganda. The Declaration plays a critical role in ensuring that fundamental human rights and freedoms of research participants are respected. Plomer has correctly observed that the Declaration complements human rights instruments in protecting the rights of disadvantaged populations and participants in

20 As above.
21 Art 4(2)(h).
22 Principle A(1).
23 Principle A(5).
24 Principle 8.
25 Principle B(10).
26 Principle B(21 & 20).
27 Principle B(11).
28 Principle B(18).
29 Principle B(19).

biomedical research.[30] It may be argued that norms in the Declaration have acquired the status of customary international law, which is directly applicable to states, including Uganda.[31]

3.3 The UNESCO Declaration

The Declaration recognises the fact that scientific and technological developments can be of great benefit to humankind in improving the quality of life.[32] However, it cautions that such developments should promote 'the recognition of the human person and universal respect for, and observance of human rights and fundamental freedoms' contained in key fundamental documents such as the CESCR, CRC, CEDAW, and ICCPR.[33]

The aims of the Declaration are inter alia, 'to provide a universal framework of principles and procedures to guide states in the formulation of their legislation, policies or other instruments in the field of bio-ethics'[34] and 'to promote respect for human dignity and protect human rights by ensuring respect for the life of human beings, and fundamental freedoms consistent with international human rights law'.[35] The Declaration also aims at the promotion of

> equitable access to medical, scientific and technological developments as well as the greatest possible flow and the rapid sharing of knowledge concerning those developments and the sharing of benefits with particular attention to the needs of developing countries.[36]

The Declaration calls for respect of human dignity, autonomy, consent and other human rights and the need to maximise benefits and minimise harm to patients, research participants, and other affected individuals.[37]

On the question of consent, the Declaration provides that any preventive, diagnostic and therapeutic medical intervention must

> be carried out with the prior, free and informed consent of the person concerned, based on adequate information. The consent should where

30 A Plomer 'In Defence of Helsinki and Human rights' (2012) 5 *South African Journal of Bioethics & Law* 83.
31 See art 38(1)(b) of the Statute of the International Court of Justice. As illustrated in Chapter 1, declarations, which belong to the category called 'soft law' may not be binding as such but the norms contained therein may form part of customary international law, if they have been subjected to intensive state practice.
32 Preamble to the Declaration.
33 As above.
34 Art 2(a).
35 Art 2(c).
36 Art 2(f).
37 Arts 3 - 6.

> appropriate, be express and may be withdrawn by the person concerned any time and for any reason without prejudice or disadvantage.[38]

Prior, free, express and informed consent is also required for any scientific research.[39] The information must be adequate and provided in a comprehensive form and include modalities for withdrawal of the consent.[40] In cases of research carried out on a group of persons or a community, efforts should be made to obtain an additional agreement of the legal representative of the group or community.[41] However, this agreement should never substitute individual consent.[42]

It should be noted that there are people who may lack the capacity to give informed consent. According to the Declaration, any authorisation of the research should take into account the best interests of the person concerned.[43] That person should be involved to the greatest extent possible in the decision making process and in any process of withdrawing consent.[44] The research should be for his or her direct health benefit with exposure to minimal risk and burden.[45] His or her refusal to take part in the research should be respected.[46] The Declaration calls for protection of individuals and groups with special vulnerability and stresses the promotion of equity, justice, non-discrimination and non-stigmatisation.[47]

It should also be noted that research in developing countries creates a greater risk of exploitation.[48] Whereas individuals and communities in these countries assume the risk of the research, most of the benefits go to the developed world where big pharmaceutical companies and other entities engaged in clinical research are based.[49] Consequently, the Declaration addresses the question of sharing the benefits of research in order to minimise the possibilities of exploitation. It provides that the benefits from scientific research should be shared with society and the international community as a whole in particular with developing countries.[50] Any scientific and technological progress should advance, inter alia, access to quality health care and essential medicines.[51] Professionalism, honesty, integrity and transparency should be promoted

38 Art 6(1).
39 Art 6(2).
40 As above.
41 Art 6(3).
42 As above.
43 Art 7(a).
44 As above.
45 Art 7(b).
46 As above.
47 Arts 9 - 11.
48 Mason (n 2 above).
49 See P Wilmshurst 'Scientific imperialism: If they won't benefit from the findings, poor people in the developing world should not be used in research' (1997) 314 *British Medical Journal* 840; SR Benator 'Avoiding exploitation in clinical research' (2000) 9 *Cambridge Quarterly of Healthcare Ethics* 526.
50 Art 15.
51 Art 14(2)(a).

in the decision making process.[52] It can be stated that the Declaration adopts a human rights based approach and is thus an important document for regulation of research involving human subjects.[53]

3.4 The CIOMS International Ethical Guidelines

The CIOMS Guidelines recognise the fact that the Declaration of Helsinki has influenced the formulation of international, regional and national legislation and codes of conduct in both developed and developing countries. Consequently, the major concern of the Guidelines is how the Declaration can be applied in developing countries given their peculiar socio-economic circumstances. The Guidelines focus on the human rights of research subjects paying particular attention to respect for autonomy and the protection of vulnerable persons. According to the Guidelines, vulnerability refers to

> a substantial incapacity to protect one's own interests owing to such impediments as lack of capability to give informed consent, lack of alternative means of obtaining medical care or other expensive necessities, or being a junior or a subordinate member of a hierarchical group.[54]

The document is divided into two parts: general ethical principles and the guidelines as presented below.

3.4.1 General ethical principles

The Guidelines are based on three general ethical principles. The first is the principle of *respect for persons*, which covers respect for autonomy and capacity for self-determination, and protection of persons with impaired or diminished autonomy. The second is the principle of *beneficence*, which refers to the obligation to maximise benefit and to minimise harm. This principle requires that the risks of research should be reasonable in light of the expected benefits; the research design should be sound; the investigators should be competent; and the welfare of the research subjects should be safeguarded. The principle also prohibits the deliberate infliction of harm on persons (*non-malfeasance*). The third is the principle of *justice*, which refers to the obligation 'to treat each person in accordance with what is morally right and proper, to give each person what is due to him or her'.[55] This principle underlines *distributive justice*, which calls for the equitable distribution of both the burdens and the benefits of participation

52 Art 18.

53 See V Garaffa et al 'Between the needy and the greedy: The quest for a just and fair ethics of clinical research'(2010) 36 *Journal of Medical Ethics* 500. See also CC Macpherson 'Global ethics: Did the universal declaration on bioethics miss the boat?' (2007) 33 *Journal of Medical Ethics* 588.

54 CIOMS (n 10 above) 18.

55 CIOMS (n 10 above)18.

in research. The principle of *justice* also requires that the research project should benefit developing countries or communities where the research is carried out: it should positively respond to their health needs and priorities by ensuring that any product developed is reasonably available to them.[56]

3.4.2 The Guidelines: An overview

There are twenty one guidelines and each is accompanied by a commentary. The first guideline is to the effect that biomedical research involving human subjects must be ethically justified and scientifically valid. The ethical justification for such research is the prospect of discovering new ways of benefiting people's health. The research must respect, protect and be fair to the research subjects. The research must also be morally acceptable within the communities where it is carried out. The second guideline is that all proposals to conduct research involving human subjects must be submitted for review for their scientific merit and acceptability to one or more scientific and ethical review committees. The third guideline requires that externally sponsored research protocols should be submitted for ethical and scientific review in the country of the sponsoring organisation. The fourth guideline addresses the critical question of informed consent and provides as follows:

> For all biomedical research involving humans, the investigator must obtain the voluntary informed consent of the prospective subject or, in the case of an individual who is not capable of giving informed consent, the permission of a legally authorized representative in accordance with the applicable law. Waiver of informed consent is to be regarded as uncommon and exceptional, and must in all cases be approved by an ethical committee.[57]

According to the commentary to this guideline, informed consent

> is a decision to participate in research, taken by a competent individual who has received the necessary information; who has adequately understood the information; and who, after considering the information, has arrived at a decision without having been subjected to coercion, undue influence or inducement, or intimidation.[58]

The fifth guideline outlines essential information that must be provided to prospective subjects in order for them to give or refuse or withdraw consent. The information must be in a language or another form of communication the individual can understand. Such information should include the fact that participation is voluntary; the right to refuse to participate in the research; the right to withdraw from the research; and the purpose of the research and any foreseeable risks. The sixth guideline lays

56 As above.
57 CIOMS (n 10 above) 31.
58 CIOMS (n 10 above) 32.

down the obligations of sponsors and investigators in respect of informed consent. They must refrain from deception, undue influence or intimidation and ensure that the subject has adequate understanding of relevant facts about the proposed research and the consequences of participation.

The seventh guideline concerns inducement to participate in research. Research subjects may be reimbursed lost earnings, travel costs and other expenses incurred in taking part in the study and may also receive free medical services. They may also be compensated for the income and time lost. The eighth guideline is about the benefits and risks of the study population. The investigator must ensure a balance between potential risks and benefits and that the former are minimised. The ninth guideline places special limitations on risk when research involves individuals who are not capable of giving informed consent. The tenth guideline addresses the special situation of poor populations and communities. Before undertaking research, a sponsor or investigator must ensure that the research is responsive to the health needs and the priorities of the population or community in which it is to be carried out. The sponsor or investigator must also ensure that any intervention or product developed, or knowledge generated, will be made available for the benefit of the population or community.

The tenth guideline deals with choice of control in clinical trials while the twelfth guideline concerns the equitable distribution of burdens and benefits in the selection of groups of subjects in research. The exclusion of groups or communities that might benefit from participation in the research must be justified. Given that vulnerable individuals may lack power, intelligence, education or resources or attributes to protect their rights or interests, the thirteenth guideline calls for special justification for inviting vulnerable individuals to participate in the research. If vulnerable individuals are selected, their rights and welfare must be strictly protected. Research involving vulnerable individuals may for example be justified where the research will yield knowledge that will lead to improved diagnosis, prevention or treatment of diseases or health problems unique to the vulnerable group.

The fourteenth guideline deals with research involving children. The investigator must ensure that the purpose of the research is to obtain knowledge relevant to the health needs of children; a parental or legal representative of each child has given permission; the assent or cooperation of each child has been obtained to the extent of his or her capabilities; and a child's refusal to participate in the research should be respected.[59] The fifteenth guideline is about research involving persons with mental or behavioural disorders. The guideline recognises that persons with mental or behavioural disorders are capable of giving consent. However, some of these persons may be incapable of giving adequately informed consent. Consequently, such persons will not participate in research that might as well be carried out on persons who are capable of giving the requisite consent. The purpose of the research must be to obtain knowledge relevant to the specific health needs of persons with mental or behavioural disorders. The consent of each subject must be obtained to the extent of his or her capabilities and his or her right of refusal must be respected. Where the person lacks capacity to consent, permission may be obtained from a responsible family member or a legally authorised representative.

The Guidelines recognise that women have over the years been excluded from biomedical research and have therefore lost out on the benefits of research. Consequently, the sixteenth guideline enjoins investigators, sponsors or ethical review committees to include women of reproductive age in biomedical research. According to the seventeenth guideline, pregnant women are presumed to be capable of participating in research. However, they should be adequately informed about the risks and benefits to themselves and their fetus. The research to be carried out should be relevant to the specific needs of the pregnant woman or her fetus or to the health needs of women in general.

There have been instances of research subjects suffering injury as a consequence of their involvement in research.[60] Consequently, the nineteenth guideline tackles the question of compensation of subjects who have been injured as the result of their participation in the research. The guideline obliges investigators to ensure that injured subjects receive free medical treatment. They should also be provided with financial or other assistance that would compensate them equitably for any impairment or disability. In case of death of a research subject, the dependents are entitled to compensation. In no circumstances should subjects be required to waive their right to compensation. The twentieth guideline is about strengthening the capacity for ethical and scientific review and biomedical research. The last guideline requires external sponsors to provide health services that are essential to the safe conduct of the research and for treatment of subjects who suffer injury as a result of the research.

59 It should be noted that under common law, whether a child has a right to be included in the clinical trial is a bit uncertain. Perhaps the courts may apply the test in *Gillick v West Norfolk & Wisbech AHA* (1985) 3 All ER 402. Where a child lacks sufficient maturity to personally give consent, researchers have to obtain consent from a parent or guardian. Thus, one of the challenges of research involving children as participants is assessing the capacity of individual children to give genuine consent. See DS Wendler 'Assent in paediatric research: Theoretical and practical considerations' (2006) 32 *Journal of Medical Ethics* 229.

60 See Washington (n 2 above); Mason (n 2 above).

3.5 UNAIDS/WHO Guidance Document

The UNAIDS/WHO Guidance Document (Guidance Document) enjoins researchers and trial sponsors to ensure that the affected community participates in the proposed research. The community should be consulted

> through a transparent and meaningful participatory process which involves them in an early and sustained manner in the design, implementation, monitoring, and distribution of the results of biomedical HIV prevention trials.[61]

Researchers and trial sponsors should carry out such trials only in countries and communities that possess the capacity to carry out independent and competent scientific and ethical reviews.[62] Participation in the trials should be voluntary and the selection of the participants must be fair in accordance with the goals of the research.[63] On informed consent, the Guidance Document provides as follows:

> Each volunteer being screened for eligibility for participation in a biomedical HIV prevention trial should provide voluntary informed consent based on complete, accurate, and appropriately conveyed and understood information before s/he is actually enrolled in the trial. Researchers and research staff should take steps to ensure throughout the trial that participants continue to understand and to participate freely as the trial progresses. Informed consent with pre-and post-test counselling, should also be obtained for any testing for HIV status conducted before, during, and after the trial.[64]

The research protocol should pay particular attention to the rights, the safety, dignity, and welfare of vulnerable participants.[65] Women should be included in clinical trials in order to benefit from future safe and effective biomedical HIV prevention interventions. Women should be provided with adequate information about possible risks to themselves as well as to their foetuses or breastfed infants, where applicable.[66] Children and adolescents should be recruited into clinical trials in order to benefit from future biomedical HIV prevention interventions. Researchers and trial sponsors should pay specific attention to the safety, ethical, and legal considerations relevant for children and adolescents. Their rights and welfare should be safeguarded during participation in the research.[67]

The research protocols should specify the potential harms resulting from participation in the research and the possible measures to minimise

61 Guidance Point 2.
62 Guidance Point 4.
63 Guidance Point 7.
64 Guidance Point 16.
65 Guidance Point 8.
66 Guidance Point 9.
67 Guidance Point 10.

and mitigate or remedy the harm.[68] The protocols should also provide an accurate statement of the anticipated benefits of the trial.[69] Participants who may acquire HIV infection during the trial should be provided access to internationally recognised treatment regimens.[70]

4 The national framework

It is important to point out here that the Constitution is the primary legal instrument that contains human rights and freedoms, which apply to research involving human beings as participants. Thus, researchers, sponsors and others must observe such rights as health;[71] equality and non-discrimination;[72] the right to life;[73] liberty;[74] privacy and confidentiality;[75] and freedom from cruel, torture, inhuman and degrading treatment.[76] In addition to the Constitution, this section considers other instruments, which are critical for the research under scrutiny.

4.1 The Uganda National Council for Science and Technology Act

The Act[77] establishes the Uganda National Council for Science and Technology (UNCST), which is mandated to clear all research to be undertaken in the country.[78] Any person or organisation intending to carry out research in Uganda should register with the council. One of the functions of the UNCST is to advise and coordinate the formulation of an explicit national policy in all fields of science and technology.[79] The UNCST acts as a 'clearing house for information on research and experimental development taking place in scientific institutions, centres and other enterprises and on the potential application of their results'.[80] The council is also mandated 'to work in close cooperation with and coordinate all scientific and technological activities of persons, institutions, sectors and organizations'.[81]

The UNSCT has the power to 'establish specialized committees, research councils, organizations and experimental and development

68 Guidance Point 11.
69 Guidance Point 12.
70 Guidance Point 14.
71 For a discussion of the fundamental right to health, see Chapter 2.
72 Art 21
73 Art 22.
74 Art 23.
75 Art 27.
76 Art 24.
77 Cap 209.
78 Sec 2 of the Act.
79 Sec 4(a).
80 Sec (b)(d).
81 Sec 4(h).

activities or other scientific and technological services'.[82] The Act establishes specialised committees to assist the UNCST execute its mandate and they include, a medical sciences committee, which is responsible for human and veterinary medicines, and a social sciences and humanities committee and such other committees as the council may deem necessary.[83]

4.2 The National Drug Policy and Authority Act

The main purpose of the Act[84] is to ensure the availability of essential, efficacious and cost-effective drugs to the Ugandan population. The Act provides for a national drug policy, which shall inter alia, intensify research in all drugs, including traditional medicines.[85] The Act also establishes a National Drug Authority (NDA), whose functions include the development and regulation of drugs in the country, and encouraging research and development of herbal medicines.[86] According to the Act, the NDA may issue a certificate to any person for the purpose of carrying out clinical trials in respect of a drug that may be specified in the certificate.[87] The Act prohibits any person from carrying out clinical trials in respect of any drug unless he or she is in possession of a certificate issued by the authority.[88]

4.3 The HIV and AIDS Prevention and Control Act 2014

The Act specifically provides for biomedical research in the context of HIV/AIDS and empowers the minister in collaboration with other relevant agencies to

> institute clinical trials on HIV and AIDS vaccines, medicines and other related bio-products within the country provided that such trials shall not endanger the health of persons undergoing such trials.[89]

The research must be in conformity with UNCST guidelines above 'or any other written law in force',[90] which, in my view, include the legal instruments outlined above. The Act requires that the bio-medical research should 'be with the written informed consent of persons on whom research is to be carried out'.[91] In the case of a minor, the parent or guardian should provide the written informed consent.[92] The person should 'be adequately

82 Sec 5(e).
83 Sec 15.
84 Cap 206.
85 Sec 2(g).
86 Sec 5(a) & (g).
87 Sec 40(1).
88 Sec 40(2).
89 Sec 29(1).
90 Sec 29(2).
91 Sec 30(1)(a).

informed of the aims, methods, anticipated benefits and the potential hazards and discomforts of the research'.[93] The participant should also be facilitated.[94]

4.4 The UNCST National Guidelines

The major purpose of the Guidelines, whose design was largely guided by the legal, ethical and administrative frameworks considered above, is to 'provide a national framework for harnessing the benefits of research while ensuring that the rights, interests, values and welfare of research participants are protected'.[95] According to the Guidelines, research involving humans as research participants includes: clinical investigations; social-behavioural studies which involve interaction with or observation of people; basic scientific research to study the biology of persons or organs and specimens; and systemic collection, storage and analysis of data on humans.[96]

The rights of the research participants include: to participate in ethically acceptable research; respect for autonomy, culture, beliefs and values; information about the research; protection against research related injuries, harm and other forms of abuse; privacy and confidentiality; decision whether to participate in the research or not, or withdraw at any time without penalty; access to quality standard of available health care; and compensation for research related injuries and costs.[97] The Guidelines provide that the welfare of research participants can be attained through provision of health care beyond research related care; optimisation of collateral benefits to the research communities; provision of good client care during study investigations and procedures; and taking measures to ensure that the community accesses the test drug or device, if proven beneficial. In order to protect the rights and welfare of the research participants, the Guidelines call for observance of the ethical principles of respect for persons, beneficence, non-malfeasance, and justice.[98]

The Guidelines provide for regulation of research projects by Institutional Review Committees (IRCs), whose main function is to review and approve the projects with the aim of protecting the rights and welfare of research participants. The IRCs have a special role of monitoring research activities to ensure compliance with scientific and ethical

92 Sec 30(1)(b).
93 Sec 30(2).
94 Sec 30(3).
95 UNCST (n 3 above)1. A number of African countries such as Nigeria and Kenya have also developed guidelines for conducting research involving humans. On Nigeria see C Onyemelukwe, 'Regulating research involving humans in Nigeria: Some recent improvements' (2008) 16 *Health Law Review* 36.
96 UNCST (n 3 above) 3.
97 As above.
98 UNCST (n 3 above) 4.

requirements. According to the Guidelines, Scientific Committees may be set up within institutions to review and evaluate all scientific aspects of the research projects paying particular attention to the suitability, relevance and feasibility of the study. According to the Guidelines, study sponsors may establish a Data and Safety Monitoring Board (DSMB) to review data during a clinical trial. The functions of the DSMB are to ensure safety of the study participants; preserve the integrity and credibility of the trial; ensure availability of definitive and reliable results in a timely manner; and make safety related decisions and recommend whether the study should continue or not.

According to the Guidelines, research should be scientifically and ethically valid. The informed consent process should be observed.[99] The potential participants should be accurately informed of the purpose, methods, risks, benefits and alternatives to research so as to make a voluntary decision whether or not to participate. Participants must have an adequate understanding of all the material facts and of the consequences of participation in the research. On consent, the Guidelines provide as follows:

> Seeking consent shall be carried out under circumstances that provide the prospective research participant or the representative sufficient opportunity to consider whether or not to participate and that minimize(s) the possibility of coercion or undue influence. The information that is given to the research participant or the representative, whether it is conveyed orally, in writing or other delivery mechanism, shall be in a language and form understandable to the participant or the representative. No informed consent, oral or written shall include any exculpatory language through which the research participant or representative is: (1) made to waive or appear to waive any of the research participant's rights, or (2) appears to release the investigator, the sponsor, the institution, or its agents from liability.[100]

The Guidelines oblige researchers and trial sponsors to pay particular attention to the rights, interests and welfare of vulnerable persons and groups such as children, mentally ill persons, and disabled children. Before involving a child in research, the risk should be justified by the anticipated benefits to the child and the 'relation of the anticipated benefit to the risk is at least favourable to the research participants [children] as that presented by available alternatives'.[101] It must be shown that the participation of the child is indispensable and is in his or her best interests. It is stressed in the Guidelines that there should not be any financial or other inducements to the child to participate in the research except for reimbursements or a token after completion of the study. For mentally ill persons, consent of each potential research participant should be obtained

99 UNCST (n 3 above) 22-24.
100 UNCST (n 3 above) 23 para 6.2.
101 As above.

to the extent of his or her abilities. For those who are incapable of giving consent, it can be obtained from the guardian or representative.

The Guidelines prohibit research on pregnant women and their fetuses unless appropriate studies have been done on animals and non-pregnant individuals and have been completed and the risk to the fetus is minimal. It must be shown that the purpose of the research project is to meet the health needs of the particular fetus and the parents are legally competent and have given informed consent.

4.5 The Uganda Guidelines for AIDS Research

The main objective of the Guidelines[102] is to provide overall guidance for scientific, legal, ethical and policy issues in HIV/AIDS research, development and evaluation in Uganda. The Guidelines describe Uganda's policy, ethical and legal frameworks for conducting HIV/AIDS research in the country. The Guidelines call for careful consideration of human rights, ethical and legal aspects of conducting HIV/AIDS research.

According to the Guidelines, researchers and trial sponsors should pay particular attention to issues such as informed consent; health care for volunteers; confidentiality; and compensation of volunteers. Individual volunteers should be provided with pre-test counselling each time an HIV test is administered. Post-test counselling including appropriate referrals should also be provided to HIV-infected individuals identified during the screening process. Prevention counselling should also be provided to HIV-free individual volunteers. The Guidelines require written, individual informed consent, which is an on-going process that begins with community outreach and consultation, and continues with one-on-one counselling sessions during the screening and enrolment process. The informed consent must be revisited and reviewed at every study visit.

5 Liability in research involving human as participants

In Chapter 8, we saw that a health care professional such as a doctor has a duty to of care to a patient and breach of that duty may give rise to a medical malpractice action. We also saw in the previous chapter that consent to treatment is at the heart of a patient's right to self-determination and dignity. In this chapter, I stress the fact that researchers, research institutions, review committees, and research sponsors have a responsibility to ensure that informed consent of research subjects is procured. They have a duty to protect human subjects from a foreseeable

102 UAC *Uganda guidelines for AIDS vaccine research: A guide for vaccine research, development and evaluation* (2005).

harm that could occur during the course of the study. Liability will arise where research is conducted without informed consent from the subjects first being obtained. I have not come across local cases on the subject of bio-medical research. However, cases such as *Halushka* and *Weiss* below are persuasive authorities for the thesis that the standard of obtaining consent in the research context is higher than the standard of consent to treatment, which we saw in the preceding chapter.

In the Canadian case of *Halushka v University of Saskatchewan & Others*,[103] the defendants were conducting research in the field of anaesthesia. The plaintiff agreed to participate in the test of a new anaesthetic drug after being assured by the doctors that their experiment was a safe test. The plaintiff was not told about the risks and never had any therapeutic benefits of the research. He sued the doctors for trespass to the person and negligence. Hall J stated that the subject of medical experimentation is entitled to a full and frank disclosure of all the facts, probabilities and options which a reasonable man might be expected to consider before giving his consent. The judge emphasised that research participants are entitled to full and frank disclosure of all 'facts, probabilities and opinions'[104] that a reasonable person would wish to consider before providing consent.

In *Weiss v Solomon*,[105] a 62 year old patient who had undergone cataract surgery was recommended by a surgeon to participate in a study on the ability of an eye drop solution to diminish the retinal swelling that tends to follow that operation. He volunteered to participate in the study. The consent form stated as follows:

> Some patients may develop a minor allergic reaction to this injection, but the majority of patients have no side effects ... I have been told the possible side effects and unfavorable reactions that can happen and what my alternatives are. I have had a chance to ask questions to the doctor and have received acceptable answers.[106]

Shortly after being injected, the patient's blood pressure dropped and he died. The deceased family sued the principal investigator, the hospital and a physician. The Quebec Supreme Court decided the case in favour of the plaintiff on grounds that the informed consent procedure was flouted. The court found that the duty to inform in matters relating to purely scientific experimentation is the most exacting possible and includes the disclosure of all known risks including those that are remote, especially if they may result in grave consequences. De Blois stated:

103 53 DLR 2d 436 (1965).
104 *Halushka* (n 103 above) 444.
105 (1988) AQ 312 (Sup Ct).
106 *Weiss* (n 105 above) 396.

> The Research Committee of the hospital must be aware of that which its participants and members know. Even if the consent form to be obtained from the research subjects does not fall under any regulations, we should ask ourselves why the risk ... was minimized in the consent form, whereas it should have been explained in detail.[107]

It should be noted that a plaintiff may decide to base his or her claim on the common law principles of malpractice under tort law. However, the plaintiff may also decide to invoke human rights law, alleging violations of the right to self-determination, human dignity, and privacy as provided in the instruments considered above. In *Gelsinger v Trustees of the University of Pennsylvania,*[108] an 18 year old male with a rare genetic liver disease, enrolled in a phase I clinical trial of gene-therapy treatment conducted at the University of Pennsylvania. A serious unfavourable reaction occurred, and Gelsinger experienced multiple organ failure and died days later. The plaintiffs sued the trustees of the university, 2 hospitals affiliated with the research, the former dean of the medical school and a bioethicist. They based the claim on wrongful death, assault and battery due to a lack of informed consent, and fraud or misrepresentation linked to the informed consent process. They alleged a conflict of interest on the part of the primary investigator in terms of pecuniary gain for trial success; failure to report previous adverse effects; the enrolment of unqualified subjects including Gelsinger; and approval of inadequate informed consent documents and procedures.[109] However, the case was settled out of court.

In *Robertson v McGhee,*[110] a Protocol for Phase I study of a cancer vaccine was approved. Many of the patients who enrolled in the study had advanced disease, were unresponsive to standard therapies and had very poor prognoses. The vaccine was received by 92 subjects but unfortunately 29 died in the course of the study. The clinical trial's nurse coordinator had advised the Institutional Review Board's Chair of problems with quality control, patient care, reporting of adverse events, and adherence to the study protocol. In 2000, the Office of Human Research Protection had also found that the IRB Chair had unilaterally approved retrospective changes to the research protocol, and that continuing review had not been properly carried out. The IRB had also failed to ensure that additional safeguards were included in the study. The consent forms also did not adequately describe the study's risks, and overstated its benefits. There were even problems of privacy and confidentiality. The plaintiffs sued the hospital, the principal investigator, the sponsor, a top university official and the bioethicist for specific, general and punitive damages. However, the court dismissed the case on a technicality: that it had no jurisdiction to hear the case. It should be noted that the *Robertson* case was based on international

107 *Weiss* (n 105 above) 315.
108 Phila Cnty Ct of CP filed18 September 2000.
109 For an elaborate discussion of the *Gelsinger* case, see MR Onixt & RL Sterling 'Institutional review board liability for adverse outcomes' (2009) 11 *Virtual Mentor* 306.
110 No 01CV00G0H (M) (ND Okla, filed 29 January 2001).

law rather than the standard medical malpractice. The plaintiffs alleged, amongst other things, the breach of the right to be treated with dignity, citing the Nuremberg Code and the Declaration of Helsinki examined above.

In *Abdullahi v Pfizer*,[111] it was alleged that the defendant improperly administered an experimental antibiotic to children in Nigeria during an outbreak of bacterial meningitis, measles and cholera in Kano, Northern Nigeria. The guardians of some of the children instituted a suit in the Southern District of New York, alleging violations of norms of international law contained in instruments such as the Nuremberg Code, the Declaration of Helsinki, the ICCPR, and the US Food and Drug Administration's regulations. They also averred that the court had jurisdiction over the matter under the Alien Torts Claim Act. The case was sent back to the District Court to determine whether the US or Nigeria was the appropriate forum for the case.

6 Conclusion

Medical research involving humans as participants has significantly contributed to the understanding of disease and other health challenges. However, the research may also present burdens and risks to the volunteers or patients who participate in the research. If not effectively regulated, medical experimentation on humans may have deleterious consequences for human health.

There are sufficient legal, ethical and administrative frameworks to regulate, monitor and evaluate research involving human participants in Uganda. These frameworks, which may be strengthened by the common law principles on consent considered in the preceding chapter, stress the importance of informed consent and the need to minimise risks and maximise benefits for research participants and their communities. Thus, researchers and sponsors must focus on the rights, interests, welfare and the general well-being of the research participants especially the vulnerable and disadvantaged members of society such as women, children and persons with mental disorders. Researchers should take into account gender differences in the study design and analysis so that women and men's special health interests are catered for. Researchers must take reasonable care not to subject the participants to harm. Participants who suffer injury or harm should be compensated and provided with the necessary health care. Participants should where possible be involved in the formulation of the research instruments so that they are able to know what the research is about and the consequences of participation. Researchers should avoid a paternalistic attitude by openly discussing the

111 77 Fed App 48 (2d Cir 2003).

benefits and risks of research with the participants. The latter should receive feedback from the researchers about the results of the research and how they will benefit from it. Researchers should be aware that failure to observe critical elements of the research process such as informed consent may give rise to an action in trespass and or negligence.

The UNCST should actively play its regulatory role by ensuring that the standards set out in the above instruments are observed. It should monitor the activities of researchers and investigators to ensure that the consent obtained from the participants is genuine and is in the latters' best interests. There is a need for UNCST to sensitise and educate potential participants about their rights so that they are able to challenge any unscrupulous actions of the researchers and their sponsors, who may seek to take advantage of poverty and the low level of awareness amongst the people. The UNCST national guidelines should be translated into local languages and distributed to communities.

UNCST should ensure that any research carried out is culturally appropriate and in the best interests of the participants and their communities. Short of this, the benefits would enrich the multinational drug companies sponsoring the research to the detriment of the country. In the long run, the government should build capacity in the field of scientific research so that it does not depend on developing countries and their pharmaceutical companies to conduct research in the field of health care.

As cases from other jurisdictions have illustrated, researchers, review boards, sponsors and doctors must ensure that research involving human as participants is carried out in accordance with norms and standards such as informed consent, dignity, privacy and confidentiality, which are outlined in the instruments considered above. Short of this, they might be arraigned in court for special, general and punitive damages, and of course this compromises the reputation of the researchers and the institutions they are attached to, including universities and hospitals.

BIBLIOGRAPHY

Abbey, FT 'An assessment of the legal securities and uncertainties of persons with disabilities in Eritrea' (2013) 19 *East African Journal of Peace and Human Rights* 60

Acheson, D (1998) *Committee of inquiry into the future development of the public health function* London: HMSO

Adila, H; Heywood, M & Berger, J (2007) *Health and democracy: A guide to human rights, health law and policy in post apartheid South Africa* South Africa: Siber Ink

Ahaibwe, G & Kasirye, I 'EPRC policy brief: Reducing the burden of malaria among children in Uganda' http://www.eprc.or.ug/pdf_files/policybrief20.pdf (accessed 5 June 2013)

Alastair Mullis & Ken Oliphant (2003) *Torts* 3rd ed New York: Palgrave Macmillan

Benator, SR 'Avoiding exploitation in clinical research' (2000) 9 *Cambridge Quarterly of Healthcare Ethics* 526

Blackstone, W *Commentaries on the laws of England (1765-1769)* http://www.lonang.com/exlibris/blackston (accessed 6 August 2013)

Bonthuys, E 'Women's sexuality in the South African Constitutional Court' (2006) 14 *Feminist Legal Studies* 391

Boyle, A 'Some reflections on the relationship of treaties and soft law' (1999) 48 *International and Comparative Law Quarterly* 901

Braiser, M & Loibojoit, M (eds) (1991) *Protecting the vulnerable: Autonomy and consent in health care* London: Routledge

Brand, D (2006) 'Socio-economic rights and courts in South Africa: Justiciability on a sliding scale' in Coomans, F (ed) (2006) *Justiciability of economic and social rights: Experiences from domestic systems* Antwerp/Oxford: Intersentia

Breslow, L 'A quantitative approach to the World Health Organization definition of health: Physical, mental and social well-being' (1972) 4 *International Journal of Epidemiology*347

Bridge, C 'Parental beliefs and medical treatment of children' (1994) *Butterworth's Family Law Journal* 131

Burns, JK 'The mental health gap in South Africa: A human rights issue' (2011) 6 *The Equal Rights Review* 99

Caldwell, JC 'The international conference on population and development, Cairo 1994: Is it important, desirable and feasible?' (1996) 6 *Forum: Health Transition Review* 71

Cameron, S & Lynch, A 'Undue influence, consent and medical treatment' (2003) 96 *Journal of the Royal Society of Medicine* 598

Choper, JH 'The political question doctrine: Suggested criteria' http://www.scholarship.law.duke/cgi/viewcontent.cgi?article=1258&content:dlj (accessed 15 March 2014)

Combrinck, H & Mute, LM 'Developments regarding disability rights during 2013: The African Charter and African Commission on Human and Peoples' Rights' (2014) *African Disability Rights Yearbook* 309

Corley, R; Robert, N; Holmes, EM & Williams, JR (1982) *Fundamentals of business law* London: Prentice Hall

Correa, C (2002) *Intellectual property rights, the WTO and developing countries: The TRIPS agreement and policy options* London & New York: Zed Books

Correa, S & Petchesky, R 'Reproductive and sexual rights: A feminist perspective' in Sen, G; Germain, A & Chen, L (1994) *Population policies reconsidered* Boston: Harvard Centre for Population and Development Studies

Detels, R; Beaghole, R; Lansang, MA & Gulliford, M (eds) (2011) *Oxford textbook of public health* 5th ed Oxford: Oxford University Press

Dimopoulous, A (2013) *Issues in human rights of intellectually disabled persons* England: Ashgate Publishing Limited

Dugard, J & Theunis, R 'The record of the South African Constitutional Court in providing an institutional voice for the poor: 1995-2004' in Gargarelle, R; Domingo, P & Theunis, R (eds) (2006) *Courts and social transformation in new democracies: An institution voice for the poor?* Burlington: Ashgate Publishing Limited

Durojaye, E 'The approaches of the African Commission to the right to health under the African Charter' (2013) 17 *Law, Democracy and Development* 393

EAC *Regional intellectual property policy on the utilization of public health-related WTO-TRIPS flexibilities and the approximation of national intellectual property legislation*http://www.cehurd.org/wp-content/uploads/downloads/2013/05/EAC-TRIPS-Policy.pdf (accessed 20 February 2014)

Fayd, E; Michelle, F; Sharon Kleintjes, S; Ofori-Atta, A; Ssembunya, J; Mwanza, J; Kim, K & Flisher, A 'An assessment of mental health policy in Ghana, South Africa, Uganda and Zambia' (2011) 9 *Health Research Systems* 17

Fregmen, BF (2009) *Medical law and ethics* New Jersey: Pearson Education, Inc

Garaffa, V; Solbakk, JH; Vidal, S & Lorenzo, C 'Between the needy and the greedy: The quest for a just and fair ethics of clinical research' (2010) 36 *Journal of Medical Ethics* 500

Gargarelle, R; Domingo, P & Theunis, R (eds) (2006) *Courts and social transformation in new democracies: An institution voice for the poor?* Burlington: Ashgate Publishing Limited

Garner, BA (ed) (2003) *Black's law dictionary* St Paul: West Publishing Co

Gostin, LO (1999) 'Public health law: Power, duty and restraint: A resource guide' http://www.turningpointprogram.org (accessed 3 July 2013)

Gostin, LO (2000) *Public health law: Power, duty, restraint*, 2nd ed California: California University Press

Gostin, LO 'Human rights of persons with mental disabilities' (2000) 23 *International Journal of Law and Psychiatry* 125

Gostin, LO (2002) 'State public health Law: Assessment report' (2002) http://www.publichealth.net/Resources (accessed 11 January 2013)

Gostin, LO & Lance Gable, 'The human rights of persons with mental disabilities: A global perspective on application of human rights principles to mental health' (2004) 63 *Maryland Law Review* http://scholarship/law.georgetown.edu/cgi/viewconte (accessed 18 December 2014)

Gostin, LO (ed) (2009) *Public health law and ethics: A reader* California: Milbank Books

Gostin, LO (2014) *Global health law* Harvard: Harvard University Press

Goh, CS (2012) 'Regulation of the practice of traditional medicine in China, India and Malaysia' unpublished PhD thesis, University of Leeds

Ham, C; Dingwall, R; Fenn, P; & Harris, D (1988) *Medical negligence, compensation and accountability* Oxford: Kings Fund Institute

Hartmut, H 'A fresh look at soft law' (1999) 3 *European Journal of International law* 499

Herr, S (2005) 'Self-determination, autonomy, and alternatives to guardianship', in Herr, S; Gostin, LO & Koh, H (eds) *The human rights of persons with intellectual disabilities* Oxford: Oxford University Press

Holland, W 'HIV/AIDS and the criminal law' (1994) 36 *Criminal Law Quarterly* 316

Huber, M; Knottnerus, JA; Green, L; Van der Horst, H; Jadad, AR; Kromhout, D; Leonard, B; Lorig, K; Loureiro, MI; Van der Meer, JW; Schnabel, P; Smith, R; Van Weel, C & Smid, H 'How should we define health?' (2011) *British Medical Journal* 343

Human, D & Fluss, S 'The World Medical Association's declaration of Helsinki: Historical and contemporary perspectives' http://www.wma.net/e/ethicsunit/pdf/draft_contemporary_perspectives.pdf (accessed on 3 February 2014)

Institute of Medicine (1988) *The future of public health* Washington DC: National Academies Press

Jeanmarie, F; Galizzi, P & Higgins, TE (2011) *The future of African customary law* Cambridge: Cambridge University Press

Jones, M (2008) *Medical negligence* 4th ed London: Sweet & Maxwell

Kabau, T & Njoroge, C 'The application of international law in Kenya under the 2010 Constitution: Critical issues in the harmonization of the legal system' (2011) 44 *Comparative and International Law Journal of Southern Africa* 3

Khabele, M; Kwesi Kwaa, P & Toulou, L (eds) (2008) *The state, democracy and poverty eradication in Africa* Johannesburg: Global Print

Kabumba, B 'The application of international law in the Ugandan judicial system: A critical inquiry' in Killander, M (ed) (2010) *International law and domestic human rights litigation in Africa* Pretoria: Pretoria University Law Press

Kadaaga, HF; Ajeani, J; Ononge, S; Alele, PE; Nakasujja, N; Manabe, Y & Kakaire, O 'Prevalence and factors associated with use of herbal medicines among women attending an infertility clinic in Uganda' (2014) 14 *BMC Complementary and Alternative Medicine* 27

Kakooza, JMN 'The application of customary law in Uganda' (2003) 1 *Uganda Living Law Journal* 23

Kalson, V; Robert, V; Kalson, KMB & Webb, DJ 'The revision of the Declaration of Helsinki: Past, present and future' (2004) 57 *British Journal of Clinical Pharmacology* 695

Kamatenesi-Mugisha, M & Oryem-Origa, H 'Traditional herbal medicines used in the management of sexual and erectile dysfunction in western Uganda' (2005) 14 *Africa Health Sciences* 40

Khor, M 'Patents and access to medicines: What can be done at the national level?' (2004) *Third World Network Briefing Paper* 5

Kigozi, F (2007) 'Integrating mental health into primary health care: Uganda's experience' *South African Psychiatry Review* 10

Kigozi, F; Ssebunya, J; Kiiza, D; Cooper, S; Ndyanabangi, S & the Mental Health and Poverty Project (2010) 'An overview of Uganda's mental health care system: results from an assessment using the World Health Organization's assessment instrument for mental health systems (WHO-AIMS)' *International Journal of Mental Health Systems* 1

Killander, M (ed) (2010) *International law and domestic human rights litigation in Africa* Pretoria: Pretoria University Law Press

Kinney, ED 'The international human right to health: What does this mean for our nation and world?' (2001) 34 *Indiana Law Review* 1457

Kiwanuka, GN 'Malaria morbidity and mortality in Uganda' (2003) 40 *Journal of Vector Borne Diseases* 16

Lord, JE (2009) 'Disability rights and the human rights mainstream: Reluctant gate-crasher' in Clifford, B (ed) *The international struggle for new human rights* Philadelphia: University of Pennsylvania Press

Macpherson, CC 'Global ethics: Did the universal declaration on bioethics miss the boat?' (2007) 33 *Journal of Medical Ethics* 588

Mann, JA; Grodin, MA; Gruskin, S & Annas, GJ (1999) *Health and human rights: A reader* London: Routledge

Mason, MB 'International protection of persons undergoing medical experimentation: Protecting the right to informed consent' (2002) 20 *Berkley Journal of International Law* 513

Mbazira, C (2008) 'Public interest litigation and judicial activism in Uganda: Improving the enforcement of economic, social and cultural rights' HURIPEC Working Paper

Mbazira, C (2009) 'The legal nature of socio-economic rights: Are they capable of judicial enforcement?' in Mbazira, C (2009) *Litigating socio-economic rights in South Africa: A choice between corrective and distributive justice* Pretoria: Pretoria University Law Press

Mbazira, C (2009) *Litigating socio-economic rights in South Africa: A choice between corrective and distributive justice* Pretoria: Pretoria University Law Press

McCall-Smith, A 'Criminal negligence and the incompetent doctor' (1993) 1 *Medical Law Review* 33

McHale, J; Fox, M; Gunn, M & Wilkson, S (1997) *Health care law: Texts and materials* London: Sweet & Maxwell

McLean, S (1989) *A patient's right to know: Information disclosure, the doctor and the law* Aldershot: Dartmoth

Meena, R (ed) (1992) *Gender in Southern Africa: Conceptual and theoretical issues* Harare: SAPES Books

Mental Health and Poverty Project 'Mental health reform in Uganda' Policy Brief 3 http://r4d.dfid.gov.uk/PDF/Outputs/MentalHealth_RPC/MHPB_Uganda 3.pdf

Ministry of Health (2001) *National training curriculum for health workers on adolescent health and development: Trainee handbook* Kampala: Ministry of Health

Ministry of Health (2006) *The national policy guidelines and service standards for sexual and reproductive health and rights* Kampala: Ministry of Health

Ministry of Health (2009) *Patients' charter* Kampala: Ministry of Health

Ministry of Health (2010) *National health policy 2010*http://www.health.go.ug (accessed 20 February 2013)

Ministry of Health (2010) *Health sector strategic plan, 2010/11-14* Kampala: Ministry of Health

Ministry of Health (2010) *Uganda national malaria control strategic plan* 2010/11-2014/15 Kampala: Ministry of Health

Ministry of Health (2011) *Sero-Behavioural Survey* Kampala: Ministry of Health

Ministry of Health (2012) *The national policy guidelines and service standards for sexual and reproductive health and rights* Kampala: Ministry of Health

Ministry of Health (2012) *National strategic plan for HIV/AIDS 2011/12-2014/15 (revised)* http://www.health.go.ug (accessed 1 March 2014)

Ministry of Health 'The burden of malaria in Uganda' http://www.health.go.ug/malaria.htm (accessed 10 January 2014)

Ministry of Health (2015) *The national policy guidelines and service standards for sexual and reproductive health and rights* Kampala: Ministry of Health

Montgomery, J 'Power/knowledge/consent: Medical decision making' (1988) 51 *Modern Law Review* 245

Montgomery, J (2003) *Health care law* 2nd ed New York: Oxford University Press

Moszynski, P 'New malaria drugs need subsidy, study finds' (2008) *British Medical Journal* 12

Mubangizi, JC & Twinomugisha, BK 'Protecting the right to freedom of sexual orientation: What can Uganda learn from South Africa?' (2011) 22 *Stellenbosch Law Review* 330

Mukubwa, GP 'International human rights norms in the domestic arena' (1997) *East African Journal of Peace and Human Rights* 33

Mullis, A & Oliphant, K (2003) *Torts* 3rd ed New York: Palgrave Macmillan

Mulumba, M 'Analysis of the Uganda Mental Treatment Act from a human rights and public health perspective' http://www.pages.ssm.com/so13/papers.cfm/abstract-id=10006230 (accessed18 May 2015)

Murray, LR; Lippman, SA; Donini, AA & Kerrigan, D '"She is a professional like anyone else": Social identity among Brazilian sex workers' (2010) 12*Culture, Health and Sexuality* 293

Murthy, D 'The future of compulsory licensing: Deciphering the Doha Declaration on the TRIPS agreement and public health' (2002) 17 *American University International Law Review* 1299 http://www.auilr.org/pdf/17/17-6-4.pdf (accessed 19 June 2013)

Musungu, SF 'The right to health, intellectual property, and competition principles' in Cottier,T; Joost, P & Elisabeth, B (eds) (2005) *Human rights and international trade* Oxford: Oxford University Press

Musungu, S; Villaneva, S, & Blasetti, R (2004) *Utilizing TRIPS flexibilities for public health protection through South-South co-operation* Geneva: South Centre

Mental Health and Poverty Project 'Mental health reform in Uganda' Policy Brief 3 http://r4d.dfid.gov.uk/PDF/Outputs/MentalHealth_RPC/MHPB_Uganda 3.pdf

Micah, RO & Robyn, L Sterling 'Institutional review board liability for adverse outcomes' (2009) 11 *Virtual Mentor* 306

McLean, S *A patient's right to know: Information disclosure, the doctor and the law* (1989)

Ndeezi, A (2004) *The Disability Movement in Uganda* Kampala: NUDIPU

Ngwena, C 'The history and transformation of abortion law in South Africa' (1998) 32 *Acta Academia* 50

Ngwena, C 'Deconstructing the definition of disability under the Employment Equity Act: Legal deconstruction' (2007) 23 *South African Journal of Human Rights* 156

Ngwena, C 'Inscribing abortion as a human right: Significance of the protocol on the rights of women in Africa' (2010) 32 *Human Rights Quarterly* 783

Ngwena, C '*Western Cape Forum for Intellectual Disability v Government of the Republic of South Africa*: A case study of contradictions in inclusive education' (2013) *African Disability Rights Yearbook* 139

Ngwena, C (2014) 'Using human rights to realize access to safe, legal abortion in Uganda' CEHURD Discussion Series

Ngwena, C & Durojaye, E (eds) (2014) *Strengthening the protection of sexual and reproductive health and rights in the African region through human rights* Pretoria: Pretoria University Law Press

Novick, FL & Morrow, CB 'Historical and contemporary developments' http://www.jblearning.com/samples/076373842 (accessed 4 July 2013)

Nyandekwe, M; Nzayirambaho, M; & Kakoma, JB 'Universal health coverage in Rwanda: Dream or reality?' (2014) 17 *Pan African Medical Journal* 232

Nyombi, C 'A critical review of the mental health treatment bill (2012) 18 *East African Journal of Peace and Human Rights* 499

Nyombi, C; Kibandama, A & Kaddu, R 'A critique of the Uganda Mental Health Treatment Act, 1964' (2014) 3 *Mental Health Law and Policy Journal* 505

O'Neill Institute (2014) T-388/2009 'Conscientious objection and abortion: A global perspective on the Colombian experience' Torreblanca AG: Georgetown University

Onyemelukwe, C 'Regulating research involving humans in Nigeria: Some recent improvements' (2008) 16 *Health Law Review* 36

Otieno, LS; McLigeyo, SO & Luta, M 'Acute renal failure following the use of herbal remedies' (1991) 14 *East African Medical Journal* 993

Perlin, ML 'International human rights and comparative mental disability law: The role of institutional psychiatry in the suppression of political dissent' (2006) 39 *Israel Law Review* 69

Pieterse, M 'Coming to terms with judicial enforcement of socio-economic rights' (2004) 20 *South African Journal on Human Rights* 383

Plomer, A 'In defence of Helsinki and human rights' (2012) 5 *South African Journal of Bioethics & Law* 83

Prada, E; Mirembe, F; Ahmed, FH; Nalwadda, R & Kiggundu, C (2005) *Abortion and post abortion care in Uganda: a report from health care professionals and health facilities*New York: The Alan Guttmacher Institute

Republic of Uganda (2010) *National development plan 2010/11-2014/15* http://www.opm.go.ug/assets/media/resources/30/NationalDevelopmentPlan201:11-2014:15.pdf (accessed 20 March 2013)

Reynolds, C (2011) *Public and environmental health law* 3rd ed Federation Press

Robertson, G 'Informed consent to medical treatment' (1981) 97 *Law Quarterly Review* 102

Robyn, M 'Law as a tool in promoting and protecting public health: Always in our best interests?' (2007) 121 *Public Health* 846

Rogers, WVH (2006) *Winfield & Jolowicz on tort* (17th ed) London: Sweet & Maxwell

Rothstein, MA 'Rethinking the meaning of public health' (2002) 20 *The Journal of Law, Medicine and Ethics* 144

Rutebemberwa, E; Lubega, M; Katureebe, S; Abanga, O; Kiweewa, F & Mukanga, D (2013) 13 *BMC International Health and Human Rights* 1

Rosenthal, E & Rusbenstein, LS 'International human rights advocacy under the "Principles for the protection of persons with mental illness"' (1993) 16 *International Journal of Law & Psychiatry* 268

Scott, LC & Deborah, LR 'Public interest litigation: Insights from theory and practice' (2009) 26 *Fordham Urban Law Journal* 603

Sellin, J (2014) *Access to medicines: The interface between patents and human rights* School of Human Rights Series: Intersentia

Shakespeare, T 'The social model of disability: An outdated ideology?' (2002) 2 *Research in social science and disability* 9

Sharyl, JN; Levit, LA & Gostin, LO (2009) *Beyond the HIPPA privacy rule: Enhancing privacy, improving health through research* Washington DC: National Academies Press

Shelton, D 'Soft law' in Armstrong, D (ed) (2009) *Routledge handbook of international law* London: Routledge 68

Shue, H (1996) *Basic rights: Subsistence, affluence and US foreign policy* 2nd ed Princeton: Princeton University Press

Simangele, M & Ngwena, C (2014) 'Access to legal abortion for rape as a reproductive health right: A commentary on the abortion regimes of Swaziland and Ethiopia' in Durojaye, E (eds) *Strengthening the protection of sexual and reproductive health and rights in the African region through human rights* Pretoria: Pretoria University Law Press

Simma, B & Alston, P 'The source of human rights law: Custom, jus cogens, and general principles' (1992) 12 *Australian Law Book of International Law* 82

Singh, S; Prada, E; Mirembe, F & Kiggundu, C 'The incidence of induced abortion in Uganda' (2005) 31 *International Family Planning Perspectives* 183

Sonya, D 'Unintended consequences of regulating traditional medicine' (2013) 2 *World Health Organization South East Asia Journal of Public Health* 131

Sophie, H 'The dual feminisation of HIV/AIDS' (2011) 8 *Gender, Governance and Power* 213

Ssebunya, J; Kigozi, F; Kiiza, D & Ndyanabangi, S 'Integration of mental health care into primary health care in a rural district in Uganda' (2010) 13 *African Journal of Psychiatry* 128

Stanford Encyclopedia of Philosophy 'Disability: Definitions, Models, Experience' (2011) http://www.plato.stanford.edu/entries/disability/ (accessed 21 November 2014)

Szmukler, G; Daw, R & Callard, F 'Mental health law and the UN Convention on the rights of persons with disabilities' (2014) *International Journal of Law & Psychiatry* 245

Tamale, S 'The right to culture and the culture of rights: A critical perspective on women's sexual rights in Africa' (2008) *16 Feminist Legal Studies* 47

Tamale, S 'Paradoxes of sex work and sexuality in modern-day Uganda' (2009) 15 *East African Journal of Peace and Human Rights* 69

Thakur, JS; Gargi, R; Narain, JP & Menabde, N 'Tobacco use: A major risk factor for non-communicable diseases in South-East Asia region' (2011) 55 *Indian Journal of Public Health* 155

Thuo, GT 'The legal status of the Doha Declaration on TRIPS and public health under the Vienna convention on the law of treaties' (2002) 15 *Harvard Journal of Law and Technology* 291

Tobey, JA (1947) *Public health law* 3rd ed New York: Commonwealth Fund

Tullock, G 'Does punishment deter crime?' (1974) 36 *The Public Interest* 103

Turnock, BJ (2001) *Public health: What is it and how it works* (2nd ed) Gaithersburg: Aspen Publishers

Twinomugisha, BK (1996) 'The development of the law relating to the protection of the ozone layer with particular reference to the position of developing countries' unpublished LLM thesis, Makerere University

Twinomugisha, BK (2004) 'Protection of rural poor women's right of access to maternal health care in Uganda: The case of Kashambya sub-county, Kabale district' unpublished LLD thesis, Makerere University

Twinomugisha, BK 'Some reflections on judicial protection of the right to a clean and healthy environment in Uganda' (2007) 3 *Law, Environment and Development Law Journal* 246

Twinomugisha, BK 'Exploring judicial strategies to protect the right of access to emergency obstetric care in Uganda' (2007) 7 *African Human Rights Law Journal* 283

Twinomugisha, BK 'Implications of the TRIPS agreement for the protection of the right of access to medicines in Uganda' (2008) 2 *Malawi Law Journal* 253

Twinomugisha, BK (2008) 'A critique of Uganda's PEAP' in Khabele Matlosa; Kwesi Kwaa, P, & Toulou, L (eds) (2008) *The state, democracy and poverty eradication in Africa* Johannesburg: Global Print

Twinomugisha, BK (2008) 'Beyond social programmes: Protection of the right of access to malaria treatment in Uganda' HURIPEC Working Paper

Twinomugisha, BK 'African customary law and women's human rights in Uganda' in Jeanmarie, F; Galizzi, P & Higgins, TE (2011) *The future of African customary law* Cambridge: Cambridge University Press

Twinomugisha, BK (2012) 'Beyond "malaya" or prostitute: Interrogating sexual and reproductive health rights of young female commercial sex workers in the context of HIV/AIDS in Uganda' HURIPEC Working Paper

Twinomugisha, BK (2012) 'Beyond juridical approaches: What role can the gender perspective play in interrogating the right to health in Africa?' in Viljoen, F (ed) (2012) *Beyond the law: Multidisciplinary perspectives on human rights* Pretoria: Pretoria University Law Press

Uganda AIDS Commission (2005) *Uganda guidelines for AIDS vaccine research: A guide for Vaccine Research Development and Evaluation* Kampala: UAC

Uganda AIDS Commission (2010) *Uganda AIDS Indicator Survey 2011* Kampala: UAC

UBOS (2006) *Uganda demographic & health survey 2006* Entebbe: UBOS

UBOS (2012) *Uganda demographic and health survey 2011* Kampala: UBOS

UBOS & IFC Macro (2010) *Uganda malaria indicator survey 2009* Claverton: UBOS & IFC Macro

Uganda Medical and Dental Practitioners Council (UMDPC) (2002) *Guidelines in respect of complaints against medical and dental practitioners* Kampala: UMDPC

UMDPC/USAID (2013) *Code of professional ethics* Kampala: UMDPC

Uganda National Council for Science and Technology (2007) *National guidelines for research involving humans as research participants* Kampala: UNCST

UNAIDS (2009) *Guidance note on HIV and sex work* Geneva: UNAIDS

UNAIDS (2011) *Presidential malaria initiative Uganda, malaria operational plan for 2012* USA: USAID

UNDP (2012) Global Commission on HIV and the Law: Risks, Rights and Health New York: UNDP

UPIAS (1976) *Fundamental principles of disability* London: Union of the Physically Impaired against Segregation

Verweij, M & Dawson, A 'The meaning of "public" in public health' http://fds.oup.com/www.oup.co.uk/pdf/o-19-9 (accessed 4 July 2013)

Walker, N (1991) *Why punish?* Oxford: Oxford University Press

Washington, HA 'Medical apartheid: The dark history of medical experimentation on black Americans from colonial times to the present' (2007) 20 *Social History of Medicine* 620

Wendler, DS 'Assent in paediatric research: Theoretical and practical considerations' (2006) 32 *Journal of Medical Ethics* 229

White, CMN 'African customary law: The problem of concept and definition' (1965) 9 *Journal of African Law* 86

WHO (1948) *The Constitution* WHO: Geneva

WHO (1978) Declaration of Ama-Ata (International Conference on primary Health Care, Alma-Ata, USSR, 6-12 September 1978) http://who/int/publications/almaata_declaration_en.pdf (accessed 21 April 2014)

WHO (1981) *International code of marketing of breast milk substitutes* Geneva: WHO

WHO (1986) *The Ottawa charter for health promotion*. Adopted at the First International Conference on Health Promotion, Ottawa, 21 November 1986 WHO/HPR/HEP/95.1

WHO (1996) *Mental health care law: Ten basic principles* Geneva: WHO

WHO (2002) *25 Questions on health and human rights* Geneva: WHO

WHO (2002) *Traditional medicine strategy 2002-2005* Geneva: WHO

WHO (2003) *Mental health legislation and human rights* Geneva: WHO

WHO (2004) *Guidelines on developing consumer information on proper use of traditional, complementary and alternative medicines* Geneva: WHO

WHO (2004) Global strategy on diet, physical activity and health WHA 57.17

WHO (2005) *Resource book on mental health, human rights and legislation* Geneva: WHO

WHO (2006) *Defining sexual health* Geneva: WHO

WHO (2006) *Report on the mental health systems in Uganda* Geneva: WHO

WHO (2008) *UN Convention on the rights of persons with disabilities: A major step forward in promoting and protecting rights* Geneva: WHO

WHO (2009) *Action plan for the global strategy for the prevention and control of non-communicable diseases* Geneva: WHO

WHO (2010) *Mental health and development: Targeting people with mental health disabilities as a vulnerable group* Geneva: WHO

WHO (2011) *World health statistics 2011*Geneva: WHO

WHO (2011) *Unsafe abortion: Global and regional estimates of the incidence of abortion and associated mortality in 2008*Geneva: WHO

WHO (2012) *Safe abortion: Technical and policy guidance for health systems*, 2nd ed Geneva: WHO

WHO (2013) *Traditional medicine strategy 2014-2023* Geneva: WHO

WHO 'Disabilities' www.who.int/topics/disabilties/en/ (accessed 2 November 2014)

WHO *Guidelines for the promotion of human rights of persons with mental disorders* http://www.who,int/mental_health/policy/legislation/guidelines_promotion.pdf?ua=1 (accessed 24 November 2014)

WHO *Mental health: A state of well-being* http://www.who.int/features/factfile/mental_health/an (accessed 1 December 2014)

Wilmshurst, P 'Scientific imperialism: If they won't benefit from the findings, poor people in the developing world should not be used in research' (1997) 314 *British Medical Journal* 840

Winslow, CEA 'The united fields of public health' (1920) 51 *Science* 22

Yamin, AE 'Not just a tragedy: Access to medication as a right under international law' (2000) *Boston University International Law Journal* 21

Yamin, AE & Gloppen, S (eds) (2001) *Litigating health rights: Can courts bring justice to health?* Harvard: Harvard University Press

Yamin, AE & Rosenthal, E 'Out of the shadows: Using human rights to secure dignity and well-being for people with mental disabilities' (2005) 2 *PLOS Medicine* 296

Permissions

All chapters in this book were first published in FHLU, by Pretoria University Law Press (PULP) by Ben Kiromba Twinomugisha; hereby published with permission under the Creative Commons Attribution License or equivalent. Every chapter published in this book has been scrutinized by our experts. Their significance has been extensively debated. The topics covered herein carry significant information for a comprehensive understanding. They may even be implemented as practical applications or may be referred to as a beginning point for further studies.

We would like to thank the editorial team for lending their expertise to make the book truly unique. They have played a crucial role in the development of this book. Without their invaluable contributions this book wouldn't have been possible. They have made vital efforts to compile up to date information on the varied aspects of this subject to make this book a valuable addition to the collection of many professionals and students.

This book was conceptualized with the vision of imparting up-to-date and integrated information in this field. To ensure the same, a matchless editorial board was set up. Every individual on the board went through rigorous rounds of assessment to prove their worth. After which they invested a large part of their time researching and compiling the most relevant data for our readers.

The editorial board has been involved in producing this book since its inception. They have spent rigorous hours researching and exploring the diverse topics which have resulted in the successful publishing of this book. They have passed on their knowledge of decades through this book. To expedite this challenging task, the publisher supported the team at every step. A small team of assistant editors was also appointed to further simplify the editing procedure and attain best results for the readers.

Apart from the editorial board, the designing team has also invested a significant amount of their time in understanding the subject and creating the most relevant covers. They scrutinized every image to scout for the most suitable representation of the subject and create an appropriate cover for the book.

The publishing team has been an ardent support to the editorial, designing and production team. Their endless efforts to recruit the best for this project, has resulted in the accomplishment of this book. They are a veteran in the field of academics and their pool of knowledge is as vast as their experience in printing. Their expertise and guidance has proved useful at every step. Their uncompromising quality standards have made this book an exceptional effort. Their encouragement from time to time has been an inspiration for everyone.

The publisher and the editorial board hope that this book will prove to be a valuable piece of knowledge for students, practitioners and scholars across the globe.

Index

A

Absence Of Disease, 1, 26, 42-43

B

Blood Transfusion, 151, 197, 202, 206

Bodily Integrity, 4, 43, 52, 97, 200

C

Capacity To Consent, 18, 196-197, 204-205, 218

Child Mortality, 24, 26, 33

Clinical Investigations, 210, 222

Communicable Diseases, 11, 56, 87, 96-97, 101, 113, 116, 169, 235

Cultural Rights, 1, 11, 17, 20-21, 25, 28, 38, 49, 62, 75, 77, 90-91, 108, 114, 120, 123, 130, 232

Customary Law, 6, 15-16, 18, 20, 231, 236

D

Declaration Of Helsinki, 211-212, 215, 227, 231

Defendant Hospital, 175-176, 181, 183

Defendant's Negligence, 178-179, 202

Dental Education, 140, 142

Dental Practitioners, 8, 63, 139-144, 148, 150-151, 154, 157, 160, 171, 201, 208, 236

Doctor-patient Relationship, 15, 167, 174, 195

Doctor-patient Rights, 140, 208

Duty Of Care, 147, 173-175, 178, 184-185, 190-191

E

Electro-convulsive Therapy, 175-176

Emergency Obstetric Care, 32, 34-35, 40, 44, 85-86, 235

F

Family Planning, 4, 24, 27, 44, 51, 235

Food Security, 28, 67

Freedom Of Movement, 90, 120

Fundamental Rights, 17, 19, 29, 41, 71-74, 125, 193

H

Health Insurance, 63, 85, 143

Health Law, 1, 4-6, 11-13, 17, 42, 84, 88-90, 92, 98, 112, 128, 136-137, 222, 229-230, 234-235

Health Rights Issues, 6-7, 80

Human Dignity, 4, 17, 21, 26, 29-30, 74, 90, 106, 115, 125, 128, 130-131, 213, 226

Human Rights Instruments, 19, 31, 40, 42, 66-67, 71, 96, 112-114, 119, 121, 132, 138, 194, 210-212

Human Rights Violations, 80, 90, 115

Human Subjects, 5, 210-212, 215-216, 224

I

Informed Consent, 18, 105, 124, 127, 151, 186, 193-194, 198-202, 207, 209-210, 219, 221, 223-228, 232, 234

Intellectual Property Regime, 53, 59, 65

Intellectual Property Rights, 54-56, 82, 229

L

Law Of Negligence, 173-175, 190-191

Legal Abortion, 50, 53, 70, 72, 74, 77, 233, 235

M

Malaria Mortality, 32

Malpractice Litigation, 5, 173, 191

Marginalised Groups, 23, 37, 91

Material Risks, 199
Maternal Health Care, 16, 35-37, 168, 235
Mental Disability, 119, 125, 135, 137, 187, 199, 203, 234
Mental Disorder, 116, 138
Mental Health, 2, 9, 11, 18, 21, 27, 37, 48-49, 53, 56, 69, 72, 78, 90, 117, 121, 125, 127-133, 138, 204, 229-235, 237
Mental Health Legislation, 133, 137, 237
Mental Treatment Act, 8, 33, 115, 134, 136, 233
Midwifery, 153, 155, 157-159

N

National Health Policy, 17, 22, 114, 232

P

Patient In Bad Faith, 207-208
Patients' Charter, 193, 232
Patients' Rights, 18, 193-194, 208
Pharmaceutical Companies, 3, 214, 228
Political Question, 35-36, 39, 229
Premature Mortality, 37, 90
Professional Misconduct, 143-144, 147, 149, 157, 161, 164, 173
Public Health, 4-5, 8-9, 11-13, 18, 21, 33, 35, 37, 83, 98, 105, 108, 113, 115, 125, 151, 153, 160, 170, 210, 231, 237
Public Health Act, 8, 33, 88, 96, 102, 112
Public Health Legislation, 18, 88, 91-92, 96, 104, 107, 112
Public Health Policy, 83, 88

R

Relaxant Drugs, 175-176
Res Ipsa Loquitur, 182-184, 191
Restrictive Abortion Laws, 68, 78
Right To Health, 7, 27, 39, 42, 55, 67, 72, 79, 81, 83, 87, 92, 96, 102, 104, 112, 114, 116, 131, 171, 220, 230-231, 233, 236
Right To Life, 14, 20, 29-31, 35, 37, 52, 56, 68, 70, 76, 78, 90, 120, 220
Right To Refuse Medical Treatment, 97, 151
Rights Of The Child, 11, 24, 70, 114, 204

S

Sensory Impairment, 118, 126, 133
Sexual Health, 42-43, 237
Sexual Intercourse, 44, 68, 94, 101, 109
Sexual Orientation, 25, 43, 45, 91, 233
Sexually Transmitted Diseases, 43, 46, 96, 98
Social Security, 1, 143
Social Well-being, 1-2, 26-27, 42-43, 90, 229
Social-behavioural Studies, 210, 222
Socio-economic Rights, 33, 36-39, 41-42, 61, 66, 76, 229, 232, 234
Spheres Of Life, 3, 85

T

Termination Of Pregnancy, 47-48, 50, 52, 68-72, 78, 86, 199
The Nurses And Midwives Act, 8, 153, 171
The Nurses And Midwives Council, 153, 160
Treatment Of Disease, 88

W

Women's Human Rights, 15, 24, 26, 35, 39-40, 70, 236

www.ingramcontent.com/pod-product-compliance
Lightning Source LLC
LaVergne TN
LVHW051047220926
848485LV00001BA/36
9781639872091